THERE'S A
DECORATOR
IN YOUR
DOLL HOUSE

THERE'S A
DECORATOR
IN YOUR
DOLL HOUSE

WRITTEN AND ILLUSTRATED BY
Melanie Kahane, F.A.I.D.

GALAHAD BOOKS · NEW YORK CITY

Copyright © 1968 by Melanie Kahane
All rights reserved

Library of Congress Catalog Card Number: 74-77015
ISBN 0-88365-280-3

Published by arrangement with Atheneum

Printed in the United States of America

to my daughter

JOAN

Contents

	Introduction	3
CHAPTER I	What Is Decorating?	5
CHAPTER II	Materials and Tools You Will Need	9
CHAPTER III	The Living Room	14
CHAPTER IV	The Dining Room	48
CHAPTER V	The Bedrooms	76
CHAPTER VI	The Guest Room	108
CHAPTER VII	The Kitchen	123
CHAPTER VIII	How to "Build" a Doll House	142

THERE'S A DECORATOR IN YOUR DOLL HOUSE

Introduction

WHEN I WAS A little girl, I thought that "decorating" was just something you did to birthday cakes to make them look fancy. Like writing your name and putting flowers and "Happy Birthday" in delicious pink and blue icing on top of the chocolate frosting.

I was very surprised to find out that every time my mother had the walls painted or papered, or our furniture got changed around, that was called "decorating" too.

That was about a million years ago. Maybe not quite a million, but before they had TV sets anyway, and on rainy days when I couldn't go out and play, I played on the back steps of our house.

It was on one of those rainy days that I decided those steps would make lovely rooms for my dolls. There was pretty carpet on the floor, and yellow wallpaper on the sides, so I really had a head start! Each step became a *room*, and I found furniture for every room and moved my dolls in. I used to call them "step-rooms." There was only one trouble. If anyone wanted to use the back stairs, I had to *undecorate* them!

Then one Christmas I got a doll house, and I played with it all the time. I never played with my "step-rooms" again. Instead I tried to make little curtains for my doll house, and bedspreads and rugs and window shades and things. But I wanted more furniture or sometimes just new furniture even though I didn't know how to make that sort of thing. Anyway, there wasn't even a hammer or a saw or nails tiny enough to make beds or tables to fit *my house*. So I began looking around for anything that could become furniture. I started by asking mother if I could find something in her sewing room, and my father if I could search his desk drawer—then I went to the kitchen tool chest and of course to my own junk drawer.

I found wonderful things.

That's what I want to tell you about in this book. . . .

What I found.

What you can find.

And what you can *make* for *your* doll house!

What Is Decorating?

FIRST THERE ARE some things you should know about decorating—
Like what is decorating?
Decorating is not painting walls.
Decorating is not putting fancy designs on a birthday cake.
Decorating *is*—putting together lovely furniture, rugs, curtains, lamps and pictures for a certain room, in the nicest way you can—
so the room will look pretty,
so the room will be comfortable,
so your doll family will be comfortable in the room,
so the colors will be fun for you and good for the room.

A PLAN. The first thing in decorating is to make a plan.
That means that you have to decide:
1. What the room needs.
2. Then where you will put the things it needs.
For instance, if it is a bedroom:
1. It needs
   a) A bed

b) 2 night tables (one for each side of the bed)
c) 2 lamps for the night tables (so your dolls can read in bed)
d) A dresser
e) A mirror above the dresser
f) A comfortable chair
g) A table and a lamp next to the chair
h) A chair or stool (so your dolls can sit while they put on their shoes)
i) A pretty warm rug or carpet for the floor
j) Nice fresh curtains for the windows
k) A bedspread for the bed, of course.

2. Where you place all these pieces is called a PLAN.
 a) The bed of course usually goes on the longest wall so there will be room for the night tables.
 b) The dresser should go on the opposite wall. But be sure that your doll has enough room to open the drawers without hitting the bed. If she hasn't, then you must move the dresser to another wall.
 c) If the room is large enough for a comfortable chair, try to place it near a window, because it's pleasant to sit and look out of a window.
 d) The little chair or stool should be placed on the other side of the room. It is best if it is near the telephone on one of the night tables —because you know that little ladies, and even little dolls—never, never sit on a bed. It is bad housekeeping and bad manners!

It is also great fun to make a list of everything you think each room in your doll house will need.
 a) Go through your house and see what your mother has in each room.
 b) See what you have in your own room.
 c) Or ask yourself what you would *like* to have in your room.
 d) Ask your brother and your father what they would *like* to have.

COLOR SCHEME. The second step in decorating is to find a color scheme. A color scheme simply means:
1. How many colors you want to use in a room
2. How the colors fit the room
3. Which colors you will use

Once you have decided on all three, you have a color scheme.

When you are selecting colors, you will naturally use the colors you like best—everyone does. So think of your favorite colors in the whole world. Think of the colors that make you feel "good." Those are the colors you will choose from whenever you need a color scheme.

For instance, if you wanted to do a color scheme for the same bedroom that we used for the plan and you wanted it in red and pink (two of your favorite colors)—you could try:
1. Red for the rug
2. Pale pink on the walls
3. White for the bedspread and pillows
4. Red and white gingham for the ruffles under the spread
5. The same gingham for the ruffles on the canopy
6. Tiny pink and white stripe for the curtains
7. Solid pink (a little darker than the walls) for the comfortable chair at the window
8. The stripe (like the curtains) for the chair or stool
9. White for the lamps—and for fun make the shades red.

For other color schemes that you may like, turn to the next page.

Now let's begin.

Let's decorate—and have fun!

	WALLS	FLOOR	DRAPERIES	UPHOLSTERY	ACCENTS
1	pale green	blue	green & blue print	green & blue print, bright green, blue & white stripe	sharp yellow
2	pale blue	bitter green	green & blue & white check	blue & white tweed, green, blue	hot pink, white
3	white	brown	blue	blue & white print, brown corduroy, blue stripe or plaid	white, chinese red
4	pale blue	floral on black ground	blue & white print	blue (pale & clear), pale beige, yellow	acid green pink
5	mustard door-white	multi-colored	off-white with mustard braid	mustard, olive, green tweed, off-white tweed	red lacquer, orange
6	white	beige	beige	green & white, yellow, green velvet	yellow, pinks
7	pale blue	red	off-white with red braid	blue & red stripe ticking, off-white, pale pink	clear yellow, pale orange
8	white	emerald green	ice blue	aqua leather, white slipcovers blue, green & white print	chrome yellow
9	pale pink	cherry red	red & white stripe	red, off-white	orange, magenta, purple
10	blackberry	lipstick red	black & white print	lipstick red tweed, black & white print	shocking pink, orange, pale pink
11	white	bitter green	brown & white small pattern print	black & white print, turquoise, bitter green	white, salmon pink, clear red
12	yellow	gold	white	yellow check (or print), beige & white tweed, pink	clear pink, orange, bitter green, white

Materials and Tools You Will Need

TO DECORATE *YOUR* doll house (or your back stairs), there are certain things you will need. It will be much easier for you, and much more fun, if you take the time to set out all the basic tools and materials you must have to do a good job—*before* you start. This is what a good cook does—it is what a good carpenter does—it is what a good decorator must do.

I think the most important thing is first to find a good working area. A folding bridge table is the best for this and perhaps the easiest to work on, unless you are lucky enough to have a big desk or play table of your own. But the bridge table will do—not only because the surface is usually plastic and therefore will not stain, but also because all the papers, boxes and bits and pieces you will use can be stored *under* the table.

Now for the tools, materials and bits and pieces.

The tools:
1. A pair of scissors—good ones—for fabrics and trimmings.
2. A pair of scissors—old ones, so you can use them for cutting cardboard and paper.
3. Scotch tape—lots of it
4. A ruler—the metal-edged kind

5. Some sharp pencils
6. Flow pens (or brush pens)
7. Tube of glue
8. Jar of paste
9. Pins
10. Mystik cloth tape
11. Double-faced tape
12. Soft art gum eraser
13. Stapler (heavy duty kind)
14. Cutting Board
15. Razor knife with hand guard (if your mother will let you have one, but you must promise to be careful)
16. X-Acto knife
17. Clean rag

Besides the "tools" listed above, the other important needs of a decorator are the "materials." You must have both—tools *and* materials! Tools are fairly simple to find; everyone in your house knows where the scissors are supposed to be or the pencils and glue. Materials, though, are not so easy because they are not always what you *think* they are! By this I mean that to find the sort of materials you will need, you will have to use your eyes *differently* than you ever have before. For instance, when you look at an old bath towel (during your hunt), you won't just see a towel—you will "see" it as wall to wall carpeting for your doll house. Or when you look at a soda straw, you will see it cut up as logs for the fireplace! Finding such materials can be a sort of game, a real treasure hunt.

So don't forget to look in the sewing box, in the tool chest, in your father's desk drawer (if you are permitted), and of course go through *everything* in your own junk drawer and even in your school desk or locker.

Some of the things I hope you will find are:

1. paper clips

2. thumb tacks
3. upholstery tacks
4. buttons
5. plastic soda straws
6. ordinary soda straws
7. electric light chain (pull-chain)
8. pocketbook mirrors
9. ribbons
10. colored tape of all kinds
11. thimbles
12. bulletin board pins
13. map pins
14. cup hooks
15. screw bolts
16. machine screws (the ones that are flat on the bottom)
17. washers (they are made of metal and used with screws)
18. birthday candles
19. string
20. paper baking cups

And lots of "empties" like:
1. empty perfume bottle tops
2. empty plastic toothbrush cases
3. empty matchboxes (both kinds: the large kitchen matches and the small table size)
4. empty thread spools
5. empty toothpaste boxes

And old stuff like:
1. old lipstick tops (covers)
2. old glass or plastic coasters
3. tops of old saltcellars

4. an old drippy earring (for a chandelier)
5. an old bath towel (that can be cut up)
6. an old dish towel (plaid or check if possible, but also one that can be cut up)
7. old or new scraps of fabric—all that you can find
8. any piece of lace or eyelet edging
9. old printed or plaid handkerchiefs
10. an old gingham apron (one that can be cut)

Then there are also loads of wonderful things you should save (even after you have begun "decorating" your doll's house) because you will find that you need much more than you thought—and because all of us can make mistakes!

So start saving:

1. lots of lightweight cardboard (the kind that the laundry uses for men's shirts)
2. all the little white gift boxes you can find—in fact any boxes as long as they are small
3. some of those little pleated paper cups that are used for chocolates and fancy candies
4. tiny little "pictures" from old magazines—cut them out—you will need many of these in different sizes
5. all the little scraps of pretty gift wrap paper you can find
6. if you still eat Cracker Jacks, some of those little favors—they can be great for accessories.

Ask everyone in the family to save all the old toothpaste caps (or any tube cap). You will use them for "cigarette holders" and for tiny "flower arrangements." In fact, ask everyone in the family to save *everything*. You never know what you will be able to use in some very clever way for *your* doll house decorating.

Further on, I am going to tell you how to use all the gadgets and things

I have listed. But these lists are really incomplete; they only cover a few ideas—just to start you on your hunt. As you go along you will discover many things on your own. Keep looking and *never* stop using your eyes!

Although most of the other materials you must have to make the things described in this book are actually listed with the instructions and these you can collect as you start each project, this book is merely a beginning. Use your imagination—and I'll bet you can discover and invent many things yourself!

The Living Room

I LOVE TO DO living rooms.

I guess it's because I think every room should be for living, so I think of every room as a "living room." That's why I also find the living room the easiest to decorate creatively. If you will follow some more of the basic principles that I am going to give you, then perhaps you too will find it the easiest to do.

One of these basic principles in decoration is "the plan." If you remember, in Chapter I, I told you that a plan means that you should decide:

1. What the room needs.
2. Where the pieces needed will go in that room.

Another important principle, almost the most basic, is to understand the purpose of each room. Of course I know that you know a kitchen is for cooking and a dining room is the room for eating the meals that are prepared in the kitchen and so on. But besides just thinking about what the room is supposed to do, you must also think of how you and your little family will use that particular room.

Suppose your doll house does not have a den. Then your living room must do double work: it must be both a living room and a den. In which case you should plan for bookcases (see page 111), a desk and a comfortable desk chair and know exactly where you will put the TV so the furniture can be arranged for good viewing, good reading and good living. Now this is where planning is important. I think all three things are important to the room—but if the TV is going to make your room look like a theater (with all the chairs and sofa strung out in a half circle), then I think the TV is in the wrong place. Instead let's pretend that you will have your TV "built in," perhaps into your book shelves, or into a cabinet (like the one on page 21). Or try a portable TV. You could then keep it behind a handsome screen (like the one on page 68). This way it could be easily pulled out whenever you wanted to watch your favorite program. Any of these ideas will help you solve the problem of "where to put the TV" and help you create a much lovelier living room-den.

Another way to figure out what the room will need is to ask yourself some simple questions, first: Do your dolls like to play games like monopoly or checkers? Do their friends? Do the grown-up dolls like to play cards? If they do, then they should have comfortable chairs to pull up to a table in the living room. The next question could be: Will the room be used only by the family or will it be used for entertaining as well (even if it is a den-living room)? Naturally the next question then is: Does your little family entertain? Well, they should—otherwise how will they meet the other dolls in the neighborhood—how will they reciprocate and entertain the friends who have entertained them? Entertaining is an important part of most families' lives, and the living room is an important part of entertaining.

We can now finish the first half of the plan, since we know what the room should do, by deciding what it should have and how it will be used. In other words, for this living room (and den) we will probably need a sofa, some club or easy chairs, bookcases, a desk and a chair, a bridge table and chairs, lamps, tables, a rug, draperies, curtains, etc.

Where you put all these things is the second half of the plan. Here again you face a problem—I call it the plan-problem. Everybody has it, and you will, too. It is when you discover you must give up some of the things you were sure would be part of your room because they don't fit, or perhaps you must add something you never counted on.

So you must ask yourself questions like these: Is the room *really* big enough for all the pieces you want to put into it? Are there too many chairs? Are there too many straight chairs and not enough comfortable ones? Or too many tables? Is the sofa way too big? Yes? What can you leave out without spoiling the room—or what can you add to make it look cozier?

Some of the answers may not only solve your plan-problems, but may make the room more interesting. You might try using a desk as an end table next to a sofa. Or try putting the sofa at right angles to the fireplace and using the desk behind the sofa (as you would a long sofa table). In either case you save the wall space where you originally thought you would use the desk and the wall space where you would have put the sofa. Anyway, every wall doesn't have to have a piece of furniture on it.

And remember you don't always have to use the longest wall for the largest piece of furniture.

To save floor space try doing away with a cabinet or bookcase and using built-in book shelves instead. Then you can put a grouping of chairs or even the sofa in front of the shelves. To use good floor space, try the sofa coming out from the fireplace, as I just mentioned, or put it right out in the middle (well, not quite the middle) of the room *facing* the fireplace, with chairs grouped on either side. This same arrangement can be used with the sofa facing a window that has a lovely view. All of these plan-ideas will keep your room new and fresh in its layout; and most important, the furniture won't look as if it is just running around the room.

The whole point of a good plan is to make the space you have do the most for you and the most for the room. The only rule is that the arrangement must be comfortable and convenient.

Naturally a well-designed living room must have comfort, and that in turn requires comfortable seating pieces. It also requires some small chairs or benches, the kind that can easily be pulled up to a grouping of other chairs (see pages 26 and 104). Good lighting is a part of comfort too—not only for reading but for overall lighting so some parts of the room and some of your guests won't be left "in the dark." And, of course, when you turn on the lights you want *everything* to be nice and bright, not just the place where you read.

One more "must" for pleasant living is: Each chair should always have a table, either next to it or near it. The reason for this is that the table permits whoever is sitting in the chair to use an ash tray, put down a glass, or handle a cup and saucer without getting up and down all the time. This is a small example of what decorating is really all about: thoughtful ideas that help make a room comfortable as well as attractive.

But just tables and chairs won't make a room—they never do. Any room to be well done can never be done with furniture alone! It must also have: books—flowers—pictures—accessories—magazines—personal photographs—anything that will make the room look "lived in." It must look as though people (even doll people) are at home there; otherwise it will always look as if it had just come out of a store window or is just getting ready to go into one!

KNEEHOLE DESK

① USE THE BOTTOM OF A SMALL GIFT BOX Ⓐ 3¼"L x 1¼"W x 1¾"H OR (3"L x 1½"W x 1¾"H) TURN THE BOX UPSIDE DOWN.

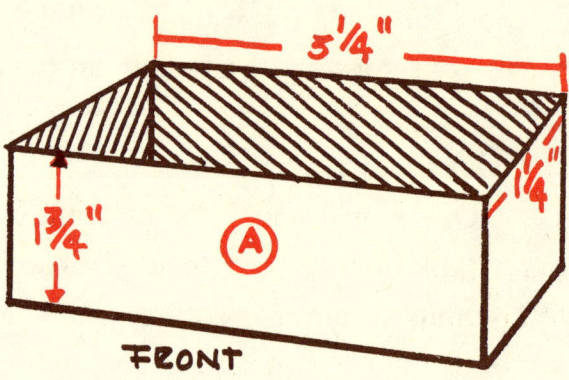
FRONT

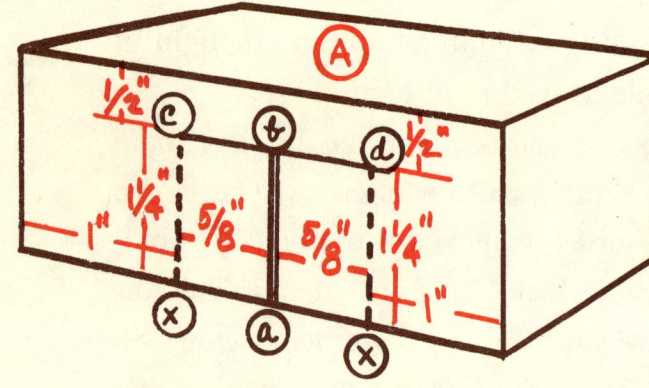

② TO MAKE THE "KNEEHOLE" PART OF THE DESK - MARK OFF PIECE Ⓐ USING THE MEASUREMENTS IN THE SKETCH AND DRAWING YOUR LINES IN THE <u>FRONT</u> AND <u>BACK</u> IN THIS ORDER:-
1. FROM Ⓧ TO Ⓐ AND Ⓐ TO Ⓧ
2. FROM Ⓐ TO ⓑ
3. FROM Ⓒ TO ⓑ AND ⓑ TO Ⓓ
4. FROM Ⓧ TO Ⓒ
5. FROM Ⓧ TO Ⓓ

③ CAREFULLY CUT THE LINES (IN THE FRONT AND BACK OF THE BOX) IN THIS ORDER:-
1. FROM Ⓐ TO ⓑ
2. FROM ⓑ TO Ⓒ
3. FROM ⓑ TO Ⓓ

NOW **FOLD-IN** ALONG THE LINES
(IN FRONT AND BACK):-
 1. FROM Ⓧ TO Ⓒ
 2. FROM Ⓧ TO ⓓ

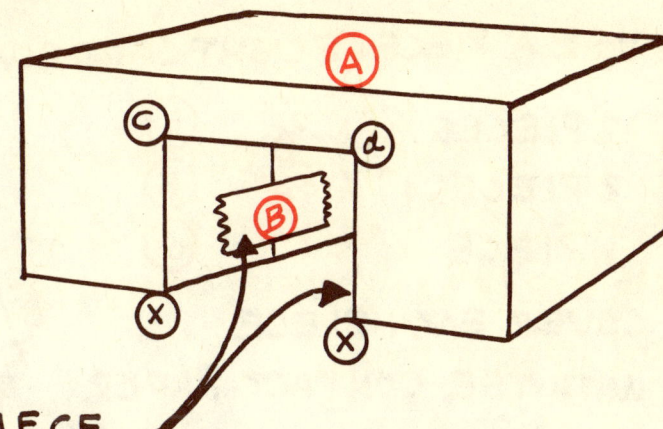

④ FASTEN **FOLDED-IN** PIECE TOGETHER WITH SCOTCH TAPE Ⓑ ON BOTH SIDES.

⑤ CUT A PIECE OF WOOD GRAIN CONTACT PAPER 4¾"W x 6¾"L CUT OUT 1¾" x 1¾" SQUARES Ⓒ FROM EACH CORNER FROM THE CENTER (FRONT) AND THE CENTER (BACK) CUT OUT 1¼" x 1¼" SQUARES Ⓓ — THEN FIT AND PASTE ON TO DESK Ⓐ

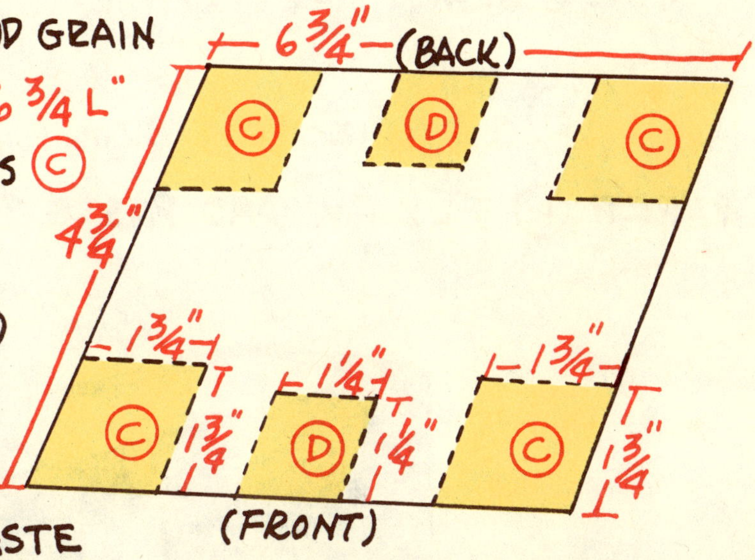

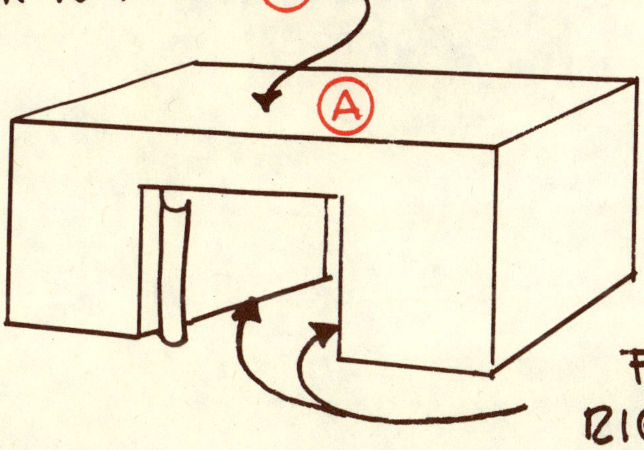

⑥ CUT 2 MORE PIECES OF CONTACT PAPER 1¼" x 1¼" AND PASTE THEM OVER THE FOLDED-IN PIECES (LEFT AND RIGHT) UNDER THE DESK Ⓐ.

⑦ TO MAKE THE DRAWER Ⓔ AND Ⓖ, AND THE DOORS Ⓕ USE A PIECE OF LIGHT CARDBOARD 1" × 2 ¾" AND CUT: —

2 PIECES ¼" × ⅝" Ⓔ
2 PIECES 1" × ⅝" Ⓕ
1 PIECE ¼" × 1"   Ⓖ

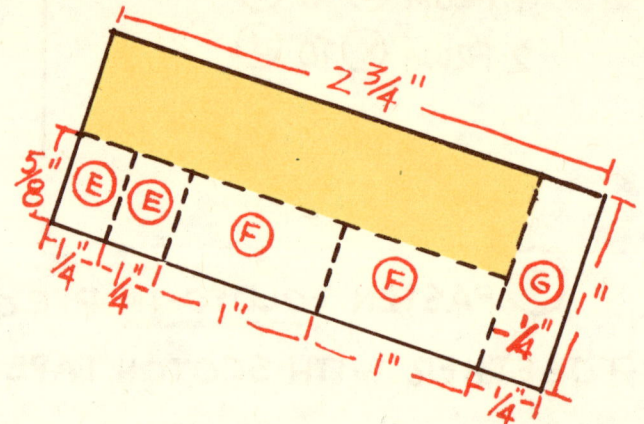

COVER EACH PIECE WITH THE CONTACT PAPER AND GLUE EVENLY ON TO THE DESK.

USE 6 BLACK MAP PINS FOR THE DRAWER AND DOOR PULLS.

⑧ CUT A PIECE OF BROWN (OR BLACK) BLOTTING PAPER Ⓗ 3" L × 1" W AND PASTE TO TOP OF DESK.

CABINET

① USE EMPTY KITCHEN MATCH BOX.

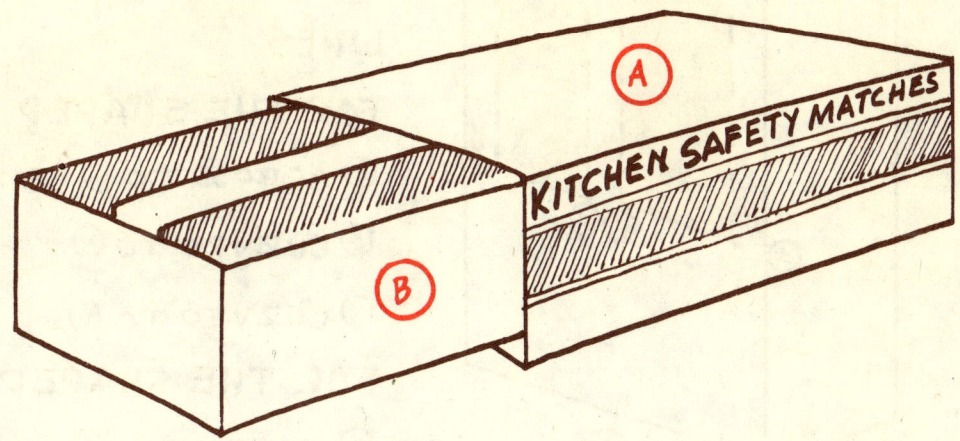

② CUT A PIECE OF WOOD GRAIN CONTACT PAPER 8½"L X 4⅜"H AND PASTE OVER ALL 4 SIDES OF BOX Ⓐ

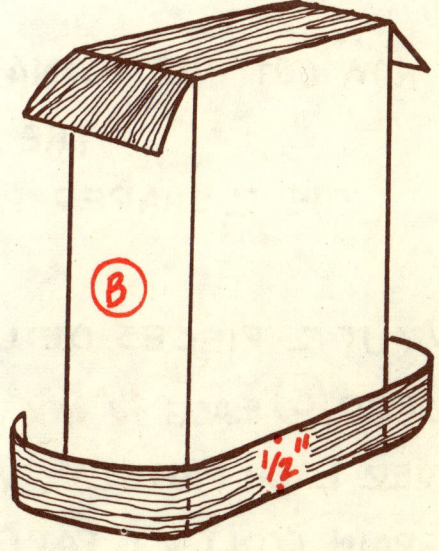

③ CUT A STRIP OF CONTACT PAPER ½"W X 5½"L AND PASTE AT BOTTOM OF BOX Ⓑ AND CUT A PIECE 4"L X 1½"W AND PASTE ON TOP OF BOX Ⓑ.

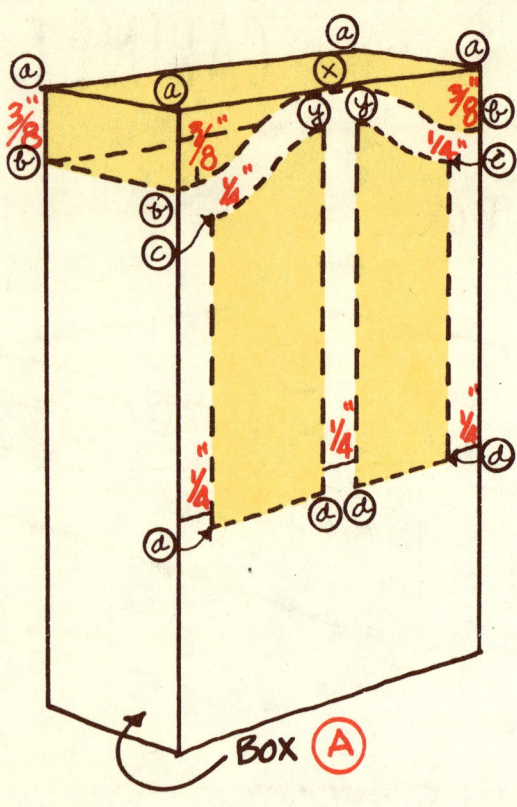

④ TO MAKE THE SHAPES SHOWN IN DOTTED LINES MARK OFF BOX Ⓐ USING MEASUREMENTS IN THE SKETCH AND DRAW YOUR LINES.

FOR THE SHAPED TOP:-
ⓑ ACROSS TO ⓑ (BOTH SIDES & BACK)
ⓑ CURVED TO ⓧ
ⓧ CURVED TO ⓑ

FOR THE SHAPED PANELS
ⓒ DOWN TO ⓓ
ⓓ ACROSS TO ⓓ
ⓨ DOWN TO ⓓ
ⓒ CURVED TO ⓨ

⑤ NOW CUT OUT ALONG THE LINES YOU HAVE DRAWN
THE SHAPED TOP
THE 2 SHAPED PANELS

⑥ CUT 2 PIECES OF LIGHT CARDBOARD Ⓒ EACH ¾"W x 1⅛"H. COVER EACH PANEL Ⓒ WITH WOOD GRAIN CONTACT PAPER. USING DOUBLE FACED TAPE PASTE ON BOX Ⓐ AS SHOWN.

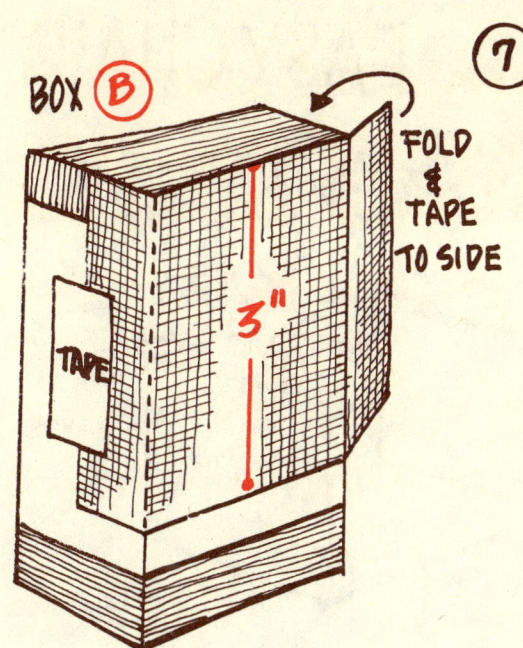

⑦ CUT A PIECE OF COARSE BRASS SCREENING. 4"L X 3"H FOLD AND WRAP SCREEN AROUND CORNERS OF BOX Ⓑ. SECURE IN PLACE WITH TAPE.

⑧ INSERT BOX Ⓑ (WITH SCREEN SIDE FACING CUT-OUT PANELS) INTO BOX Ⓐ. LEAVE ¼" OF BOX Ⓑ OUT AT BOTTOM OF BOX Ⓐ (TO MAKE BASE).

⑨ SECURE BOX IN PLACE BY PUSHING 4 GLASS-HEAD MAP PINS THROUGH BOTH BOXES - THESE BECOME THE CABINET DOOR PULLS.

CLUB or EASY CHAIR

① USE A BOX (OR BOX TOP) Ⓐ 1¾" L x 1⅜" H x 2 W" OR CUT ONE TO THIS SIZE.

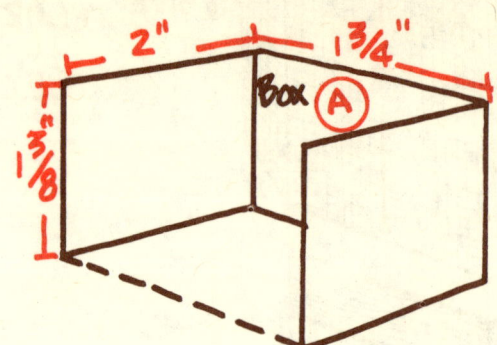

② THEN CUT A PIECE OF CARDBOARD Ⓑ 1¾" W x 4" L.

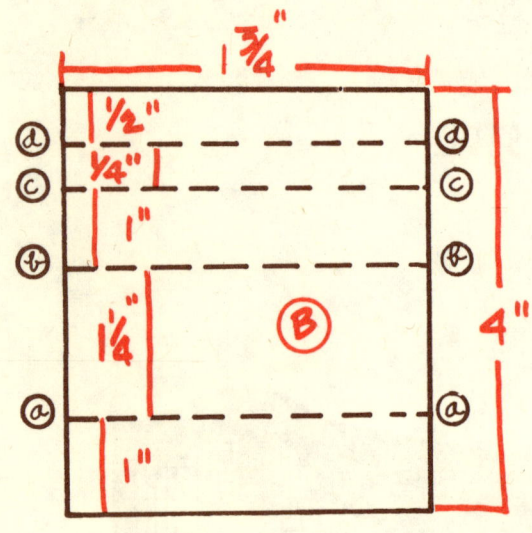

③ USING THE MEASUREMENTS SHOWN, AND WITH A RULER DRAW YOUR LINES:

FROM ⓐ TO ⓐ
FROM ⓑ TO ⓑ
FROM ⓒ TO ⓒ
FROM ⓓ TO ⓓ

④ NOW FOLD ALONG THE LINES YOU HAVE DRAWN AND PIECE Ⓑ WILL HAVE A SHAPE LIKE THIS.

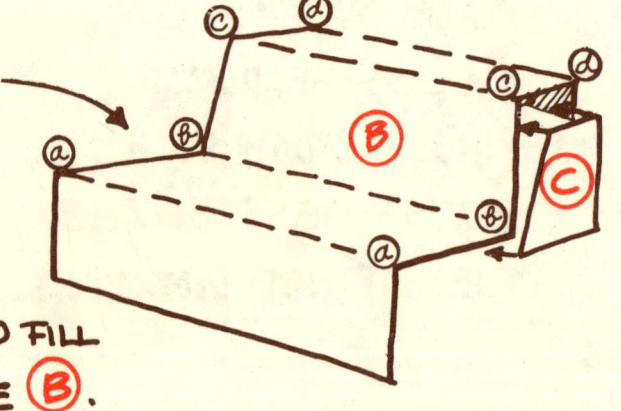

⑤ CUT 2 PIECES OF CARDBOARD Ⓒ TO FILL IN THE ENDS OF PIECE Ⓑ. FASTEN IN PLACE WITH SCOTCH TAPE.

⑥ CUT PIECES OF FABRIC OR CONTACT PAPER THE SAME SIZES AS ② AND ⑤ AND PASTE OVER PIECE Ⓑ AS SHOWN.

PIECE Ⓑ

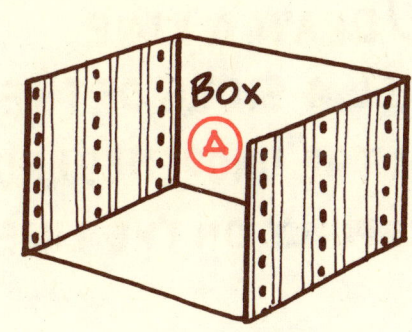
BOX Ⓐ

⑦ CUT THE SAME FABRIC OR PAPER IN A STRIP 1 3/8" W × 9 3/4" L AND PASTE IT ON BOX Ⓐ ON THE INSIDE AND OUTSIDE OF BOTH ENDS, AND ON THE OUTSIDE BACK.

⑦ CAREFULLY SLIP PIECE Ⓑ INTO BOX Ⓐ. FASTEN THEM TOGETHER WITH STRIPS OF CLEAR MENDING TAPE AT POINTS H, I, J, K, L, M.

SIDE CHAIRS

① USE AN EMPTY TOOTHPASTE BOX (LARGE SIZE).

② DRAW A LINE AROUND ALL 4 SIDES OF THE BOX 1⅛" UP FROM THE UNOPENED END. CUT THE BOX CAREFULLY ON THE LINE.

③ NOW DRAW A LINE 2¼" UP FROM THE CUT END - AND CUT THIS PIECE OFF. YOU NOW HAVE PIECES Ⓐ AND Ⓑ.

④ TAKE PIECE Ⓑ AND CUT OUT THE TOP. THROW THIS TOP PIECE AWAY. YOU THEN HAVE A PIECE Ⓒ LIKE THIS

⑤ CUT 2 PIECES OF WOOD GRAIN CONTACT PAPER AND PASTE ON BOTH SIDES OF Ⓒ THEN FOLD ON ORIGINAL FOLDS OF BOX.

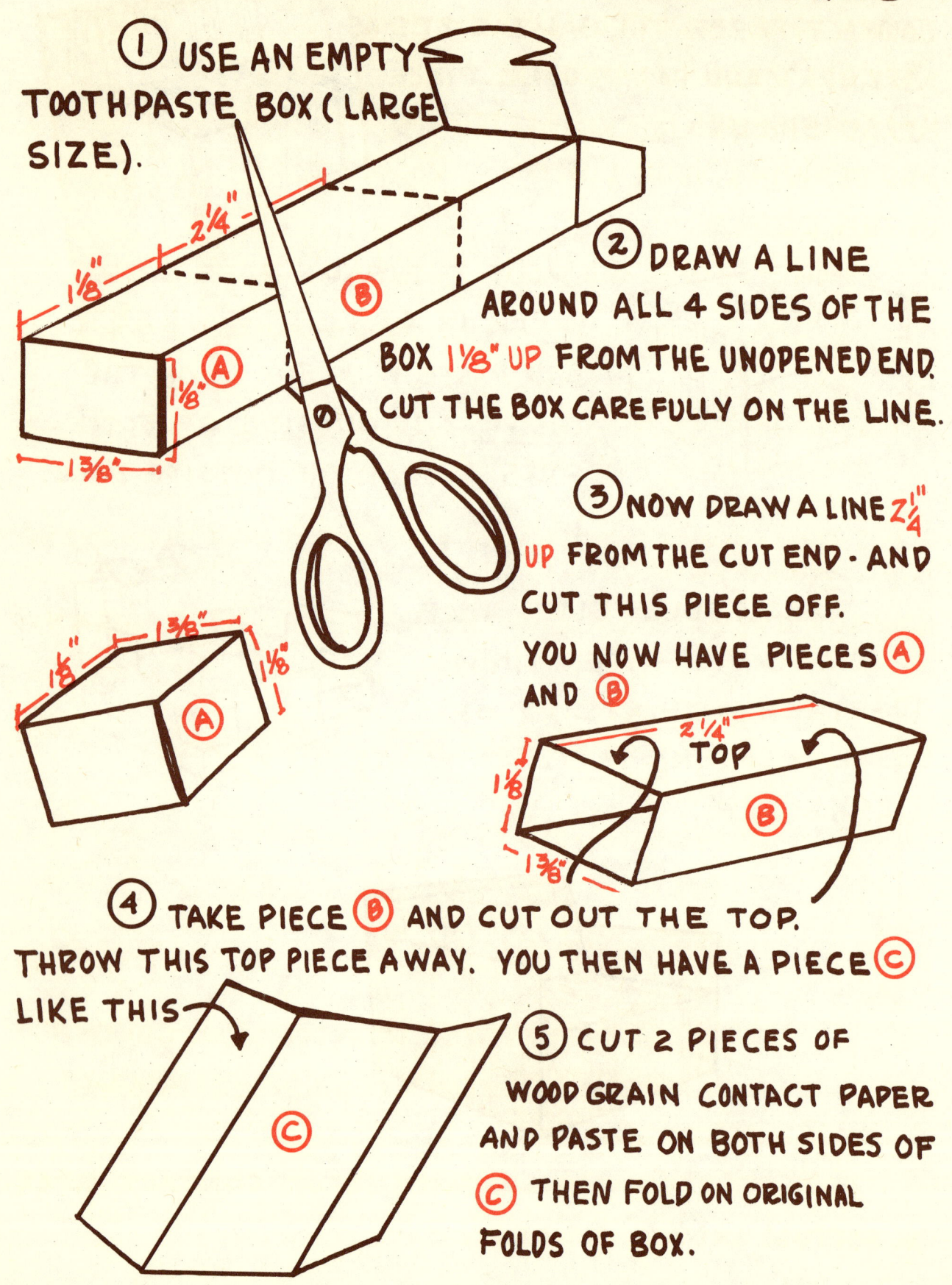

⑥ TO MAKE SHAPE SHOWN HERE IN DOTTED LINES MARK OFF PIECE Ⓒ USING THE MEASUREMENTS IN THIS SKETCH AND DRAWING YOUR LINES IN THIS ORDER:—

1 — FROM ⓐ UP TO ⓕ, AND FROM ⓒ UP TO ⓓ.
2 — FROM ⓑ UP TO ⓔ, AND FROM ⓖ UP TO ⓗ.
3 — FROM ⓔ <u>ACROSS</u> TO ⓗ.
4 — FROM ⓔ <u>ACROSS</u> TO ⓧ, AND FROM ⓨ <u>ACROSS</u> TO ⓓ.
5 — DRAW A <u>CURVED</u> LINE FROM ⓧ TO ⓨ — MAKE IT JUST TOUCH THE TOP AT CENTER ⓚ.

NOW CUT THE SHAPE ALONG THE LINES YOU HAVE DRAWN.

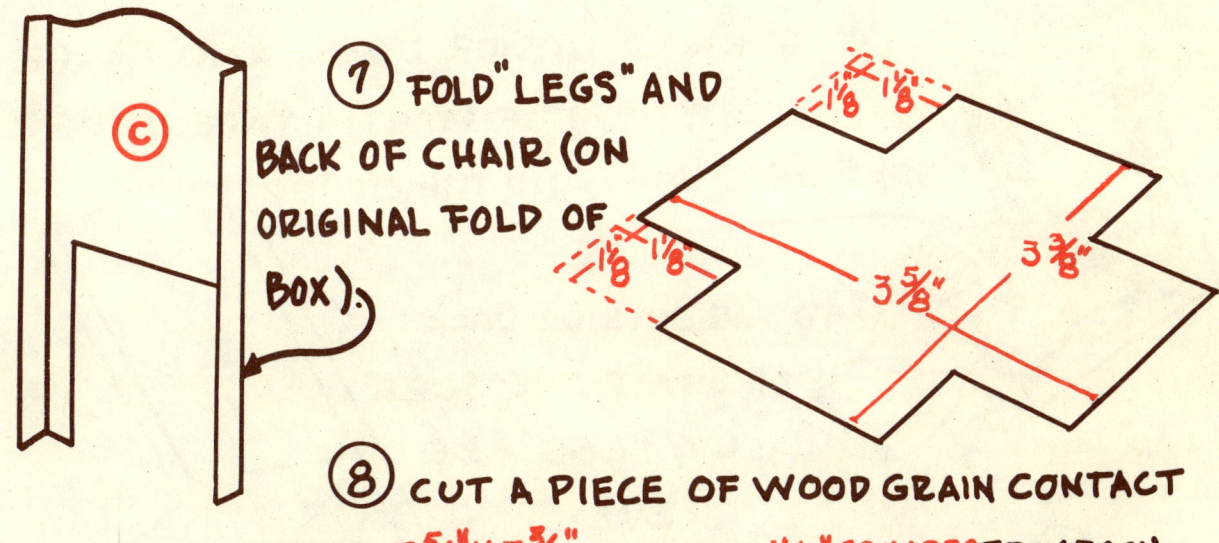

⑦ FOLD "LEGS" AND BACK OF CHAIR (ON ORIGINAL FOLD OF BOX).

⑧ CUT A PIECE OF WOOD GRAIN CONTACT PAPER 3⅝" X 3⅜" CUT OUT 1⅛" SQUARES FROM EACH CORNER.

⑨ TAKE PIECE Ⓐ AND PASTE CUTOUT CONTACT PAPER ON BOTTOM AND ALL 4 SIDES.

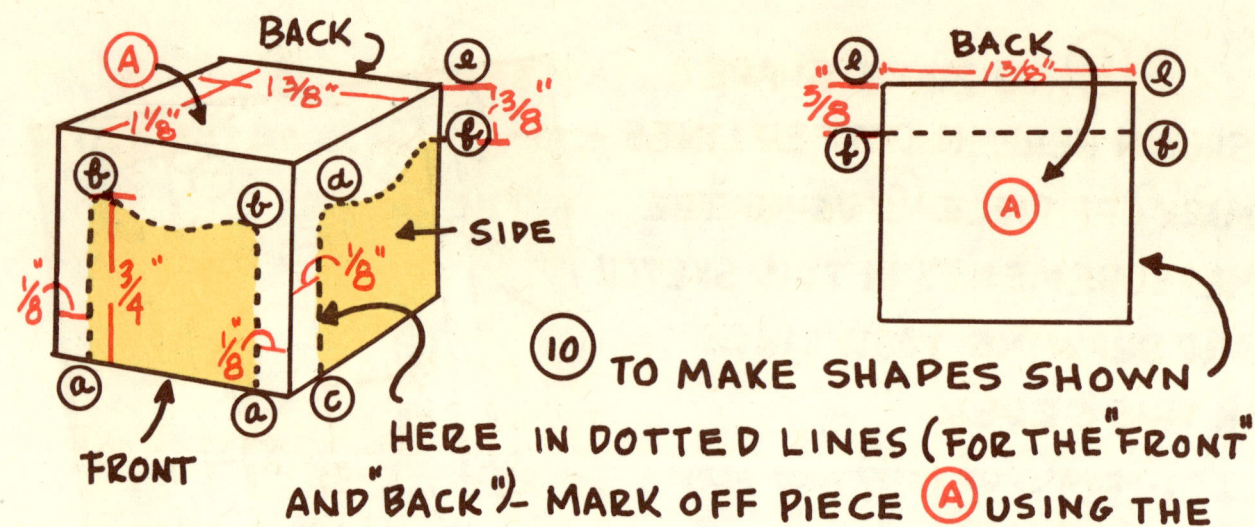

⑩ TO MAKE SHAPES SHOWN HERE IN DOTTED LINES (FOR THE "FRONT" AND "BACK") — MARK OFF PIECE Ⓐ USING THE MEASUREMENTS IN THE SKETCH, AND DRAWING YOUR LINES IN THIS ORDER:—

1. FROM ⓐ UP TO ⓑ (ON FRONT)
2. FROM ⓒ UP TO ⓓ (ON SIDES)
3. DRAW A <u>CURVED</u> LINE FROM ⓑ TO ⓑ (ON FRONT)
4. DRAW A <u>CURVED</u> LINE FROM ⓓ TO ⓕ (ON SIDES)
5. DRAW A STRAIGHT LINE FROM ⓕ TO ⓕ (ON BACK)

NOW CUT THE SHAPES ALONG THE LINES YOU HAVE DRAWN.

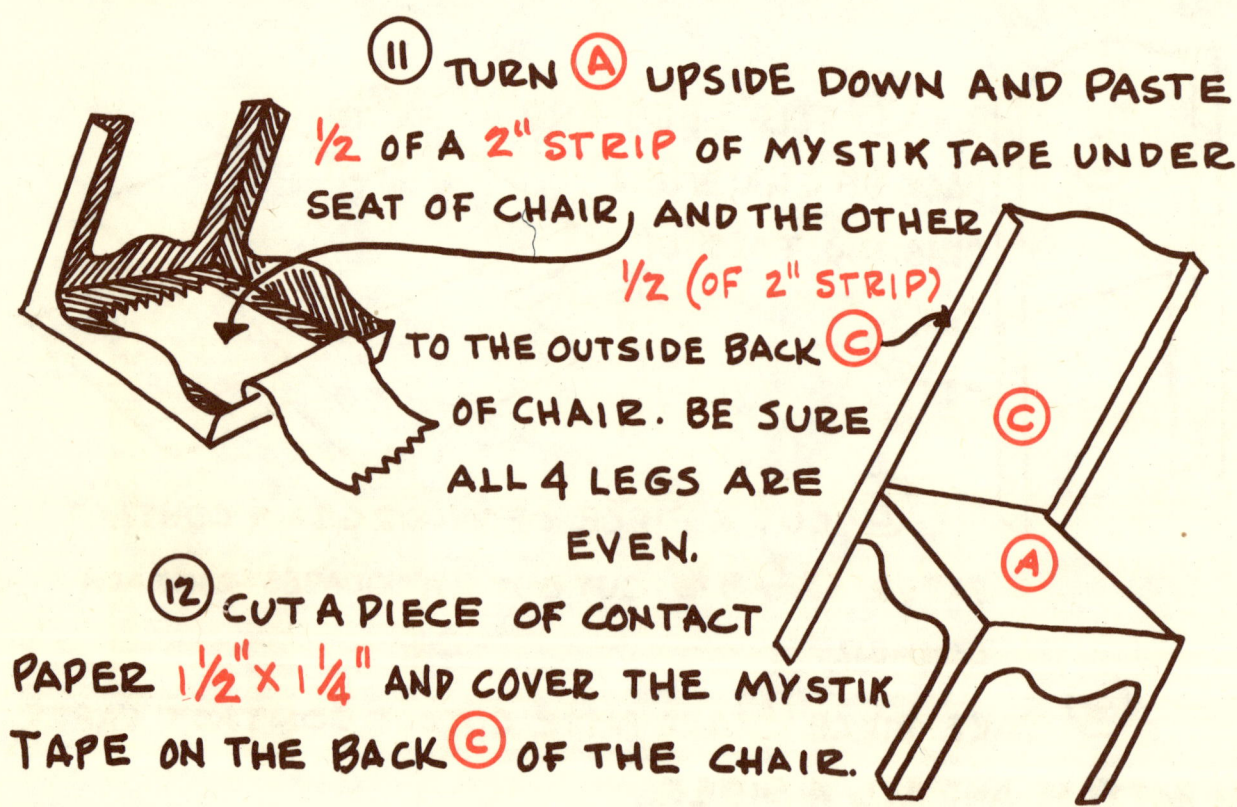

⑪ TURN Ⓐ UPSIDE DOWN AND PASTE ½ OF A 2" STRIP OF MYSTIK TAPE UNDER SEAT OF CHAIR, AND THE OTHER ½ (OF 2" STRIP) TO THE OUTSIDE BACK Ⓒ OF CHAIR. BE SURE ALL 4 LEGS ARE EVEN.

⑫ CUT A PIECE OF CONTACT PAPER 1½" × 1¼" AND COVER THE MYSTIK TAPE ON THE BACK Ⓒ OF THE CHAIR.

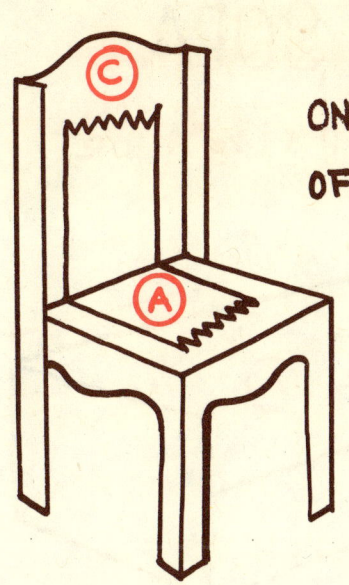

⑬ PASTE ½ OF ANOTHER 2" STRIP OF TAPE ON TOP OF THE SEAT Ⓐ AND ½ ON THE INSIDE OF THE BACK Ⓒ OF THE CHAIR.

⑭ NOW, USING A SPONGE POWDER PUFF (OR A "CELLULOSE" KITCHEN SPONGE CUT TO ⅛" THICKNESS).
CUT 1 PIECE Ⓓ ¼" SHORTER, BUT THE EXACT SHAPE OF THE INSIDE BACK Ⓒ OF THE CHAIR.

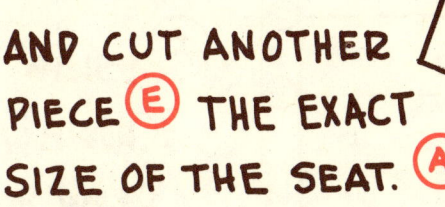

AND CUT ANOTHER PIECE Ⓔ THE EXACT SIZE OF THE SEAT. Ⓐ

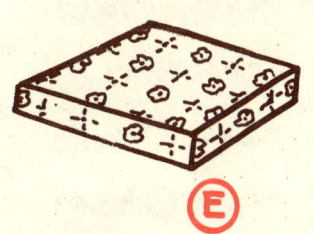

⑮ COVER EACH PIECE Ⓓ AND Ⓔ WITH PRINT CONTACT PAPER (OR PASTE ON PRINT FABRIC).

⑯ PASTE THE SEAT CUSHION Ⓔ FIRST. THEN, PASTE THE BACK CUSHION Ⓓ TO THE BACK.

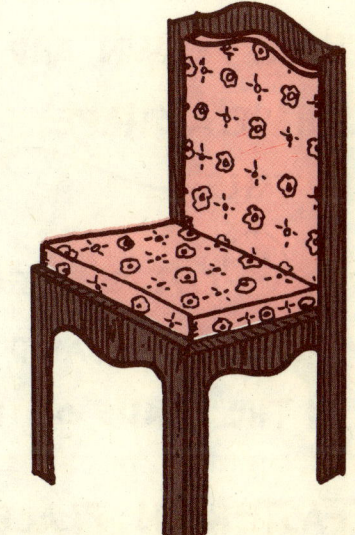

SOFA

① USE A BOX (OR BOX TOP) Ⓐ 4½" L × 2" D × 1⅜" H OR CUT ONE TO THIS SIZE.

② THEN CUT A PIECE OF CARDBOARD Ⓑ 4½" L × 4" W.

③ USING THE MEASUREMENTS SHOWN, AND WITH A RULER DRAW YOUR LINES:

FROM ⓐ TO ⓐ
FROM ⓑ TO ⓑ
FROM ⓒ TO ⓒ
FROM ⓓ TO ⓓ

④ NOW FOLD ALONG THE LINES YOU HAVE DRAWN AND PIECE Ⓑ WILL HAVE A SHAPE LIKE THIS.

⑤ CUT 2 PIECES OF CARDBOARD Ⓒ TO FILL IN THE ENDS OF PIECE Ⓑ.

FASTEN IN PLACE WITH SCOTCH TAPE.

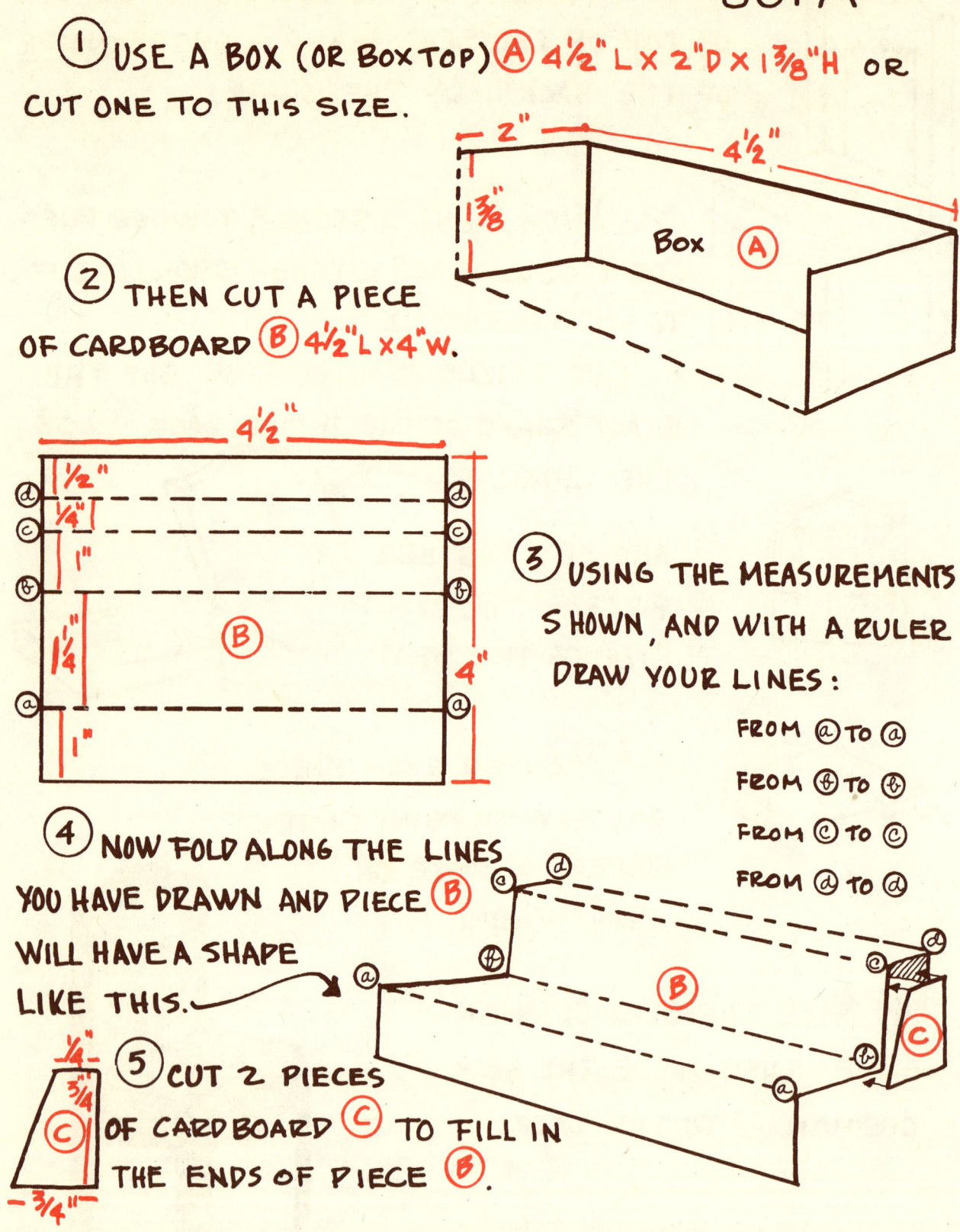

⑥ CUT PIECES OF FABRIC OR CONTACT PAPER THE SAME SIZES AS ② AND ⑤ AND PASTE OVER PIECE Ⓑ AS SHOWN.

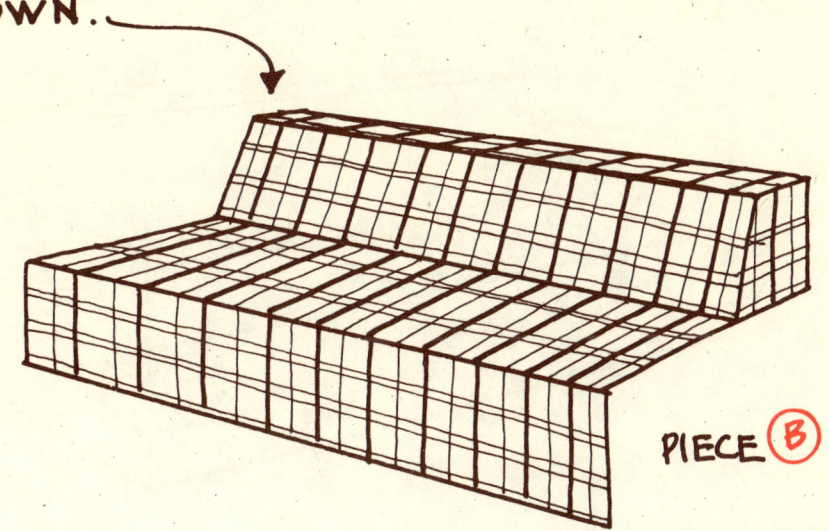

PIECE Ⓑ

⑦ NOW CUT THE SAME FABRIC OR PAPER IN A STRIP 12½" L X 1⅜" W AND PASTE IT ON BOX Ⓐ. ON THE INSIDE AND OUTSIDE OF BOTH ENDS, AND ON THE OUTSIDE BACK ONLY.

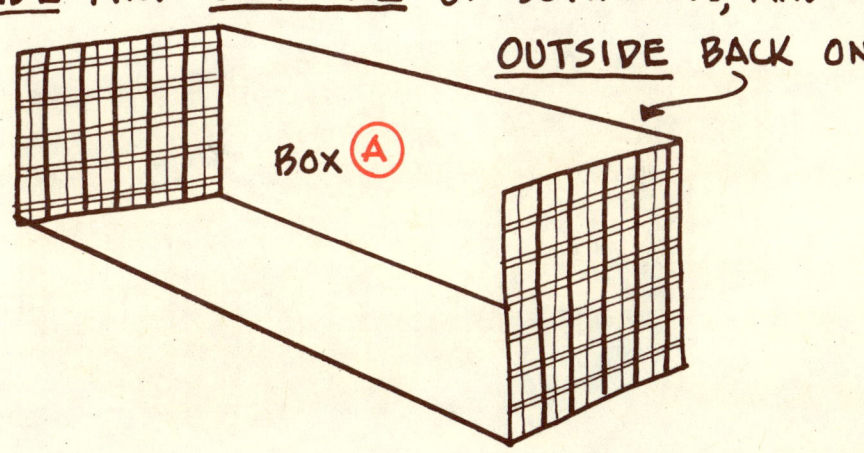

BOX Ⓐ

⑧ CAREFULLY SLIP PIECE Ⓑ INTO BOX Ⓐ.

⑨ FASTEN PIECE Ⓑ AND BOX Ⓐ TOGETHER WITH STRIPS OF CLEAR MENDING TAPE AT POINTS H. I. J. K. L. M.

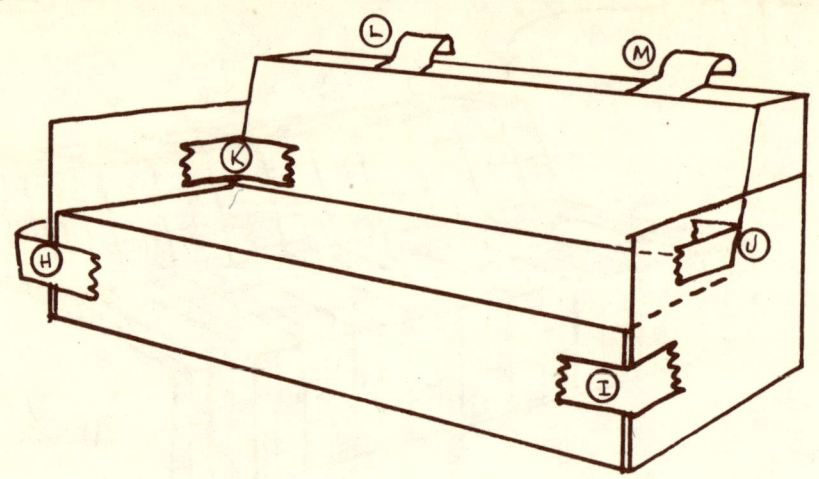

ADD CONTRASTING PILLOWS (SEE PAGE 122).

DRUM-TABLE

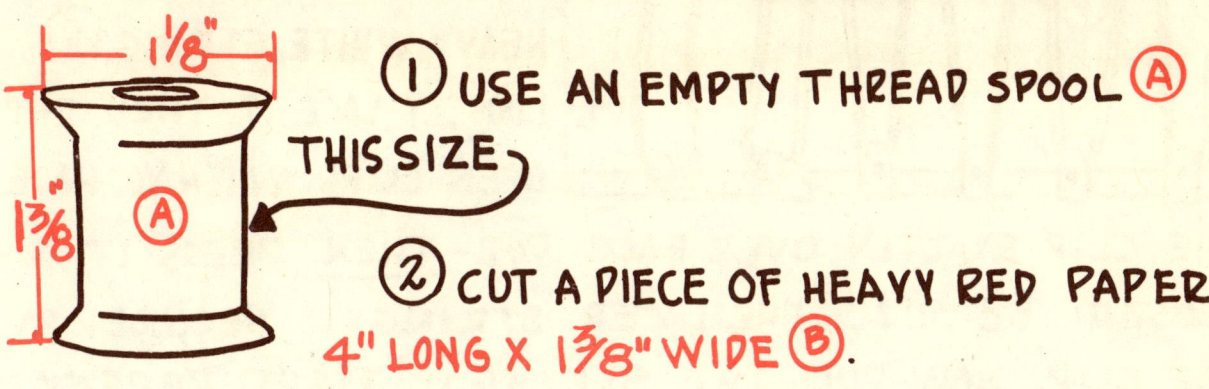

① USE AN EMPTY THREAD SPOOL Ⓐ THIS SIZE

② CUT A PIECE OF HEAVY RED PAPER 4" LONG X 1⅜" WIDE Ⓑ.

③ PASTE ¼" WIDE STRIPS OF NAVY BLUE PAPER (OR ¼" WIDE GIFT WRAP TAPE) AT THE TOP AND BOTTOM OF PIECE Ⓑ.

④ WITH A RULER AND A PENCIL, MEASURE OFF AND MARK A DOT AT EVERY ⅝" ON THE TOP OF Ⓑ. ON THE BOTTOM MARK OFF THE 1ST. DOT ⅜" IN AND THEN EVERY ⅝".

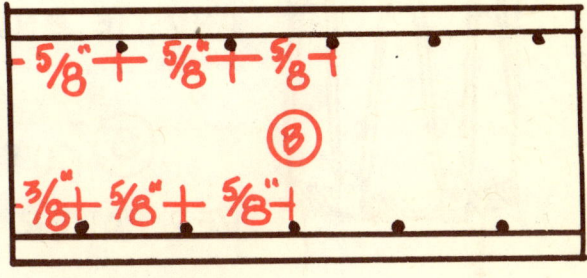

⑤ TAKE 12 METAL CLIPS Ⓒ (THE BEST SIZE FOR THE "DRUM-TABLE" IS NO. 1-B) THEN PLACE ONE CLIP AT EVERY DOT - DO NOT CLIP IT ON TO THE PAPER YET.

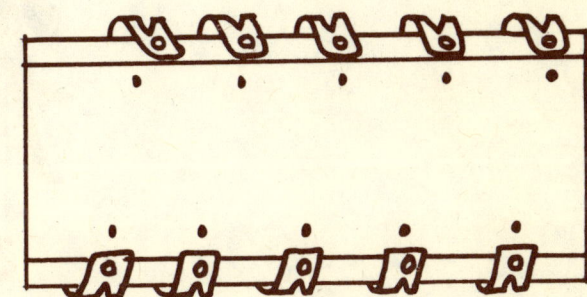

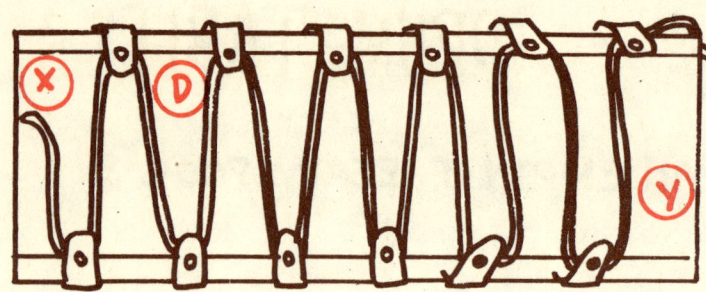

⑥ USE A PIECE OF HEAVY WHITE STRING Ⓓ LOOSELY LACE IT THRU THE OPEN CLIPS. WHEN YOU HAVE THE CLIP EXACTLY OVER EACH DOT - <u>THEN</u> PRESS IT CLOSED. BE SURE THE "LACED" STRING IS SECURED BY THE CLIP. NOW PULL THE STRING Ⓓ TIGHT. REPEAT EACH STEP UNTIL ALL 12 CLIPS ARE CLOSED OVER THE STRING AT EACH DOT.

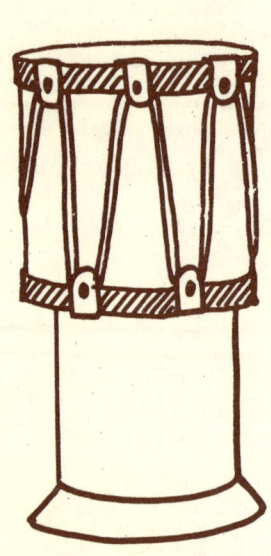

⑦ PASTE SIDES Ⓧ AND Ⓨ TOGETHER SLIP "DRUM" CYLINDER OVER SPOOL - AND TIE ENDS OF STRING TOGETHER.

⑧ CUT A ROUND PIECE OF RED PAPER 1⅛" IN DIAMETER Ⓔ. PASTE THIS PIECE Ⓔ TO THE TOP OF THE SPOOL.

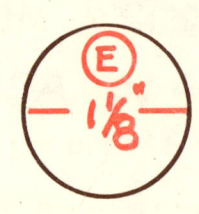

COFFEE TABLES

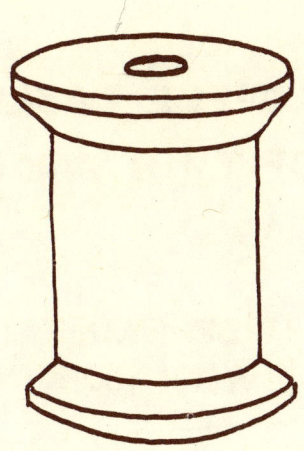

① TAKE AN EMPTY THREAD SPOOL (A LARGE ONE, ABOUT 1 5/8" H.)

② PAINT SPOOL WHATEVER COLOR WILL GO WITH YOUR ROOM.

③ GLUE ON A POCKET MIRROR TO MAKE A TOP— AND YOU HAVE A COFFEE TABLE.

— OR GLUE ON A SMALL GALLERY COASTER FOR A TOP.

AND END TABLES

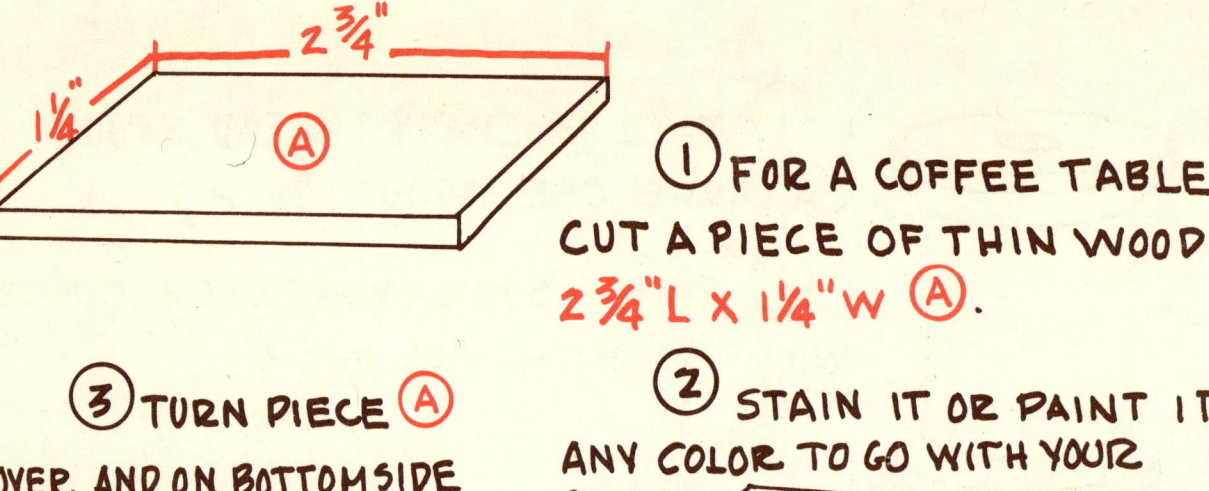

① FOR A COFFEE TABLE CUT A PIECE OF THIN WOOD 2 ¾" L X 1 ¼" W Ⓐ.

② STAIN IT OR PAINT IT ANY COLOR TO GO WITH YOUR ROOM.

③ TURN PIECE Ⓐ OVER, AND ON BOTTOM SIDE Ⓑ MARK OFF ⅜" SQUARES AND PUT A DOT IN EACH CORNER.

④ TAKE FOUR 1" FLAT TOP MACHINE SCREWS Ⓒ AND USING "EPOXY GLUE", GLUE ONE SCREW OVER EACH DOT. LEAVE TABLE UP-SIDE-DOWN UNTIL GLUE HAS SET.

⑤ TO MAKE END TABLES CUT A PIECE OF WOOD 2" L X 1 ¼" W AND REPEAT STEP ②, ③ AND ④ ABOVE.

END TABLE

COFFEE TABLE

LAMPS

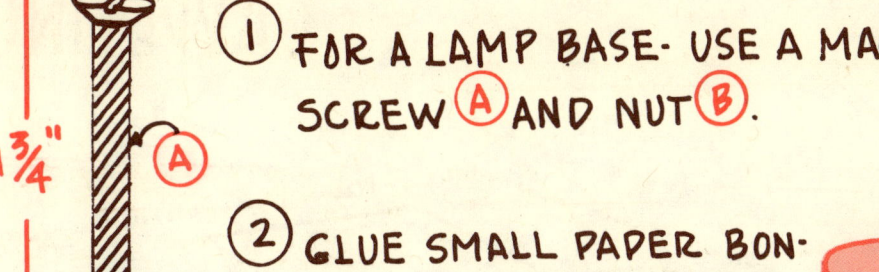

① FOR A LAMP BASE- USE A MACHINE SCREW Ⓐ AND NUT Ⓑ.

② GLUE SMALL PAPER BON-BON CUP ON TOP FOR SHADE. CUT THE "SKIRT" OF THE BON-BON CUP DOWN SO IT IS ½" HIGH.

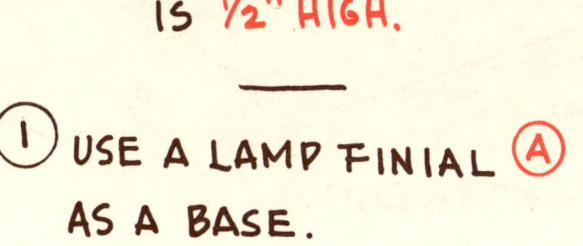

① USE A LAMP FINIAL Ⓐ AS A BASE.

② CUT A ROUND PIECE OF STYROFOAM ½" DIAMETER AND ½" THICK Ⓑ.

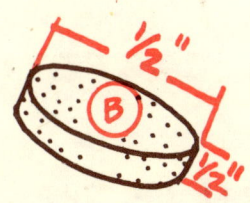

③ GENTLY FORCE THE STYROFOAM PIECE Ⓑ ONTO TOP OF THE FINIAL Ⓐ.

④ TO MAKE A LAMP SHADE CUT A PIECE OF PATTERNED PAPER ½" DIAMETER AND PASTE ON TOP OF Ⓑ. CUT ANOTHER PIECE ½" X 2" AND PASTE <u>AROUND</u> THE EDGE OF Ⓑ.

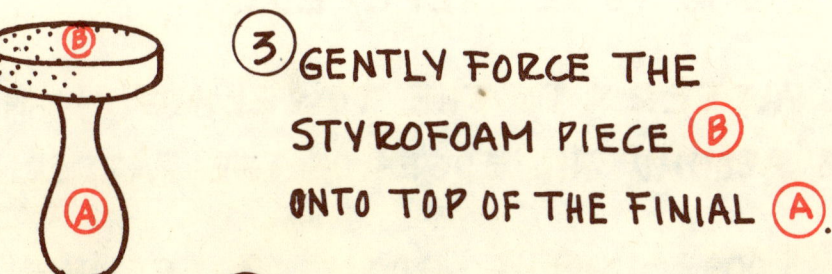

WALL TO WALL CARPETING

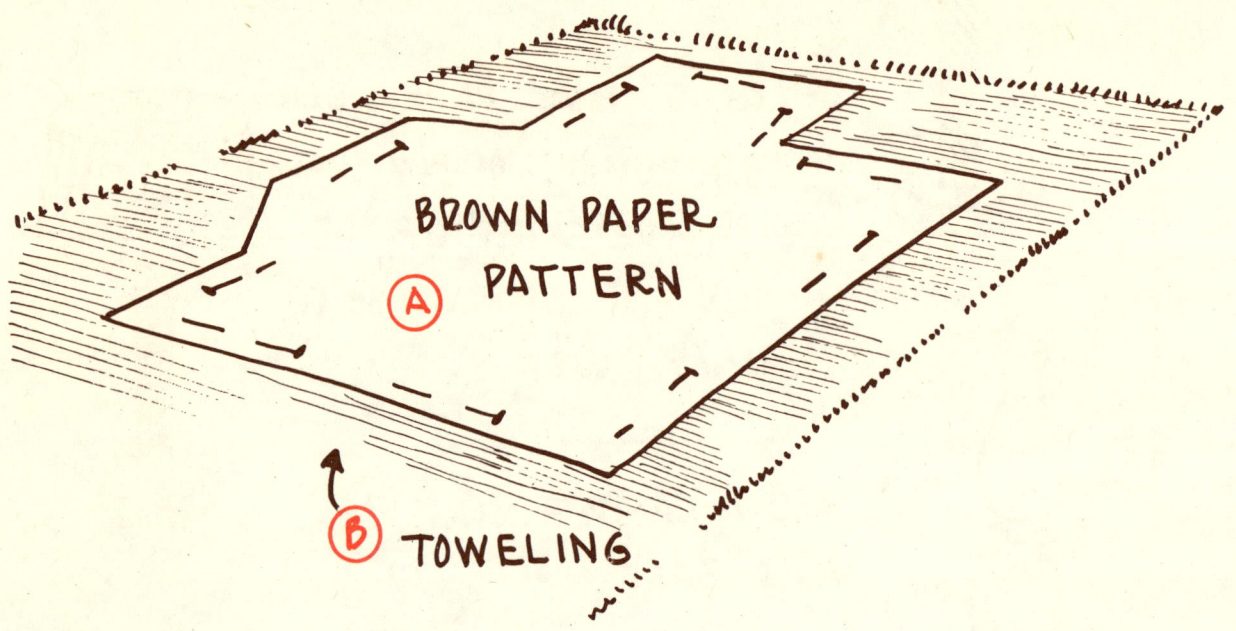

USE TOWELING FOR WALL TO WALL CARPETING.

① CUT A BROWN PAPER PATTERN OF THE FLOOR OF THE ROOMS TO BE CARPETED Ⓐ.

② PIN PATTERN TO THE TOWELING Ⓑ AND CUT TOWELING AROUND THE EDGES OF THE PATTERN.

③ LAY LOOSE IN THE ROOM OR SECURE IN PLACE WITH "DOTS" OF GLUE UNDER EACH CORNER OF THE CARPET.

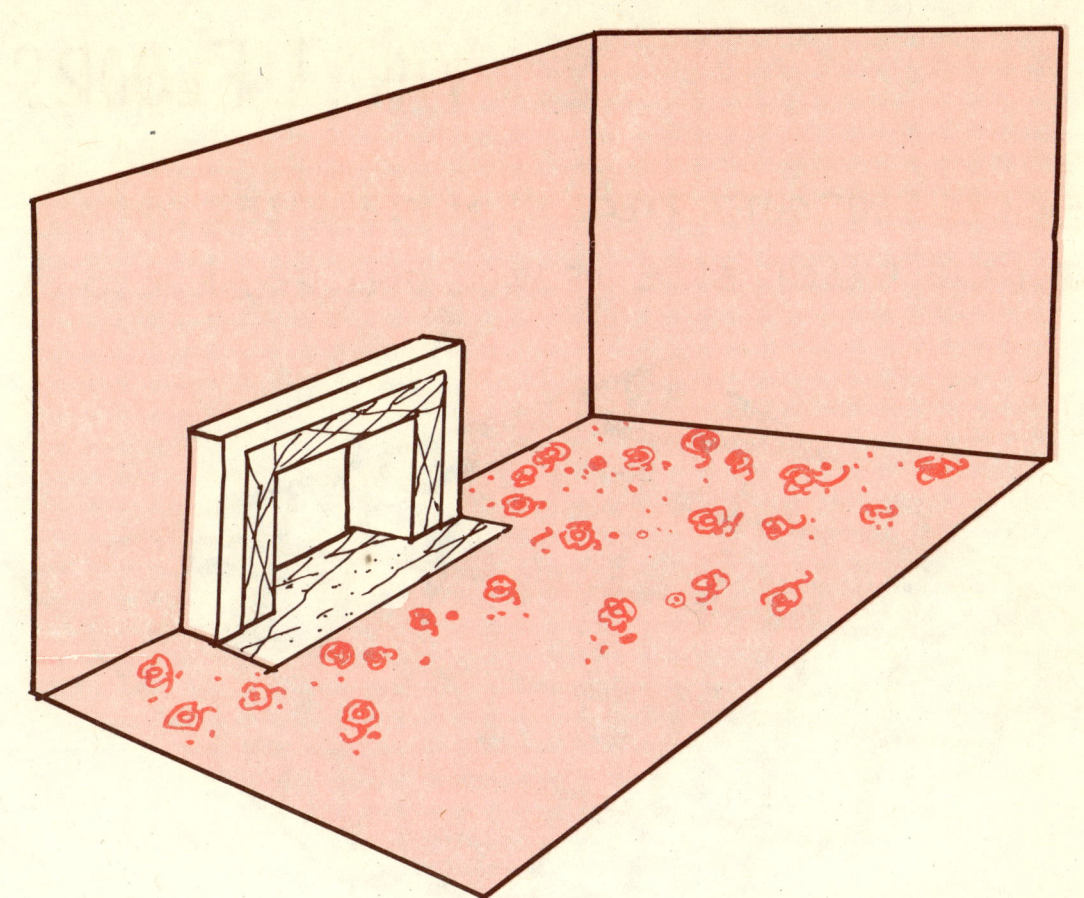

AREA RUGS

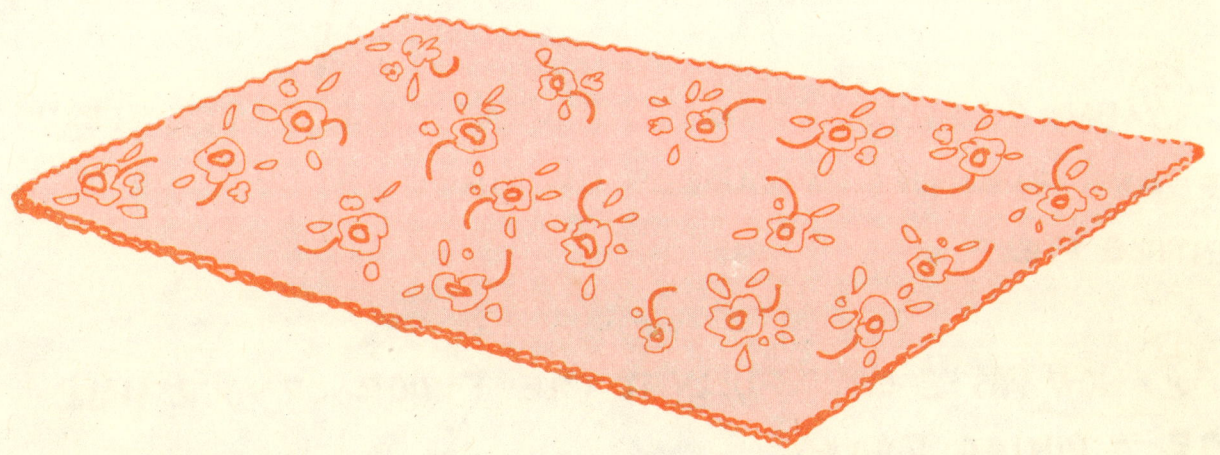

USE PRINTED WASH CLOTHES (CUT TO SIZE) FOR AREA RUGS.

VINYL FLOORS

① MEASURE & CUT OUT A PIECE OF MARBLEIZED CONTACT PAPER. (THE EXACT SIZE OF YOUR DOLL HOUSE ROOM).

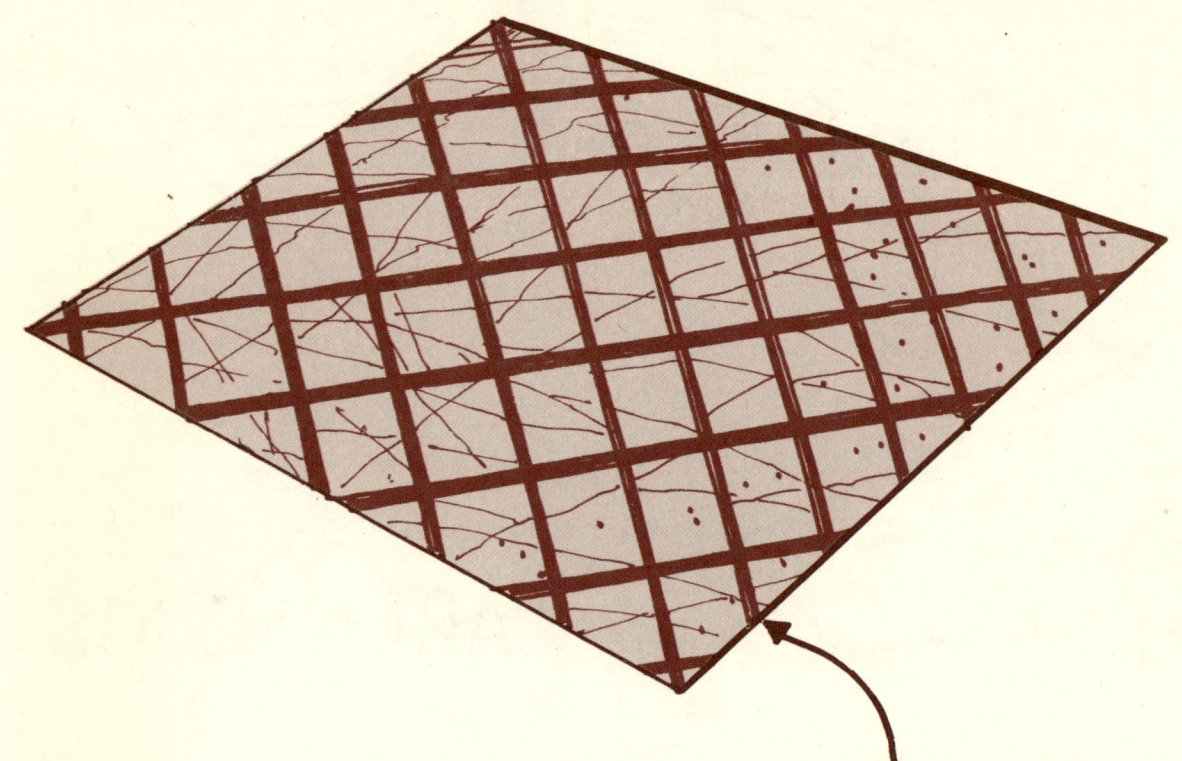

② USING <u>VERY NARROW</u> GIFT WRAP TAPE, PASTE STRIPS OF TAPE EVENLY (IN SQUARES OR DIAGONALLY) OVER THE ENTIRE PIECE.

③ NOW PASTE CAREFULLY TO THE FLOOR OF YOUR HALL OR — DINING ROOM.

DRAPERY AND CURTAINS

USE EYELET EMBROIDERY EDGING FOR CURTAINS GLUE TO TOP OF WINDOWS OR TO DRAPERY POLE (PAGE 43).

USE WIDE GIFT WRAP RIBBON FOR DRAPERIES OR CURTAINS.

CUT CORRUGATED PAPER TO LENGTH OF WINDOWS FOR DRAPERIES. GLUE RIBBON TO PAPER, PRESSING IN GROOVES FOR FOLDS.

USE UPHOLSTERY TACKS AND ELECTRIC LIGHT CHAIN TO HOLD BACK DRAPERIES.

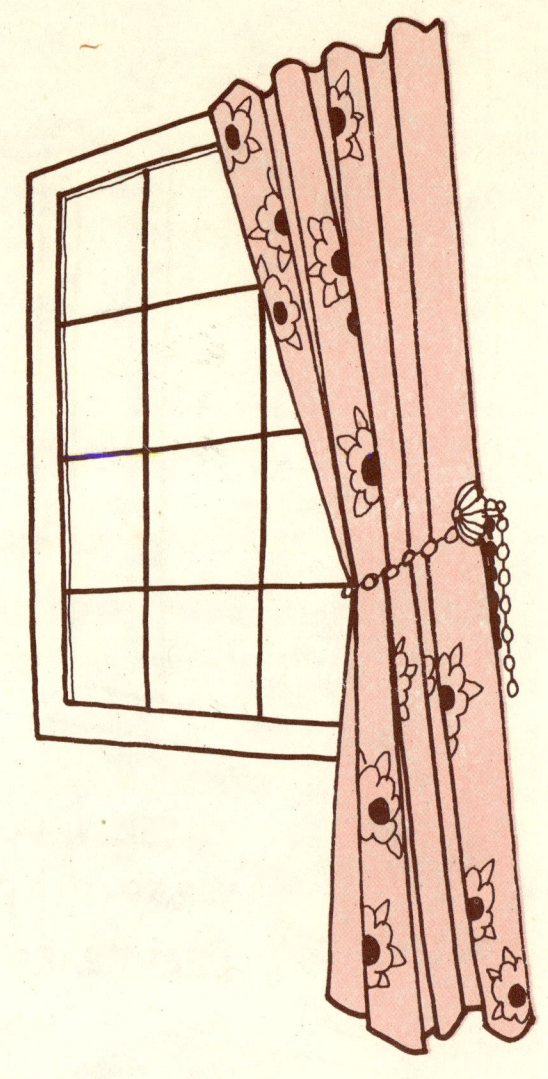

OR JUST USE UPHOLSTERY TACKS TO HOLD BACK DRAPERIES.

DRAPERY POLES

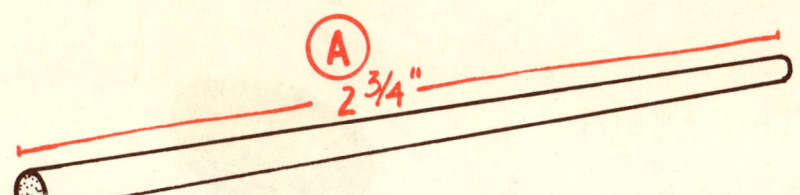

① USE LOLLIPOP STICKS Ⓐ 2¾" LONG OR CUT TO THIS SIZE.

② PAINT COLOR TO MATCH DRAPERIES OR COVER IN SAME PRINT AS "WALLPAPER" USED IN ROOM.

③ TO PUT UP DRAPERY POLES SCREW AN EYE SCREW Ⓑ ON EACH SIDE OF WINDOW (JUST ABOVE THE TOP OF THE WINDOW FRAME.)

④ SLIP THE POLE THRU BOTH SCREWS Ⓑ AND PASTE THE DRAPERIES TO THE POLE.

⑤ ADD 2 UPHOLSTERY TACKS Ⓒ FOR POLE ENDS/ OR FINIALS.

PICTURE AND FRAME

① USE A BUTTON ABOUT THE SIZE OF A NICKEL, OR A COAT BUTTON (WITH RIM) 1 1/8" SIZE.

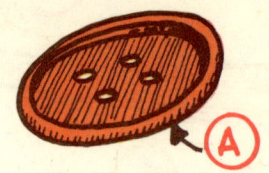

② FIND A PICTURE IN A MAGAZINE. CUT A CIRCLE TO FIT INSIDE RIM OF BUTTON.

③ PASTE PICTURE ON THE BUTTON Ⓐ, RIM WILL THEN BECOME THE FRAME OF YOUR PICTURE.

④ OR USE ALUMINUM FOIL IN PLACE OF THE PICTURE TO MAKE A MIRROR.

AND MIRRORS

① TAKE ONE OR TWO METAL DRAWER LABEL FRAMES Ⓐ.

② CUT PICTURE TO FIT FRAME (FROM A POST CARD OR MAGAZINE). Ⓑ

③ SLIP INTO FRAME AND USE AS PICTURE ABOVE MANTEL OR OVER SOFA. PIN TO WALL WITH A MAP PIN.

④ TO MAKE A MIRROR WRAP A CARD Ⓒ (TO FIT FRAME) WITH ALUMINUM FOIL Ⓓ AND SLIP INTO FRAME. USE A MAP PIN TO HANG MIRROR ON WALL OVER MANTEL, DRESSER OR SERVER.

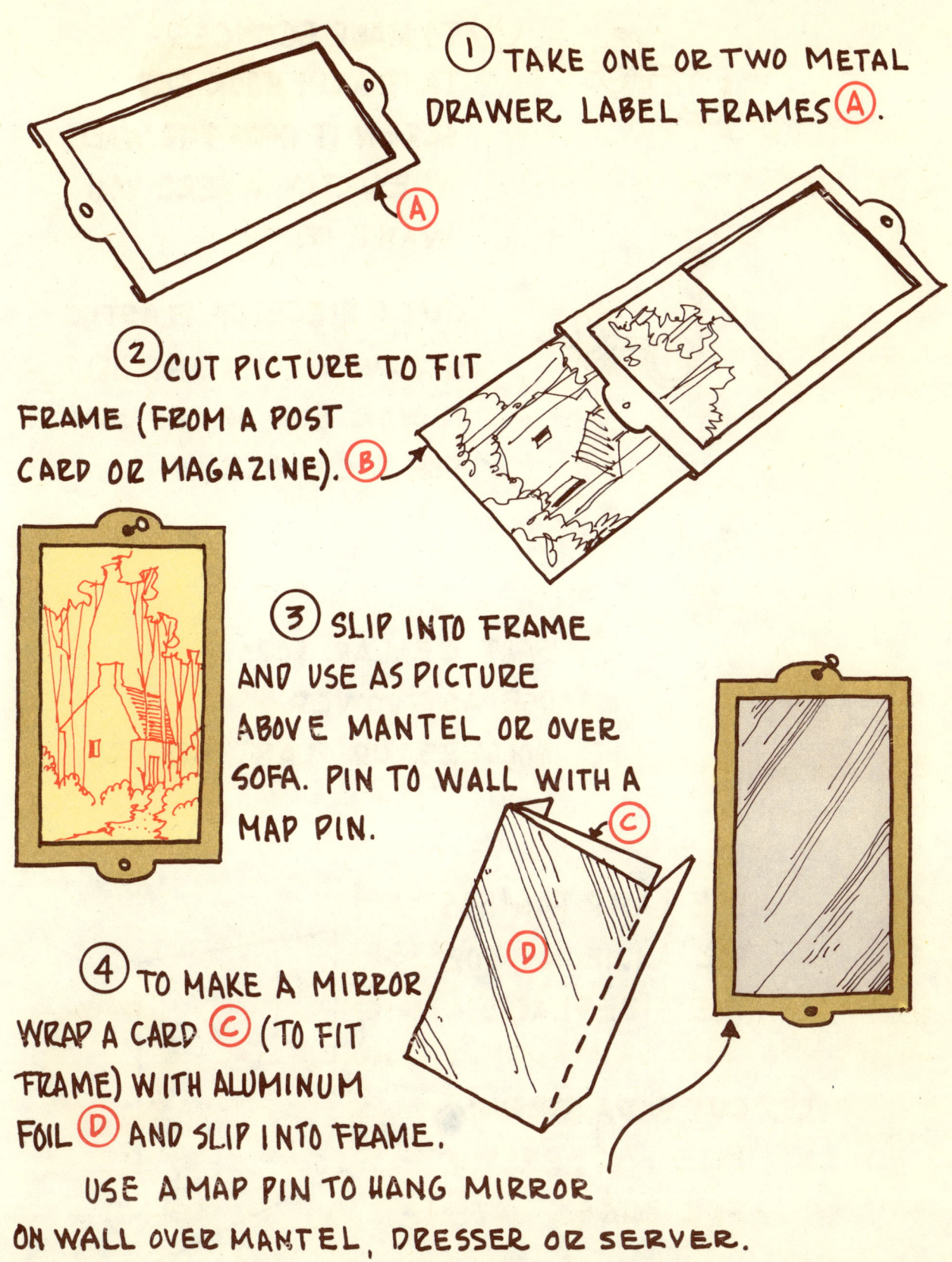

ACCESSORIES

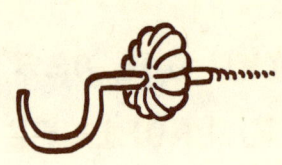

(A) TO MAKE SCONCES - TAKE A CUP HOOK AND SCREW IT INTO THE WALL AT EXACTLY WHERE YOU WANT IT.

CUT A PIECE OF PLASTIC STRAW 1" LONG AND SLIP IT OVER END OF CUP HOOK FOR A CANDLE.

(B) SALT CELLAR TOPS. USE AS FLOWER HOLDERS OR PLANT STANDS.

(C) USE LAMP FINIALS FOR ANDIRONS FOR THE FIREPLACE.

(D) CUT SODA STRAWS INTO 1½" LENGTHS FOR LOGS.

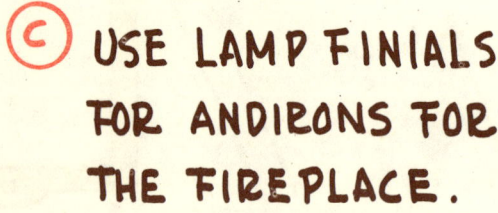

ACCESSORIES

A LIPSTICK COVER (PLASTIC OR METAL) FOR UMBRELLA HOLDER

B USE TOP OF PERFUME BOTTLE FOR:
1. WASTE BASKET
2. FLOWER CONTAINER CUT A PIECE OF STYROFOAM TO FIT CONTAINER. · STICK IN TINY STRAW FLOWERS.

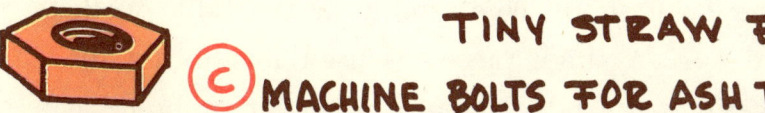

C MACHINE BOLTS FOR ASH TRAYS.

D USE DIFFERENT SIZES AND SHAPES PAINT DIFFERENT COLORS.

E USE CAP FROM PLASTIC TOOTHBRUSH HOLDER FOR FLOWER CONTAINER

F USE THIMBLE FOR:
1. WASTE BASKET
2. FLOWER CONTAINER

The Dining Room

EVERYTHING IN A dining room, that is all the furniture, is there for a purpose and always for a definite use. The table is where your dolls will eat; the chairs are what they will sit on comfortably at the table while they eat; and the cupboard (or any high piece) is used for storing the dishes, the glasses and sometimes the table linen. The server or buffet is used for serving (that's where it gets its name), and it usually has long shallow drawers for table silver storage as well.

In other words, the dining room is the one room in the house where every piece is used for dining. As a result many dining rooms look alike. And this can be a challenge, once you have decided what pieces you need—"How can you make *your* dining room look different?"

One way to accomplish this is to overcome the "woody" look in a dining room. All the pieces listed above are usually made of wood so what the room needs is fabric and lots of it. Fabric in this case can mean color, pattern, and texture—or it can mean cloth, wallpaper, marble, slate, floor tiles, carpet, rugs and so on.

Material such as chintz, plaids, checks, stripes, cotton velvets and even leather or vinyl are ideal for chair seats. Many of these can be repeated at the windows as draperies, shades, or as upholstered shutters. For the walls use any well-scaled (not too large patterned) wallpaper or use fabric or wallpaper to match the curtains, which is of course an excellent way to bring color and pattern into the room. A screen is a practical addition to a dining room (since it conceals the door to the kitchen), and always adds a very elegant touch. The screen can be made of scenic wallpaper, or be upholstered in vinyl and trimmed with nailheads, or upholstered in a fabric and trimmed with braid. A handsome piece of embroidery could be wonderful for a screen too. Or try marbleized paper cut out in sections and mounted on a plain screen like the one on page 70.

Another way to defeat the "woody" look is to add a fireplace to your dining room. At once, this gives you a setting for a pair of wing chairs or for a pair of small upholstered settees on either side of the hearth. Similarly, a bay window in the room can do the same and become the background for a comfortable upholstered seating group. Or if you prefer, place a covered table and two upholstered side chairs in the bay and you have a charming place for dinner for two, or for a small tea party.

Still another way to make your dining room "different" is to make the entire room do double work. In other words make it "a double purpose room" with part of it used for dining and the rest of it used for a living room or a family room. This is the kind of a dining room I like best—it is the kind I have.

Let me tell you about my dining room. In one corner I placed a small round table (the kind that opens out) with four armchairs at the table. On one wall is a very comfortable sofa with a small table with a lamp on it at one end and a lamp on a very long table on the other end. This long table becomes a server when we need it. In front of the sofa is a large coffee table. The wall at right angles to this grouping is a wall that is all book shelves. In front of it I placed two comfortable arm chairs with a little table between them. On the opposite wall is a fireplace with a large

This is the plan of my dining room

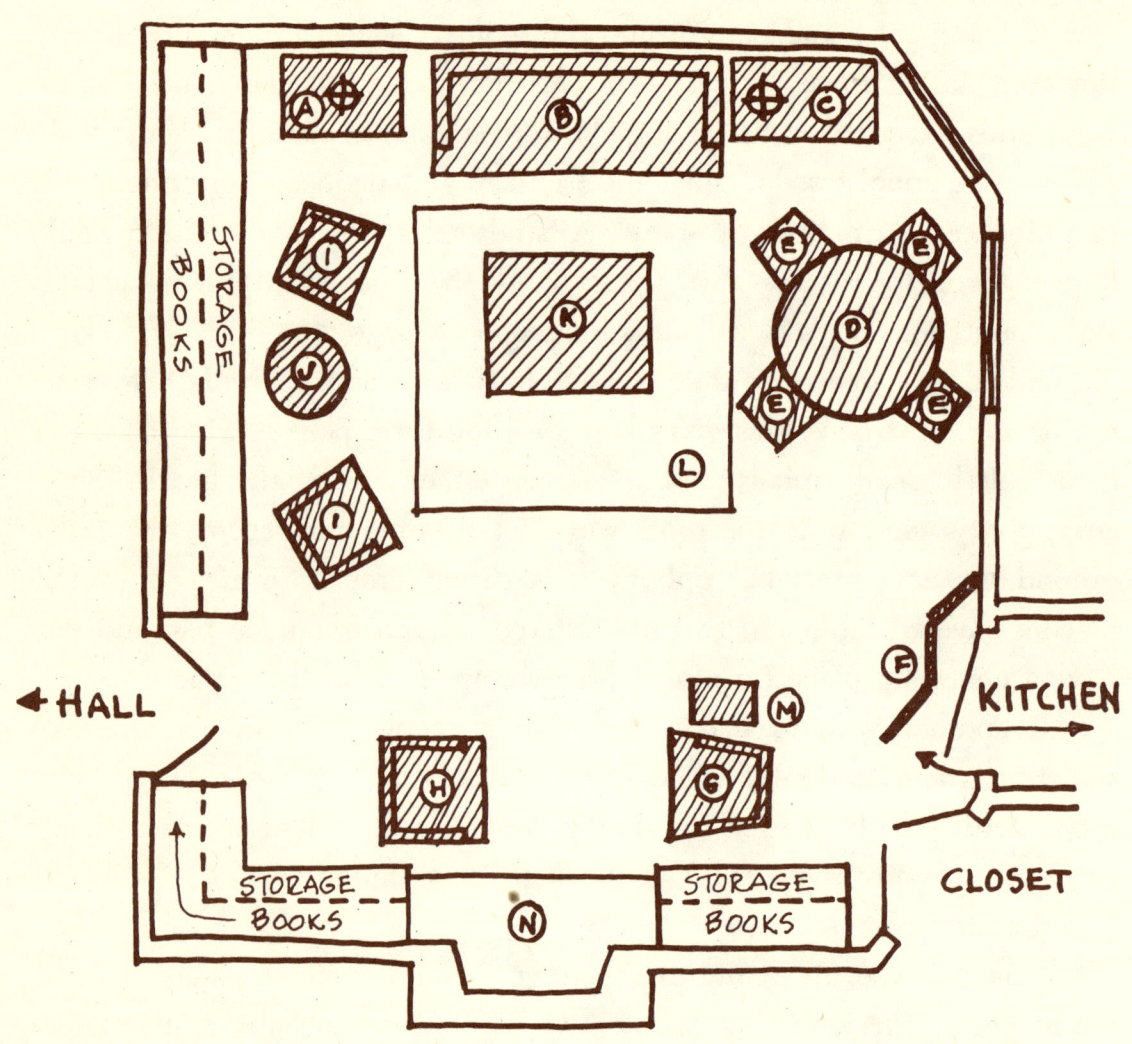

```
    A—TABLE           E—DINING CHAIRS      I—PAIR OF BERGERES
    B—SOFA            F—MIRROR SCREEN      J—DRUM TABLE
    C—LONG TABLE      G—WING CHAIR         K—COFFEE TABLE
    D—DINING TABLE    H—CLUB CHAIR         L—AREA RUG
              M—SMALL TABLE      N—FIREPLACE
```

wing chair on one side and a club chair on the other. The walls on each side of the fireplace are full of book shelves too. They were built above cabinets that hold all the linens and silver we need for our dining room. In the corner, opposite the dining table, I built a closet and arranged the interior so that the upper section would take care of all the dishes and glasses that I needed and the lower section would take our TV and Hi-Fi. After dinner the dining table is often used for games or cards. We live in our dining room. It is such a warm livable room. Why don't you try it, or one like it?

If of course you still like dining rooms just left as dining rooms, then there is another sure way of making yours look different. Try using some pieces that are not typically dining room pieces. One idea you might try is using a dresser instead of a server. The dresser could have been one that you had previously used in a bedroom or living room. You will find that it will now work very well in the dining room—since the drawers are excellent for linens and the top surface will do everything a server will do. Instead of a mirror, hang a painting above it and place a pair of wall lights (they are called "sconces") on either side of the picture. Or for a less formal look you could use a hanging wall shelf over the dresser and display some pretty dishes on the shelves. In place of the usual cupboard use a bookcase or a breakfront. If you need the book shelves for storage of dishes and glasses then stretch shirred curtains on the inside of the glass or grille doors and this way hide the mess from the rest of the room.

For the floors a colorful rug is always best, and the most practical thing, because a rug can be turned around. You don't always have to leave it in one place on the floor, as you do wall to wall carpet. This way you prevent the wear from hitting the same spot over and over. Also a heavily patterned rug will not show stains and is much easier to care for. Today of course vinyl floors are very pretty and by far the easiest to keep clean. You can get them in many styles: marble, slate, brick, French tiles or even pegged wood planks, and they come in ever so many colors. (For real vinyl you can substitute contact paper in your doll house.) Wouldn't you love to have your dining room floor in brick or slate? That would certainly be different.

BUFFET

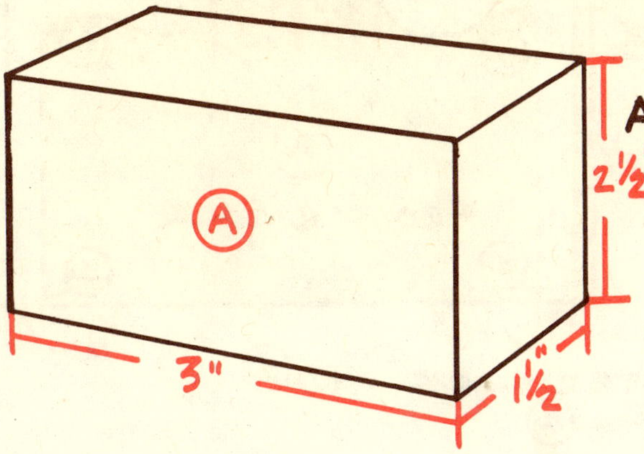

① USE A BOX (OR BOX TOP) ABOUT 3"L × 1½"W × 2½"H Ⓐ.

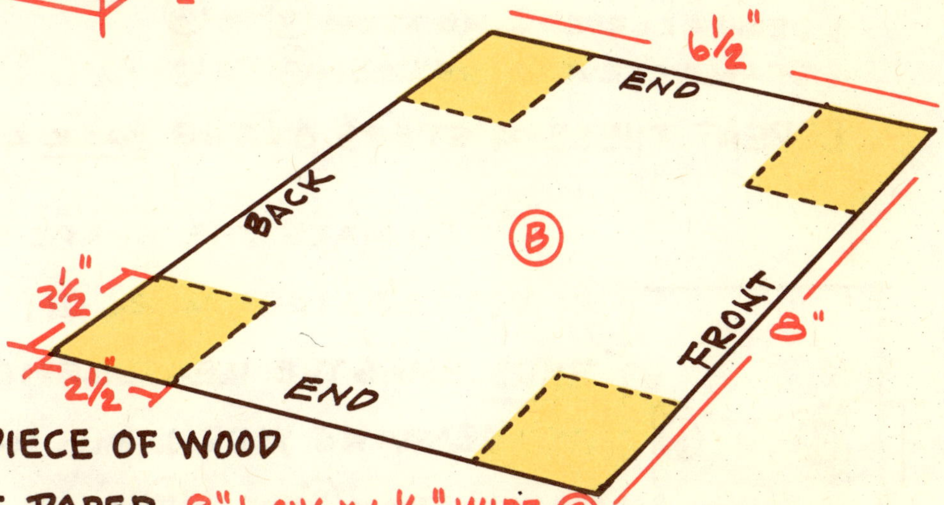

② CUT A PIECE OF WOOD GRAIN CONTACT PAPER 8" LONG × 6½" WIDE Ⓑ. CUT FROM EACH CORNER A 2½" × 2½" SQUARE.

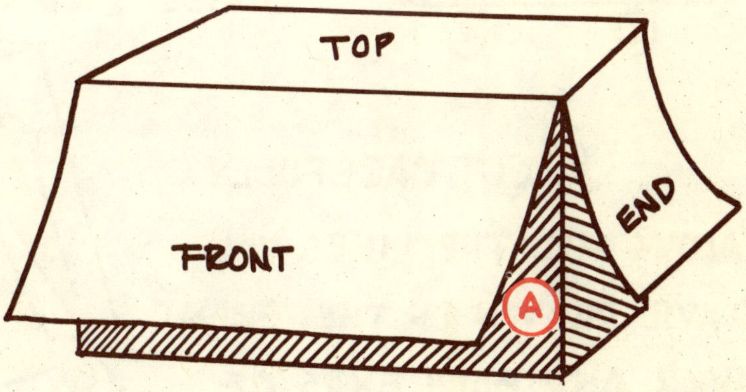

③ PASTE CONTACT PAPER TO TOP AND TO ALL 4 SIDES: FRONT, BACK AND BOTH ENDS.

④ TO MAKE THE SHAPE SHOWN HERE IN DOTTED LINES MARK OFF PIECE Ⓐ FRONT AND BACK USING THE MEASUREMENTS IN THE SKETCH AND DRAWING YOUR LINES IN THIS ORDER:—

1. FROM ⓐ UP TO ⓑ FRONT
2. FROM ⓓ ACROSS (THRU THE CENTER MARK ⓒ TO ⓓ
3. DRAW A CURVED LINE FROM ⓑ TO ⓓ
4. DRAW A CURVED LINE FROM ⓓ TO ⓑ

REPEAT THESE 4 STEPS ON THE BACK OF PIECE Ⓐ.

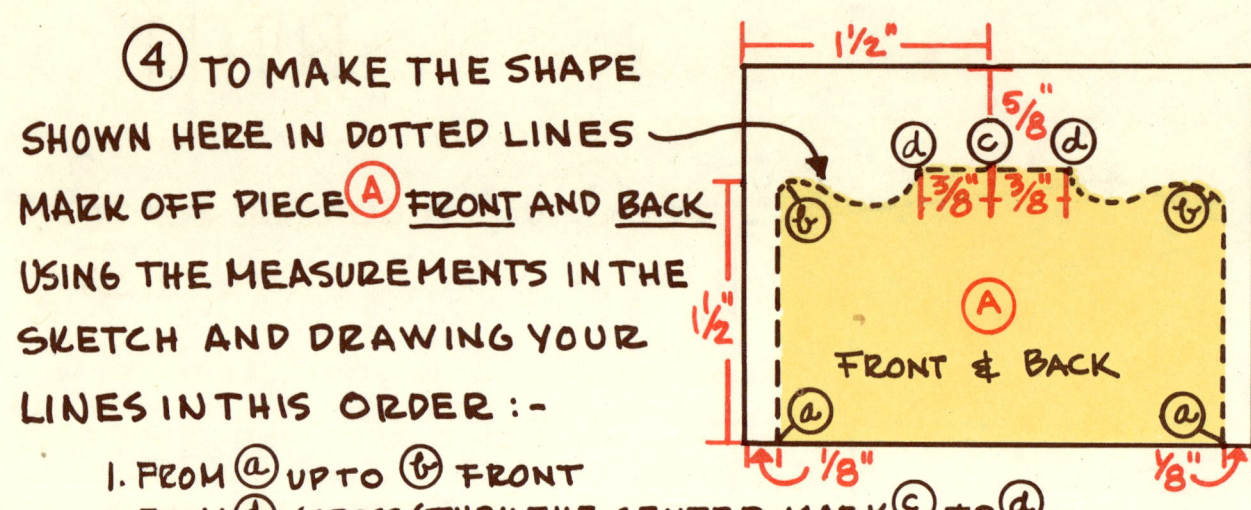

⑤ TO MAKE THE SHAPE SHOWN HERE IN DOTTED LINES, MARK OFF PIECE Ⓐ BOTH ENDS USING THE MEASUREMENTS IN THE SKETCH AND DRAWING YOUR LINES IN THIS ORDER:—

1. FROM ⓔ UP TO ⓑ
2. DRAW A CURVED LINE FROM ⓑ TO ⓑ

REPEAT THESE 2 STEPS ON THE OTHER END OF PIECE Ⓐ.

⑥ CUT CAREFULLY ALONG ALL THE LINES YOU HAVE DRAWN IN THE FRONT, BACK AND BOTH ENDS OF PIECE Ⓐ.

⑦ TO MAKE THE "DRAWERS" CUT 3 PIECES OF CARDBOARD EACH ¾" LONG × ⅜" WIDE Ⓑ.

 ⑧ PASTE THE SAME CONTACT PAPER ON EACH OF THE 3 PIECES.

⑨ THEN GLUE EACH ONE TO THE FRONT OF THE BUFFET AS SHOWN PUSH 2 WHITE MAP PINS THROUGH EACH DRAWER FOR DRAWER-PULLS.

DINING TABLE

① TAKE A GIFT BOX Ⓐ ABOUT 2½"W × 4½"L × 1¾"H OR CUT IT DOWN TO 1¾"H

② CUT A PIECE OF WOOD CONTACT PAPER 6"W × 8"L Ⓑ. CUT OUT 1¾" × 1¾" SQUARES AT EACH CORNER.

③ PASTE CONTACT PAPER Ⓑ ON TOP AND ALL 4 SIDES OF BOX Ⓐ

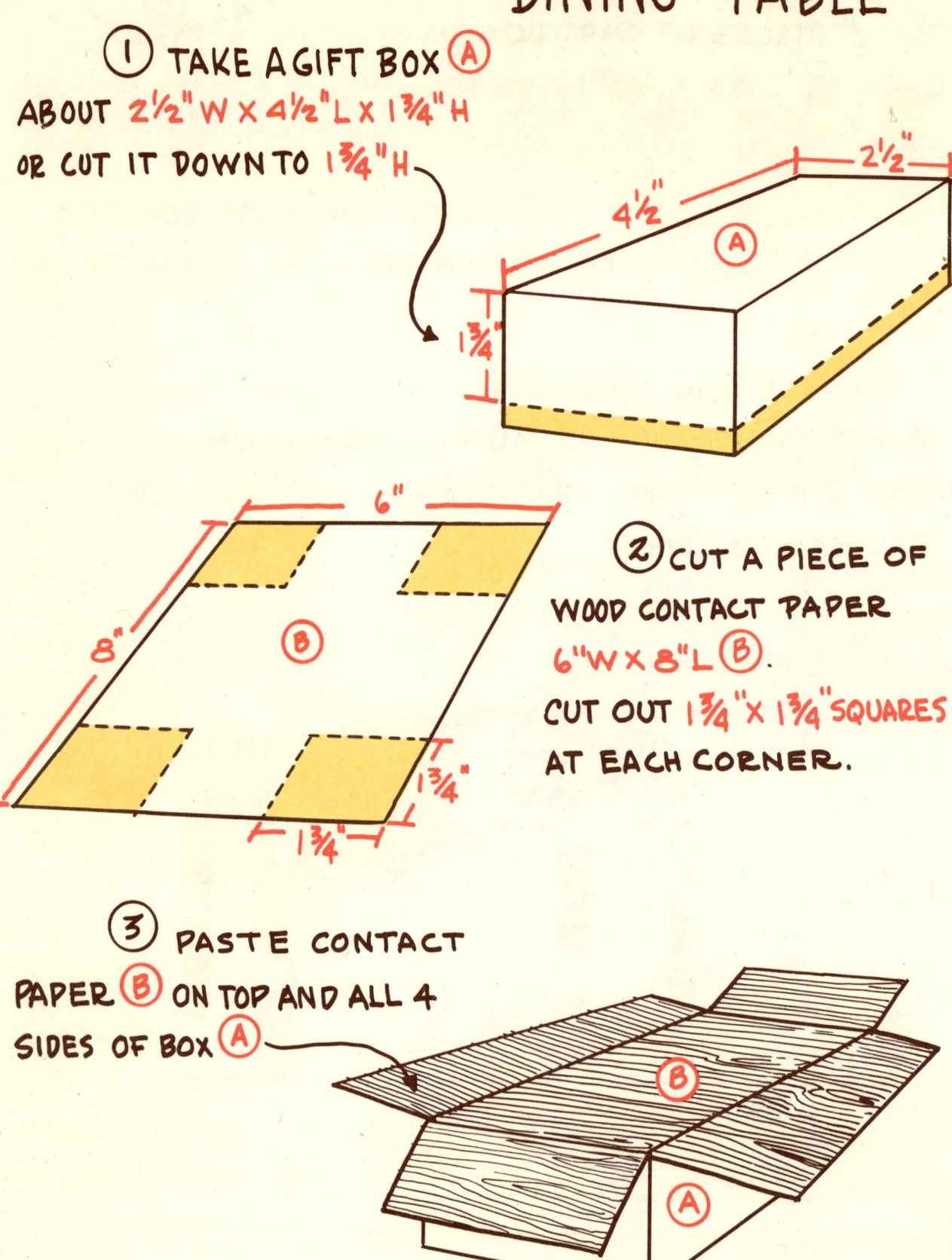

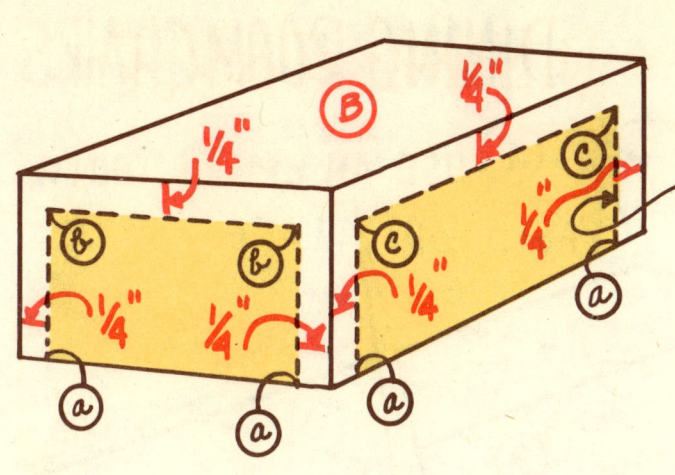

④ TO MAKE SHAPE SHOWN HERE IN DOTTED LINES, MARK OFF BOX Ⓑ USING MEASUREMENTS IN THE SKETCH AND DRAWING YOUR LINES IN THIS ORDER

1. FROM ⓐ TO ⓑ (BOTH ENDS)
2. FROM ⓑ ACROSS TO ⓑ (BOTH ENDS)
3. FROM ⓐ TO ⓒ (FRONT & BACK)
4. FROM ⓒ TO ⓒ (FRONT & BACK)

⑤ NOW CUT ALONG THE LINES YOU HAVE DRAWN AND YOU WILL HAVE A DINING TABLE THAT WILL SEAT 6.

57

DINING ROOM CHAIRS

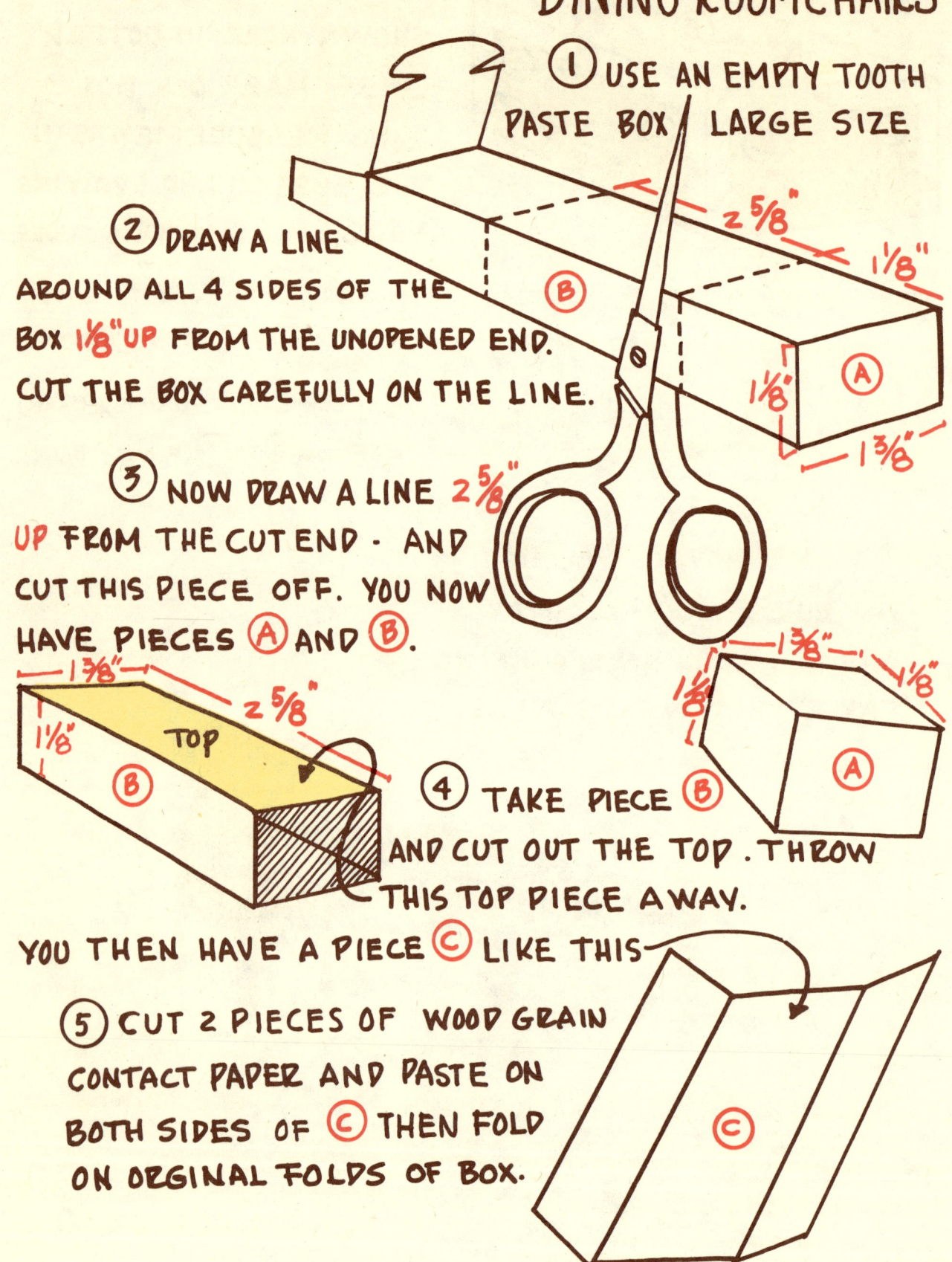

① USE AN EMPTY TOOTH PASTE BOX — LARGE SIZE

② DRAW A LINE AROUND ALL 4 SIDES OF THE BOX 1⅛" UP FROM THE UNOPENED END. CUT THE BOX CAREFULLY ON THE LINE.

③ NOW DRAW A LINE 2⅝" UP FROM THE CUT END - AND CUT THIS PIECE OFF. YOU NOW HAVE PIECES Ⓐ AND Ⓑ.

④ TAKE PIECE Ⓑ AND CUT OUT THE TOP. THROW THIS TOP PIECE AWAY. YOU THEN HAVE A PIECE Ⓒ LIKE THIS

⑤ CUT 2 PIECES OF WOOD GRAIN CONTACT PAPER AND PASTE ON BOTH SIDES OF Ⓒ THEN FOLD ON ORGINAL FOLDS OF BOX.

⑥ TO MAKE THE SHAPE SHOWN HERE IN DOTTED LINES. MARK OFF PIECE Ⓒ USING THE MEASUREMENTS IN THE SKETCH AND DRAWING YOUR LINES IN THIS ORDER:-
  1. FROM Ⓒ UP TO ⓐ (BOTH)
  2. FROM ⓐ ACROSS TO ⓐ
  3. FROM ⓐ TO ⓑ (BOTH)
  4. DRAW A <u>CURVED</u> LINE FROM ⓑ TO ⓔ CONTINUE THE <u>CURVED</u> LINE FROM ⓔ TO ⓑ. TRY TO MAKE BOTH CURVED LINES LIKE THOSE IN THE SKETCH.

NOW CUT THE SHAPE ALONG THE LINES YOU HAVE DRAWN.

⑦ FOLD "WINGS" AND "LEGS" ON THE ORIGINAL FOLDS OF THE BOX.

⑧ CUT A PIECE OF WOOD GRAIN CONTACT PAPER 3⅝" X 3⅜" AND CUT OUT 1⅛" SQUARES FROM EACH CORNER.

⑨ TAKE PIECE Ⓐ AND PASTE CUT OUT CONTACT PAPER ON BOTTOM AND ON ALL 4 SIDES.

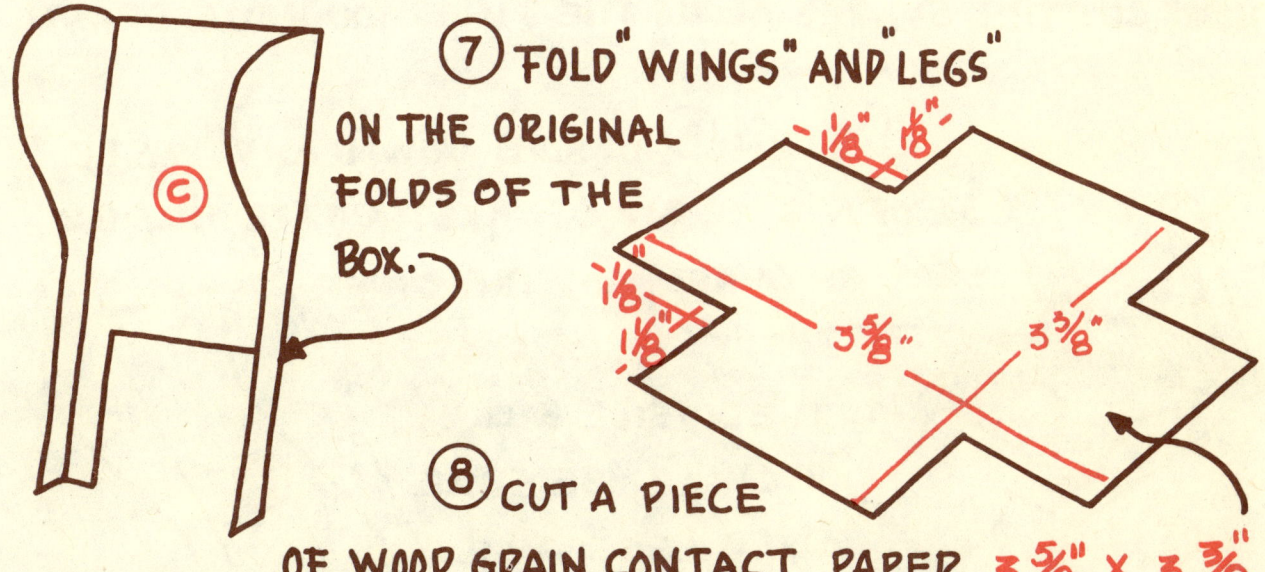

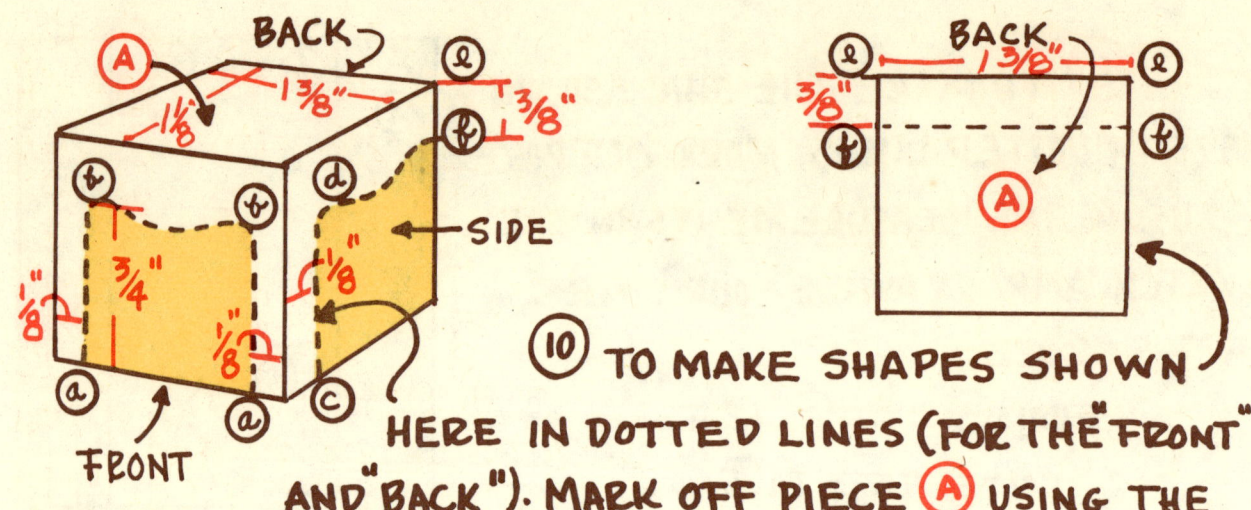

⑩ TO MAKE SHAPES SHOWN HERE IN DOTTED LINES (FOR THE "FRONT" AND "BACK"). MARK OFF PIECE Ⓐ USING THE MEASUREMENTS IN THE SKETCH, AND DRAWING YOUR LINES IN THIS ORDER

1. FROM ⓐ UP TO ⓑ (ON FRONT)
2. FROM ⓒ UP TO ⓓ (ON SIDES)
3. DRAW A <u>CURVED</u> LINE FROM ⓑ TO ⓑ (ON FRONT)
4. DRAW A <u>CURVED</u> LINE FROM ⓓ TO ⓑ (ON SIDES)
5. DRAW A <u>STRAIGHT</u> LINE FROM ⓑ TO ⓑ (ON BACK)

NOW CUT THE SHAPES ALONG THE LINES YOU HAVE DRAWN.

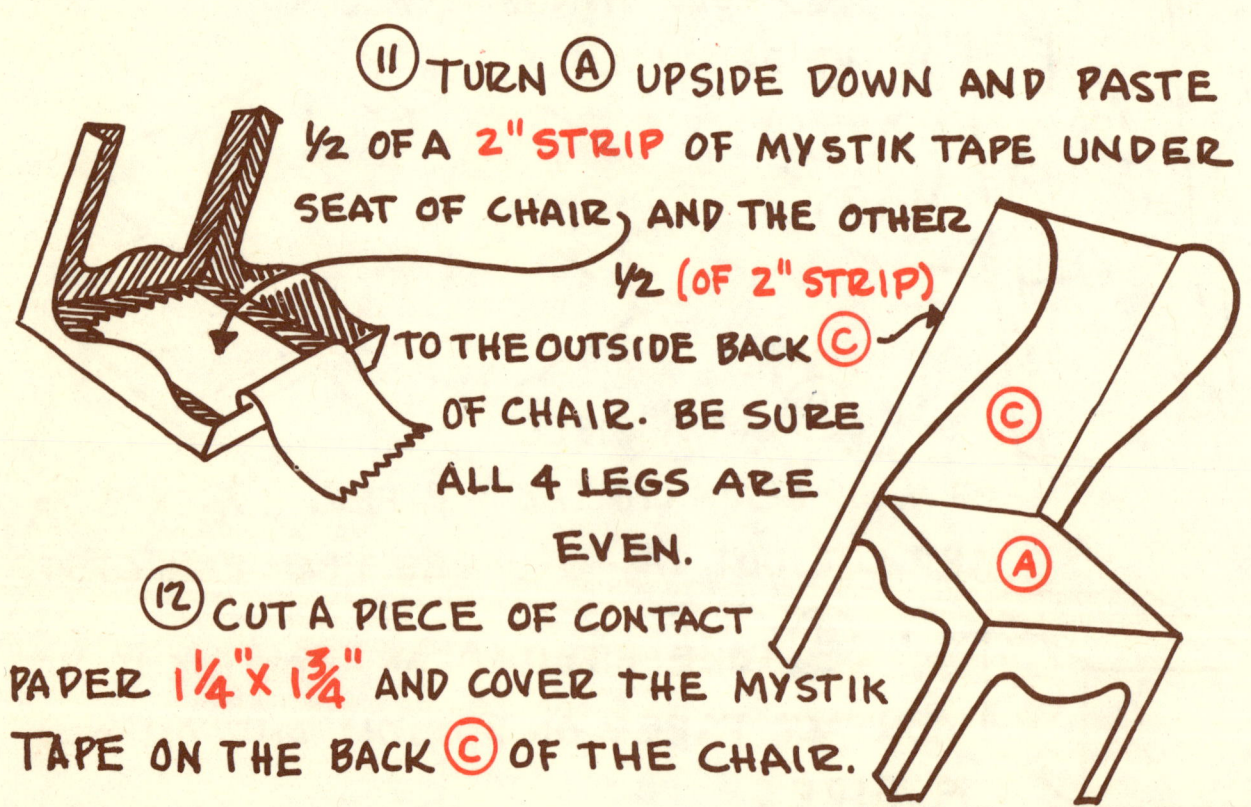

⑪ TURN Ⓐ UPSIDE DOWN AND PASTE ½ OF A 2" STRIP OF MYSTIK TAPE UNDER SEAT OF CHAIR, AND THE OTHER ½ (OF 2" STRIP) TO THE OUTSIDE BACK Ⓒ OF CHAIR. BE SURE ALL 4 LEGS ARE EVEN.

⑫ CUT A PIECE OF CONTACT PAPER 1¼" X 1¾" AND COVER THE MYSTIK TAPE ON THE BACK Ⓒ OF THE CHAIR.

(13) PASTE ½ OF ANOTHER 2" STRIP OF TAPE ON TOP OF THE SEAT Ⓐ AND ½ ON THE INSIDE OF THE BACK Ⓒ OF THE CHAIR.

(14) CUT A PIECE OF PRINT CONTACT PAPER 1¼" WIDE AND 3" LONG. PASTE THIS PIECE ON THE TOP OF THE SEAT Ⓐ AND UP THE INSIDE BACK Ⓒ OF THE CHAIR

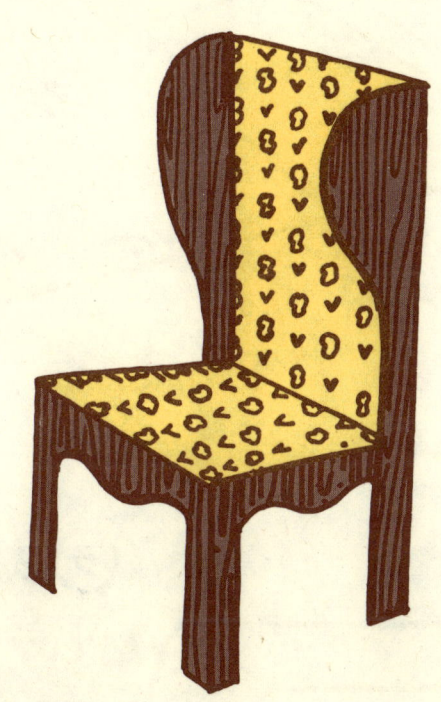

SERVER

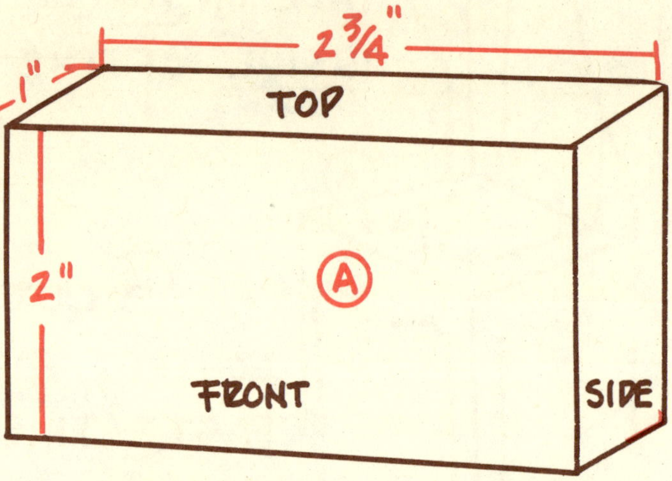

① TO MAKE A "SERVER" TAKE A BOX Ⓐ ABOUT 2¾ L × 1" W × 2" H. (YOU WON'T NEED THE BOX COVER).

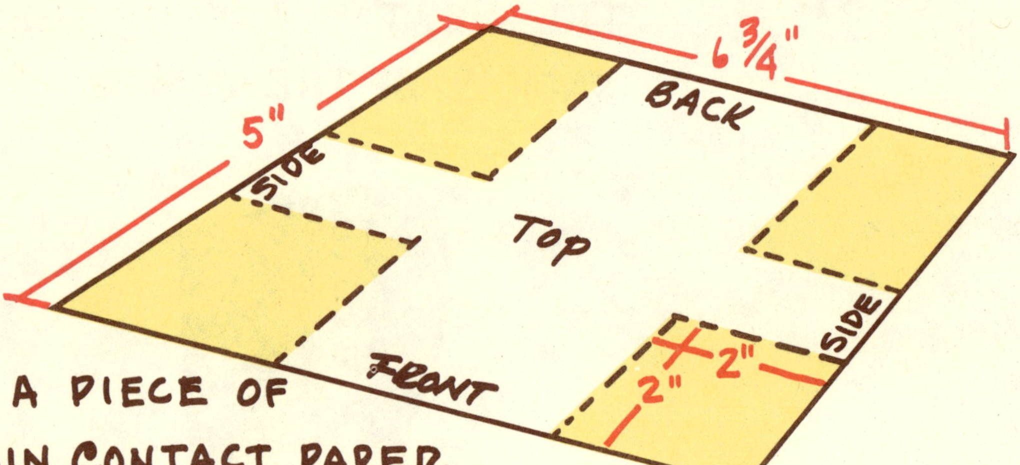

② CUT A PIECE OF WOOD GRAIN CONTACT PAPER 6¾" × 5" — CUT OUT 2" × 2" SQUARES FROM EACH CORNER.

③ PASTE CONTACT PAPER AS CUT OUT — WITH TOP TO TOP OF BOX. FRONT TO FRONT OF BOX. SIDES TO EACH SIDE AND BACK TO BACK OF BOX.

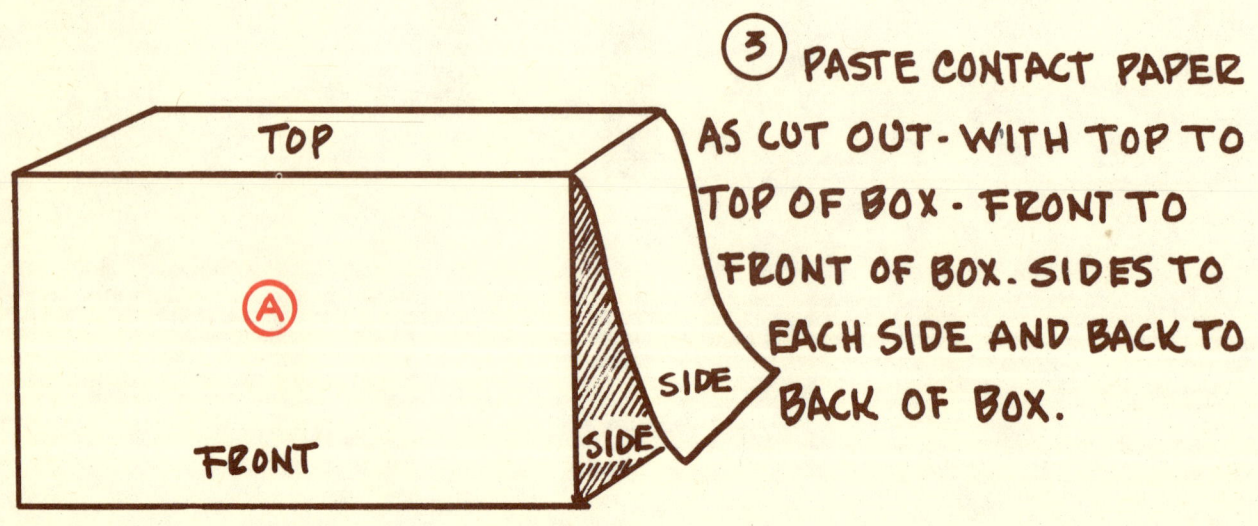

④ TO MAKE SHAPE SHOWN HERE IN DOTTED LINES - MARK OFF PIECE Ⓐ USING MEASUREMENTS IN THE SKETCH AND DRAWING YOUR LINES IN THIS ORDER :-

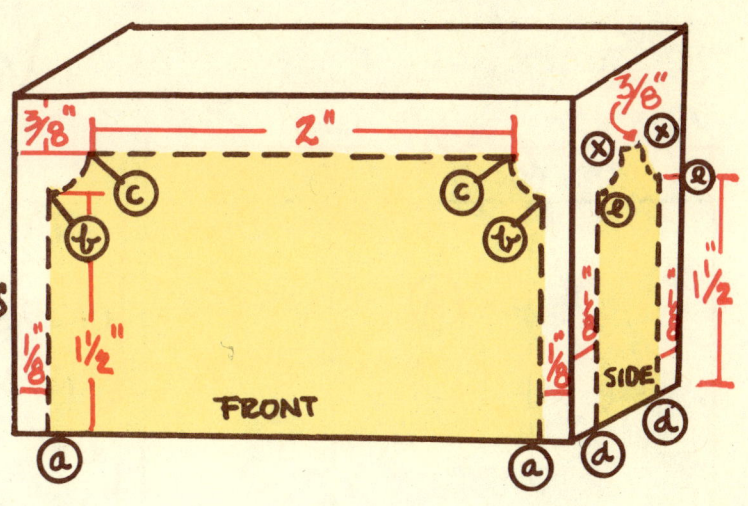

1. FROM ⓐ UP TO ⓑ (BOTH)
2. FROM Ⓒ ACROSS TO Ⓒ
3. DRAW A CURVED LINE FROM ⓑ TO Ⓒ BOTH.

REPEAT THE SAME 3 STEPS ON THE BACK.

4. FROM ⓓ UP TO ⓔ (BOTH)
5. FROM Ⓧ ACROSS TO Ⓧ
6. DRAW A CURVED LINE FROM ⓔ TO Ⓧ (BOTH).

REPEAT THE SAME 3 STEPS (4 THRU 6) ON THE OTHER SIDE.

NOW CUT THE SHAPE ALONG THE LINES YOU HAVE DRAWN.

⑤ WITH A FLOW PEN MARK OFF "DRAWERS" AS SHOWN IN THE SKETCH. ADD 2 MAP PINS FOR "HANDLES" OF EACH DRAWER

WING CHAIR

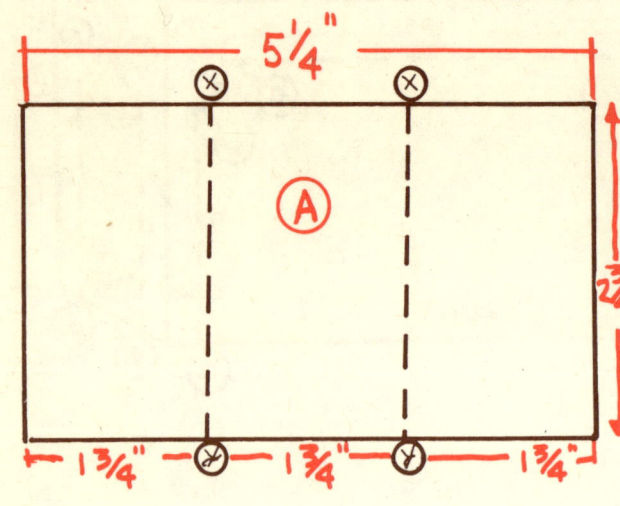

① CUT A PIECE OF CARDBOARD Ⓐ 5¼" L × 2¾" W AND WITH A RULER MARK OFF THREE EQUAL 1¾" SECTIONS AS SHOWN IN DOTTED LINES. FROM ⓧ TO ⓨ

② TO MAKE THE "WINGS AND ARMS" OF THE CHAIR. MARK OFF PIECE Ⓐ, USING THE MEASUREMENTS IN THE SKETCH AND DRAWING THE LINES IN THIS ORDER:

FROM ⓑ ACROSS TO ⓒ
FROM ⓒ A CURVED LINE TO ⓓ

REPEAT ON THE LAST SECTION

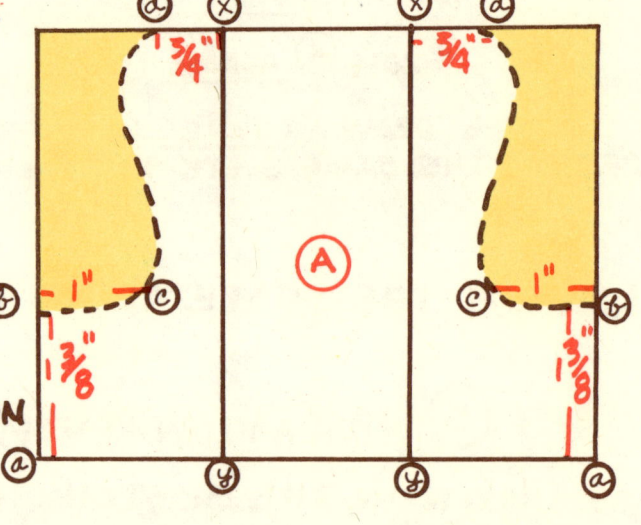

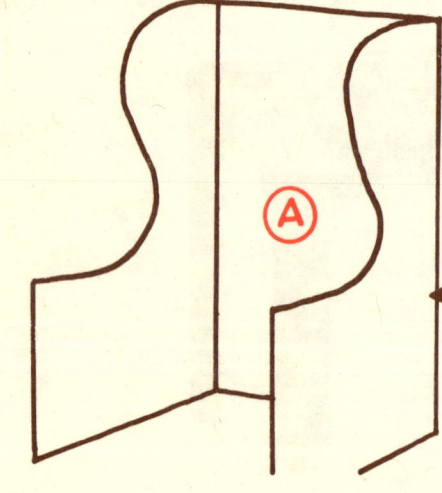

③ CUT OUT (BOTH SIDES) ALONG DOTTED LINES FROM ⓑ TO ⓒ AND FROM ⓒ TO ⓓ. NOW FOLD IN BOTH SIDES ALONG ⓧ TO ⓨ LINES.

④ CUT 2 PIECES OF FABRIC OR WOODGRAIN CONTACT PAPER EACH 5¼" L X 2¾" W.

USING ③ AS A PATTERN, CUT BOTH PIECES OF FABRIC (OR PAPER) INTO THE SAME SHAPE.

NOW PASTE ONE PIECE OF THE FABRIC (OR PAPER) ON THE INSIDE OF Ⓐ AND THE OTHER PIECE ON THE OUTSIDE

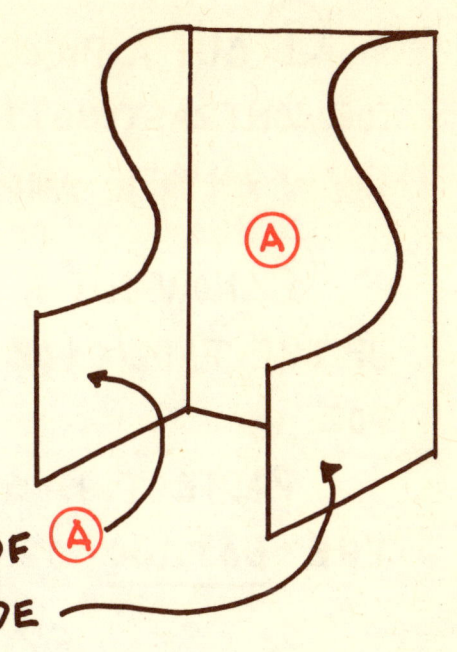

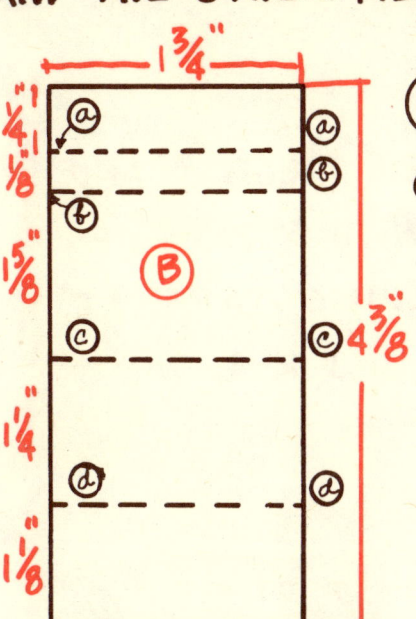

⑤ NOW CUT ANOTHER PIECE OF CARDBOARD Ⓑ 1¾" W × 4⅜" L. AND USING THE MEASUREMENTS SHOWN DRAW YOUR LINES :—

FROM ⓐ TO ⓐ
FROM ⓑ TO ⓑ
FROM ⓒ TO ⓒ
FROM ⓓ TO ⓓ

⑥ NOW FOLD ALONG THE LINES YOU HAVE DRAWN AND PIECE Ⓑ WILL HAVE A SHAPE LIKE THIS.

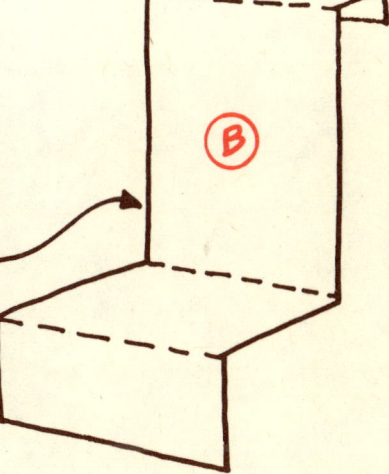

⑦ CUT A PIECE OF PRINTED (OR CONTRASTING) FABRIC OR PAPER 1¾"W x 4⅜"L AND PASTE ON Ⓑ.

⑧ NOW CUT A STRIP ⅝"W x 1¾"L OF THE FABRIC (OR PAPER) YOU USED FOR Ⓐ

PASTE THIS STRIP ALONG THE BOTTOM OF Ⓑ

⑨ FASTEN PIECE Ⓐ AND Ⓑ TOGETHER WITH STRIPS OF CLEAR MENDING TAPE AT POINTS: H, I, J, K, L, M.

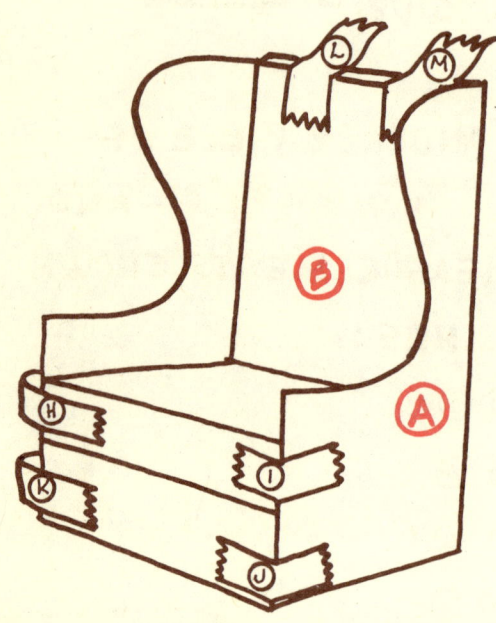

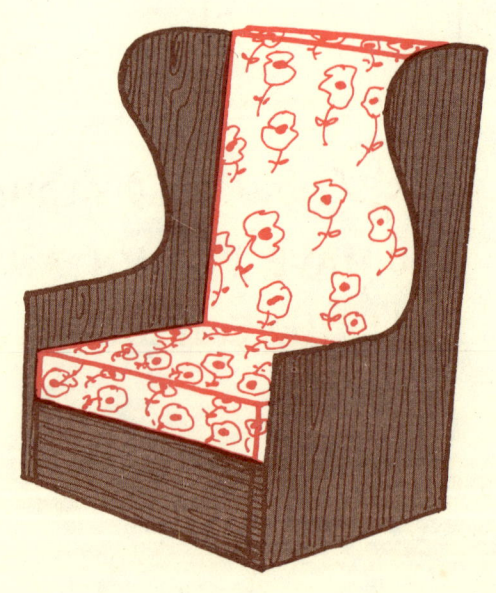

COVERED TABLE

① USE AN EMPTY THREAD SPOOL Ⓐ ABOUT 1¼" HIGH.

FOR A LARGER TABLE, FOR THE KITCHEN USE A TOP Ⓑ 2¾" DIAMETER. COVER TOP Ⓑ AND SPOOL Ⓐ IN WOODGRAIN CONTACT PAPER.

② CUT A ROUND PIECE OF THIN CARD BOARD Ⓑ, THE SIZE OF THE BOTTOM OF A PAPER BAKING CUP.

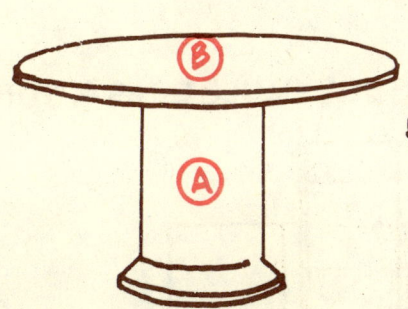

③ PASTE THE CARD BOARD PIECE Ⓑ ON TOP OF SPOOL Ⓐ.

④ PLACE A PAPER BAKING CUP OVER THE TOP AND YOU HAVE A "COVERED TABLE".

SCREENS

① TAKE THE COVER OF A GIFT BOX (OR ANY PART OF THE BOX) - CUT OUT A FLAT PIECE 4"× 5" Ⓐ.

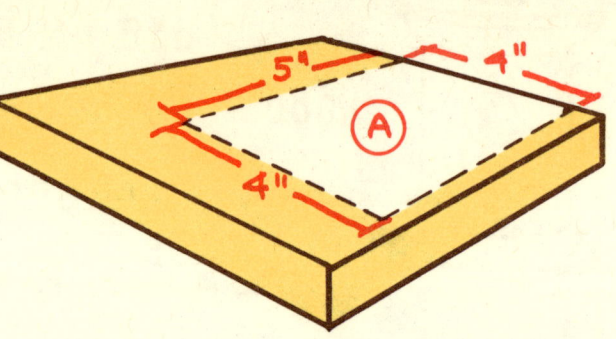

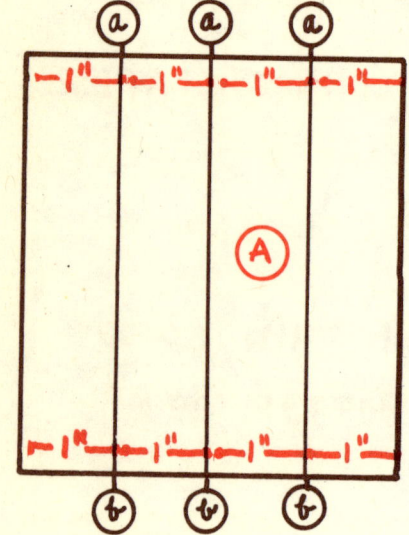

② USING A RULER, START FROM LEFT AND MARK OFF <u>THREE</u> 1" SPACES ON THE TOP ⓐ AND BOTTOM ⓑ.

MARK OFF FOUR 1" PANELS BY DRAWING STRAIGHT LINES FROM ⓐ TO ⓑ.

③ USING A METAL EDGE RULER AS A GUIDE CAREFULLY AND <u>LIGHTLY</u> DRAW AN X-ACTO KNIFE ALONG THE RULERS EDGE DOWN EACH LINE YOU HAVE DRAWN.

BE SURE YOU DO <u>NOT</u> CUT ALL THE WAY THROUGH.

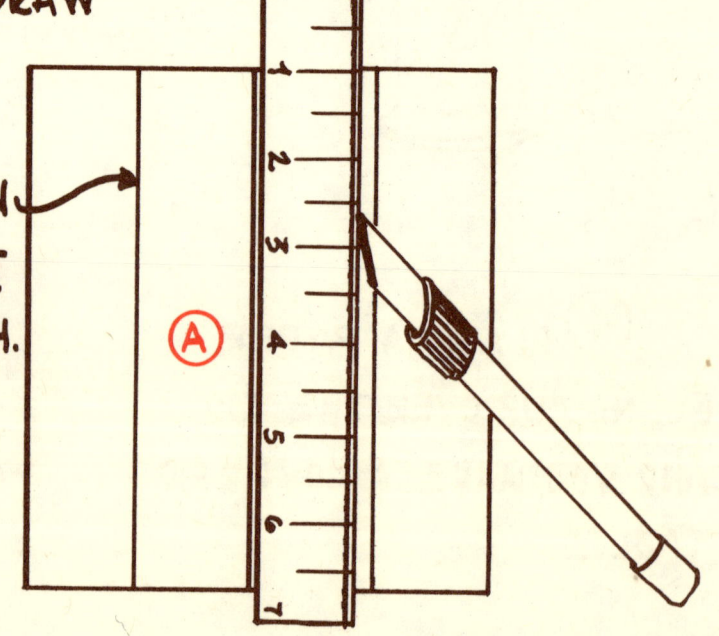

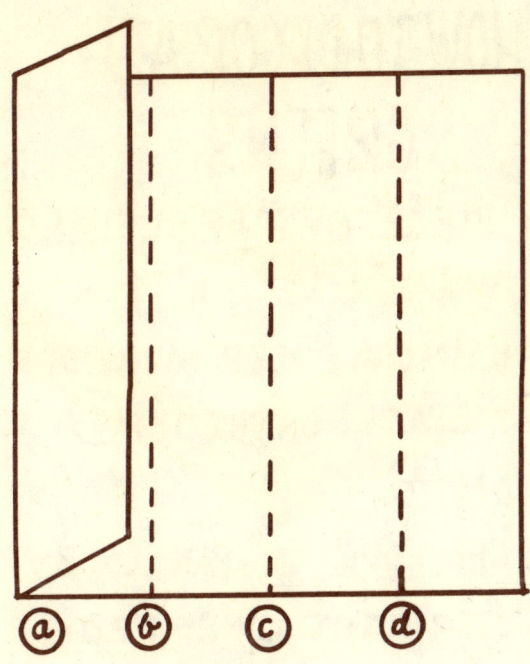

④ FOLD THE FIRST PANEL FORWARD (ON THE ⓐ LINE).

FOLD THE THIRD PANEL BACK, IN THE OPPOSITE DIRECTION (ON THE ⓑ LINE) AND —

FOLD THE FOURTH PANEL FORWARD (ON THE ⓒ LINE).

⑤ WHEN YOU HAVE FINISHED PRESS ALL THE PANELS TOGETHER FIRMLY — AND THE SCREEN WILL LOOK LIKE THIS.

⑥ CUT A PIECE OF FLORAL OR STRIPE CONTACT PAPER 4"X 5" AND PASTE IT ON ONE SIDE OF THE SCREEN. THEN FOLD ALL THE PANELS TOGETHER AGAIN. VERY TIGHTLY.

⑦ GENTLY OPEN THE FOLDED PANELS — AND YOU HAVE A SCREEN THAT WILL STAND BY ITSELF.

HOW TO DECORATE SCREENS

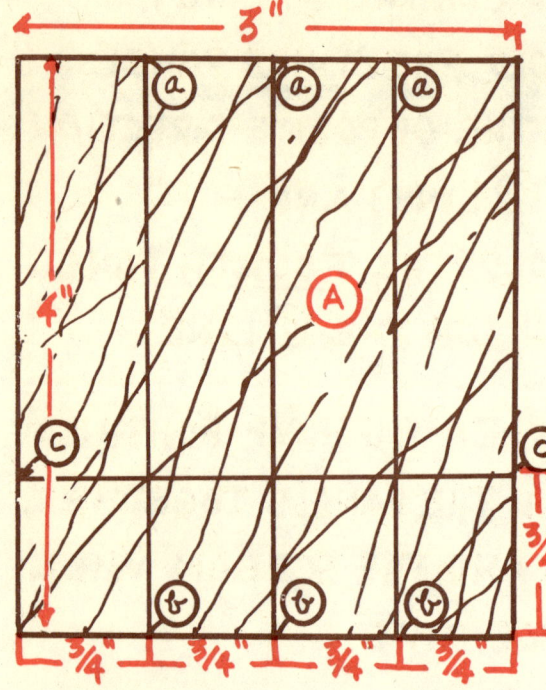

① CUT A PIECE OF MARBLEIZED PAPER 3"W X 4"L Ⓐ.

THEN USING A RULER MARK OFF THREE 3/4" SPACES ON THE TOP ⓐ AND BOTTOM ⓑ.

MARK OFF FOUR 3/4" PANELS BY DRAWING STRAIGHT LINES FROM ⓐ TO ⓑ. MEASURE 3/4" UP FROM THE BOTTOM ⓑ ON BOTH EDGES ⓒ. DRAW A LINE FROM ⓒ TO ⓒ.

② CUT ALONG THE LINES YOU HAVE DRAWN.
   1. FROM ⓐ DOWN TO ⓑ
   2. FROM ⓒ ACROSS TO ⓒ

YOU WILL THEN HAVE 4 PIECES Ⓑ LIKE THIS

AND 4 PIECES Ⓒ LIKE THIS.

③ TO MAKE THE SHAPE SHOWN HERE IN DOTTED LINE - MARK OFF PIECE Ⓑ USING THE MEASUREMENTS IN THE SKETCH.
   1. FROM ⓑ TO ⓐ ON THE LEFT.
   2. FROM ⓐ TO ⓑ ON THE RIGHT.

CUT THE CORNERS OUT ALONG THE DOTTED LINES. REPEAT FOR THE THREE OTHER Ⓑ PIECES.

④ TAKE A SCREEN AND OPEN IT.

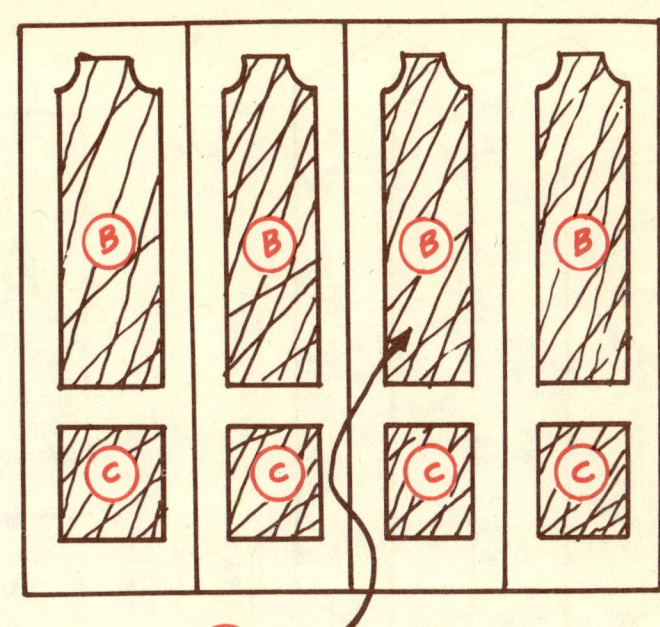

⑤ PASTE THE Ⓑ PIECES 3/8" DOWN FROM THE TOP OF EACH PANEL OF THE SCREEN. LEAVE A 1/8" MARGIN ON EACH SIDE.

NOW PASTE THE Ⓒ SQUARES 1/8" DOWN FROM THE PIECES Ⓑ ON EACH PANEL.

⑥ CAREFULLY FOLD BACK IN POSITION AS A SCREEN.

① TAKE A SCREEN AND OPEN IT.

② USE A SMALL LANDSCAPE (CUT FROM A MAGAZINE OR A LARGE POST CARD).

③ CUT THE PICTURE TO THE SIZE OF THE SCREEN 4" X 5" - AND PASTE ON THE SCREEN.

④ FOLD BACK AND FORTH TO FIT THE FOLDS OF THE SCREEN.

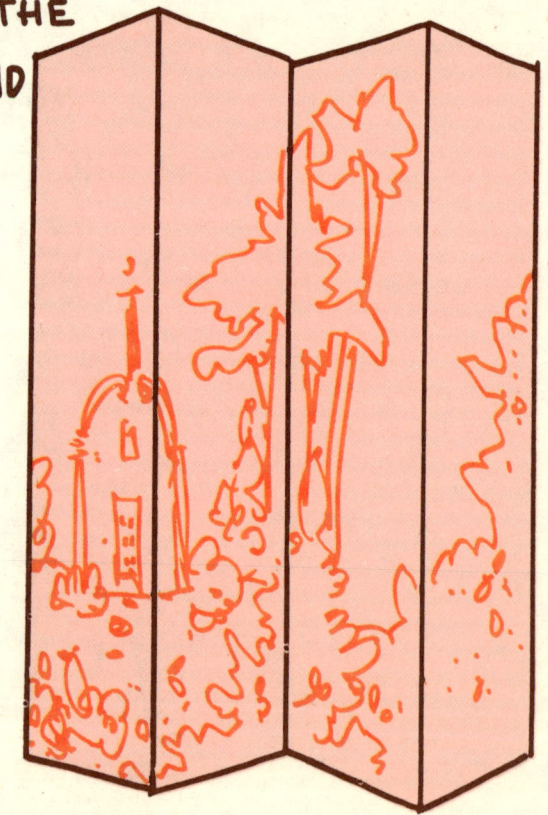

CHANDELIER

① TAKE A LARGE "HOOK & EYE" (THE SIZE USED FOR LADIES COATS). YOU WILL USE THE "EYE" PART Ⓐ ONLY — IT MEASURES ABOUT 3/8"W x 1/2"L.

② THEN TAKE A 9" LONG PIPE CLEANER Ⓑ AND CUT IT INTO THREE 3" LONG PIECES.

③ BEND EACH PIECE OF Ⓑ #1, #2, #3, EVENLY — LIKE THIS.

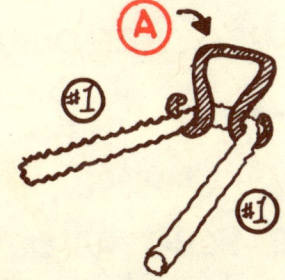

④ NOW PUSH THE ENDS OF PIECE #1 THROUGH EACH HOLE OF Ⓐ.

⑤ PUSH THE ENDS OF PIECE #2 THROUGH THE SAME HOLES BUT IN THE <u>OPPOSITE</u> DIRECTION.

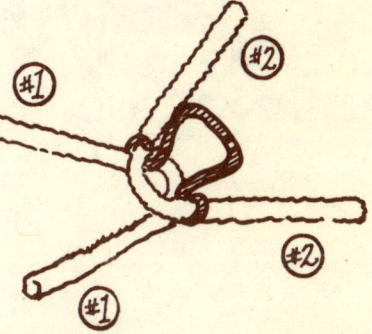

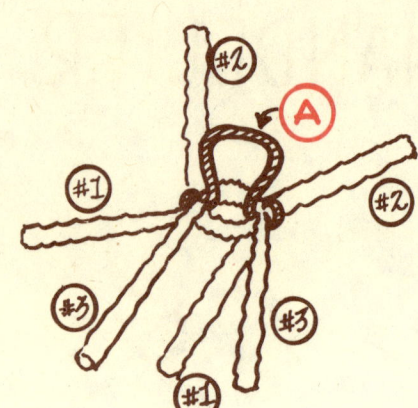

⑥ PUSH THE ENDS OF PIECE #3 THROUGH THE SAME HOLES BUT THIS TIME IN THE SAME DIRECTION AS PIECE #1.

⑦ PULL ALL THE ENDS STRAIGHT OUT, ONE BY ONE SO THEY ARE ALL TIGHTLY SECURED TO Ⓐ.

NOW SPREAD THE 6 STEMS SO THEY ARE EVENLY SPACED. THEN FROM THE CENTER Ⓐ MEASURE ½" OUT, AND AT THAT POINT, BEND EACH STEM UPRIGHT.

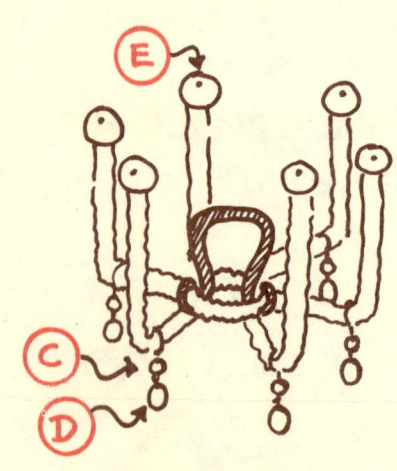

⑧ USING THREAD AND A NEEDLE THREAD ONE SMALL BEAD Ⓒ AND THEN ONE LARGE BEAD Ⓓ. NOW TIE BOTH TO A STEM, AT THE POINT WHERE IT BENDS.

DO THE SAME ON THE OTHER 5 STEMS.

THEN TAKE 6 WHITE (OR CRYSTAL) BEADS Ⓔ AND STICK ONE ON THE END OF EACH STEM.

⑨ TAKE A **2" LONG** RED RUBBER BAND.

LACE IT THROUGH THE LOOP OF Ⓐ (AS SHOWN). THEN PULL THE ENDS Ⓧ TIGHT ON ITSELF.

AND WITH A BRASS UPHOLSTERY TACK PUNCHED THROUGH THE RUBBER BAND Ⓧ SECURE THE CHANDELIER TO THE CENTER OF THE CEILING.

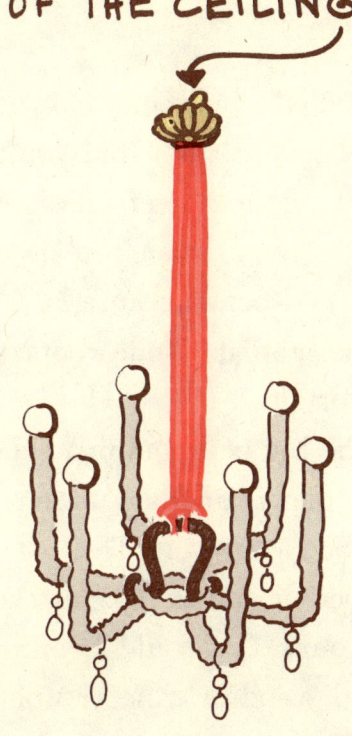

The Bedrooms

FOR MANY FAMILIES THE bedroom has become the second living room. I like that! I like it because (as I told you in Chapter III) I believe every room should be for living and every room should therefore be a living room. And the favorite "living room" in my house is the bedroom. I also enjoy decorating the bedroom because it is one room in the house that can be quite feminine, and it is one room where you can use your imagination and be most original.

Suppose we start with the big bedroom first (the mother and father bedroom) or what most floor plans call the "master bedroom." The first step is to decide what kind of bed you want. This usually decides what kind of room it will be. For instance, if you should choose a four-poster or canopy bed (see page 83) then your room could be Provincial, Colonial or English. If the beds are carved wood or cane or upholstered with some wood trim, the room could be French, whereas if the beds are plain wood or metal, then the bedroom could be Modern. Actually the choice is yours, and you can always mix periods or styles of furniture in the bedroom just as easily as you can in any other room of your doll house.

But it is with the beds that bedroom furniture begins and ends. Once you have selected the beds, you can stop thinking about bedroom furniture, unless you want your dolls' bedroom to look like everyone else's. If you want it to look different, then start looking at different furniture. By that I mean instead of using ordinary night tables for the beds, you might try a small chest of drawers on one side of the beds and a desk (or a table large enough to use as a desk) on the other side. Each will hold a lamp and each will do exactly what a night table will do, except that the chest will have many extra and useful drawers and the desk will give your dolls a pleasant place to write, a place for the telephone and an extra chair in the room for the desk. Beside all these added comforts, the entire setting will be more original and more interesting than just a bed with a pair of tiny night tables and a pair of matching lamps holding it together would be, don't you think?

Nice big comfortable chairs are great for a bedroom; and if the room is lucky enough to have a fireplace—well, I can't imagine anything more pleasant than a pair of comfy chairs on either side of the fireplace. One chair could have a large ottoman, and your dolls could enjoy hours of sewing or reading and not disturb the bed or the rest of the room. If there is no fireplace, the same grouping could be used in front of a nice window. Or a pair of armchairs and a table could be a most attractive arrangement in front of a window, just right for snacks or TV dinners.

If the bedroom is very large, then a small settee or a loveseat could be used at the foot of the bed with a tiny coffee table in front of it, and with small armchairs on either side of the loveseat—very much as you would in a living room. If the room won't take quite so much furniture, then try to place a bench at the foot of the bed. Suppose you don't have a bench, then take a blanket box, upholster it in the same fabric as your doll's spread and add a full length cushion (also upholstered in the same fabric) and nail or sew the cushion to the lid. Not only is this a very pretty touch for any bedroom, it is also very useful—the bench or the blanket box is a perfect place for the spread when your doll turns the bed down for the night. The blanket box, of course, will give lots of additional storage space for extra bed pillows or blankets.

Of course there are other things to be stored besides blankets and bedspreads in a well planned bedroom. You must also have a place for shirts, socks, pajamas, sweaters, hankies and all the things your dolls wear every day. A dresser or commode is still the best for this purpose. But suppose one dresser is not enough. Don't add another dresser, think of something else that will be useful and make the room prettier too. How about a highboy? A highboy is a piece of furniture that originally came to us from England and was used a great deal in America in Colonial times. This is what it looks like:

The highboy has lots of drawers which are good for shirts and sweaters. It is ideal for an English or Early American room.

The French, to take care of their storage, used an armoire (it's pronounced arm-wa) and it looks like this:

They used the armoire as a closet too, because they did not have closets built into their rooms as we do today—so they had to keep everything in them. Today old armoires or copies of old ones are very charming to use in a bedroom. They are quite large and are only to be used in large rooms. But because of its size an average armoire can handle so much storage that it sometimes can replace at least two or three other pieces in a room. For example, many are now made with drawers and shelves enough to hold all the personal linens two dolls would need, and leave room for a TV (I love a TV in the bedroom).

Or you might use a tall cabinet (see page 21) for storage, or even a secretary. Either one is splendid for a bedroom and they have a great deal of storage space. But since both these pieces traditionally have glass or grille on the doors, in the upper sections, you will have to stretch curtains on the inside of the doors just as you did for the pieces in the dining room (Chapter IV) so the shelves that you use for storage won't show.

Now you have seen how interesting the big bedroom can be, with beds, a dresser, a desk, small chests, tables, chairs and perhaps even a small sofa, club chairs, tall pieces, TV and everything to make it a comfortable sitting room as well.

Now let's "do" the children's bedroom for your little dolls. Here again I feel this room should have its very own special pieces because children need different things from grown-ups. In the first place, the room should have as much play space as possible, therefore this is the one room where it is considered "good planning" if the furniture does "run around" the room. An easy way to do this is to use the beds as though they were sofa beds (see page 116) and place them along the walls with a big table in the corner.

The big square table in the corner is very important because it serves as a headboard for each bed and also is big enough to hold two lamps—one for each bed—and still has room enough for your dolls' radio and books.

If the room is quite small then bunk beds with drawers in the base are by far the best to use. With them you can do without a dresser in the room, and you will have a wall free to use for a desk or even for a worktable with a good surface for games. Over the desk or over the worktable you can hang bookshelves and a large pin-up board. Under the windows or on either side of the windows there may be space for more shelves, for toys and games, and later on for more books. A cheerful, washable color painted on the walls, nice clean, crisp curtains, two chairs or stools in front of the desk or worktable and gay, bright vinyl on the floors and your "children's room" is complete. Complete for your littlest dolls' comfort and fun.

The nursery, too, is part of bedroom planning and decorating. If it is properly planned in the beginning, it can grow and grow just as the baby doll will, and in fact will grow right along with the "baby." By this I mean that if you select the right kind of crib you can later use the two ends of the crib for the headboard and footboard of a youth bed. If you choose two small dressers, just high enough for the doll to reach when she is old enough to put her things away, then as she grows up you can stack one dresser on top of the other. This is called a chest-on-chest, and your little doll can use this for years. A chest-on-chest looks like this:

A rather large comfortable chair, or a rocker, is also important in the nursery and can always be used by the doll when she "grows up" too. One more thing the well equipped nursery should have is a little table and little chairs or stools, even for the tiniest tots, for their meals or snacks, as well as for play. The table can be used as an end table or even as a little coffee table when the room "grows up." Actually it is only the little chairs that can't be used again. The bed, the chests, the comfortable chair and the table can go from the nursery to the bigger doll's room. That is what I mean by a room that can "grow!"

To finish the room as a nursery, use gay paper for the walls or paste cutout animals to painted walls. Add curtains made of tiny patterned fabric or of gingham to the windows. Then use the same fabric for the crib cover and for the lamp shades, just for fun. The floors, of course, should always be washable—so it is best to use vinyl or something that looks like vinyl such as contact paper—and always in a bright cheerful color.

Now your room is complete, and you have a perfect little nursery for your best and littlest doll.

Four Poster Bed
(Canopy Bed)

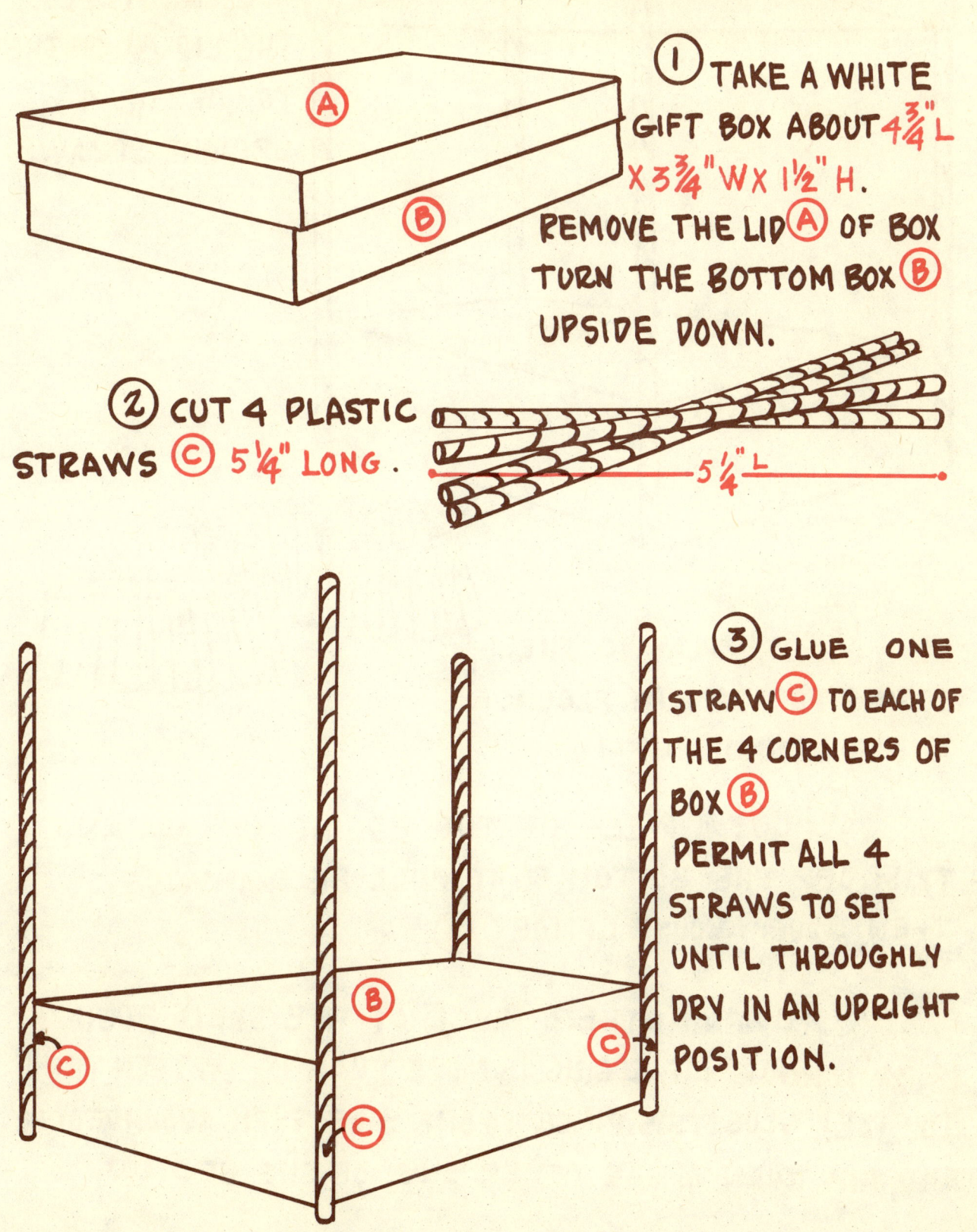

① Take a white gift box about 4¾" L x 3¾" W x 1½" H. Remove the lid Ⓐ of box turn the bottom box Ⓑ upside down.

② Cut 4 plastic straws Ⓒ 5¼" long.

③ Glue one straw Ⓒ to each of the 4 corners of box Ⓑ. Permit all 4 straws to set until throughly dry in an upright position.

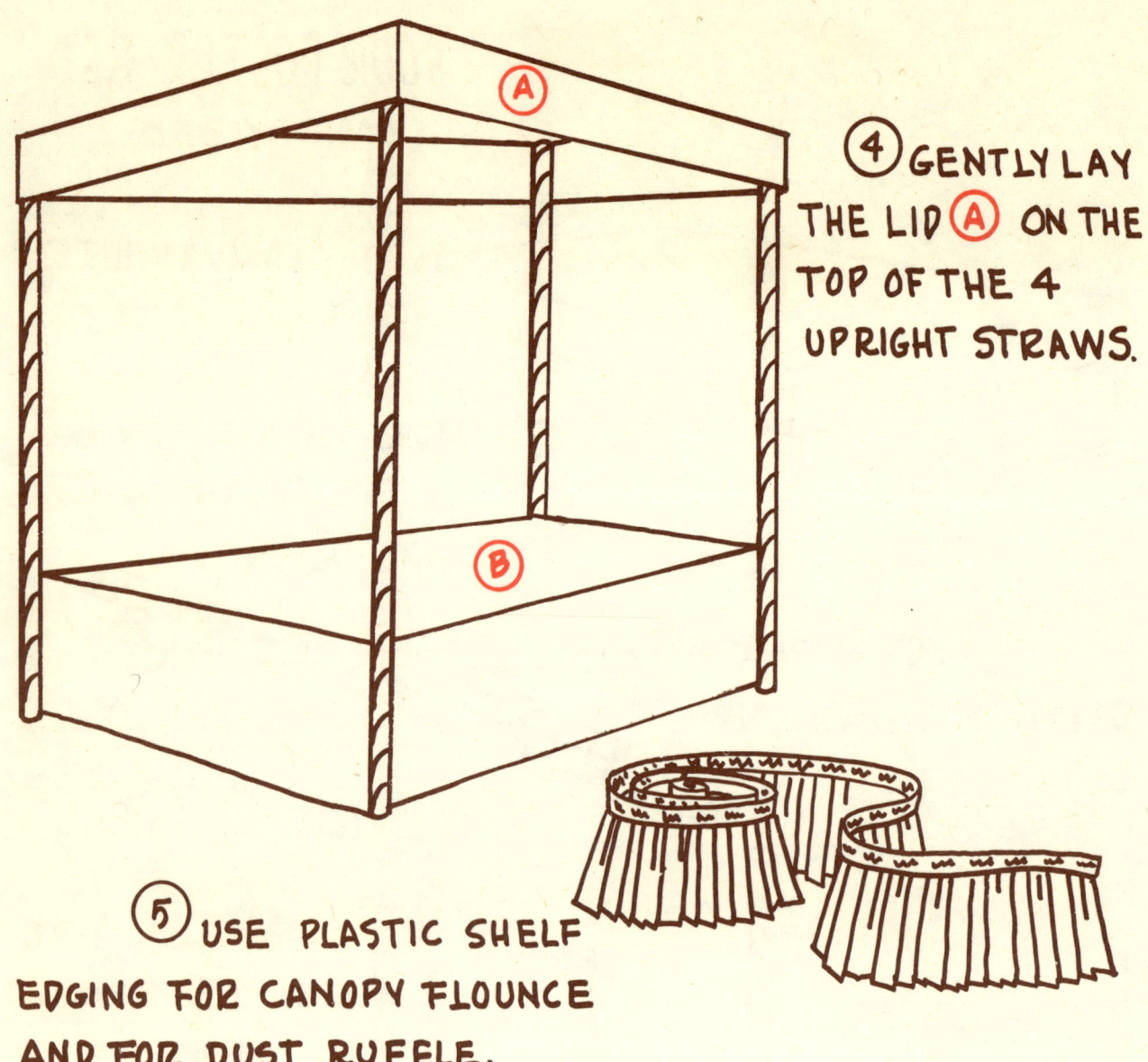

④ GENTLY LAY THE LID Ⓐ ON THE TOP OF THE 4 UPRIGHT STRAWS.

⑤ USE PLASTIC SHELF EDGING FOR CANOPY FLOUNCE AND FOR DUST RUFFLE.

⑥ CUT A PIECE OF THE EDGING 17" LONG AND TRIM OFF THE BOTTOM SO IT WILL BE 3/4" WIDE. THEN GLUE AROUND CANOPY Ⓐ.

⑦ CUT ANOTHER PIECE OF THE SHELF EDGING 12 3/4" LONG Ⓔ (IF EDGING IS MORE THAN 1 1/2" W. THEN TRIM TO SIZE). GLUE THIS PIECE TO ONE SIDE, THEN AROUND TO ONE END, AND THEN TO THE OTHER SIDE OF THE BED Ⓑ.

⑧ TO MAKE THE BED-SPREAD - CUT A PIECE OF FABRIC (OR A PRINTED HANKIE) 5¾" L X 5½" W CUT 1" SQUARES FROM EACH CORNER. COVER BED Ⓑ WITH SPREAD Ⓕ THEN PIN Ⓖ EACH CORNER OF THE SPREAD TO SIDES AND ENDS OF BED.

⑨ MAKE A BOLSTER Ⓗ 3¾" LONG. CUT A PIECE OF THE SPREAD FABRIC Ⓕ AND MAKE AND COVER BOLSTER AS SHOWN (ON PAGE 106).

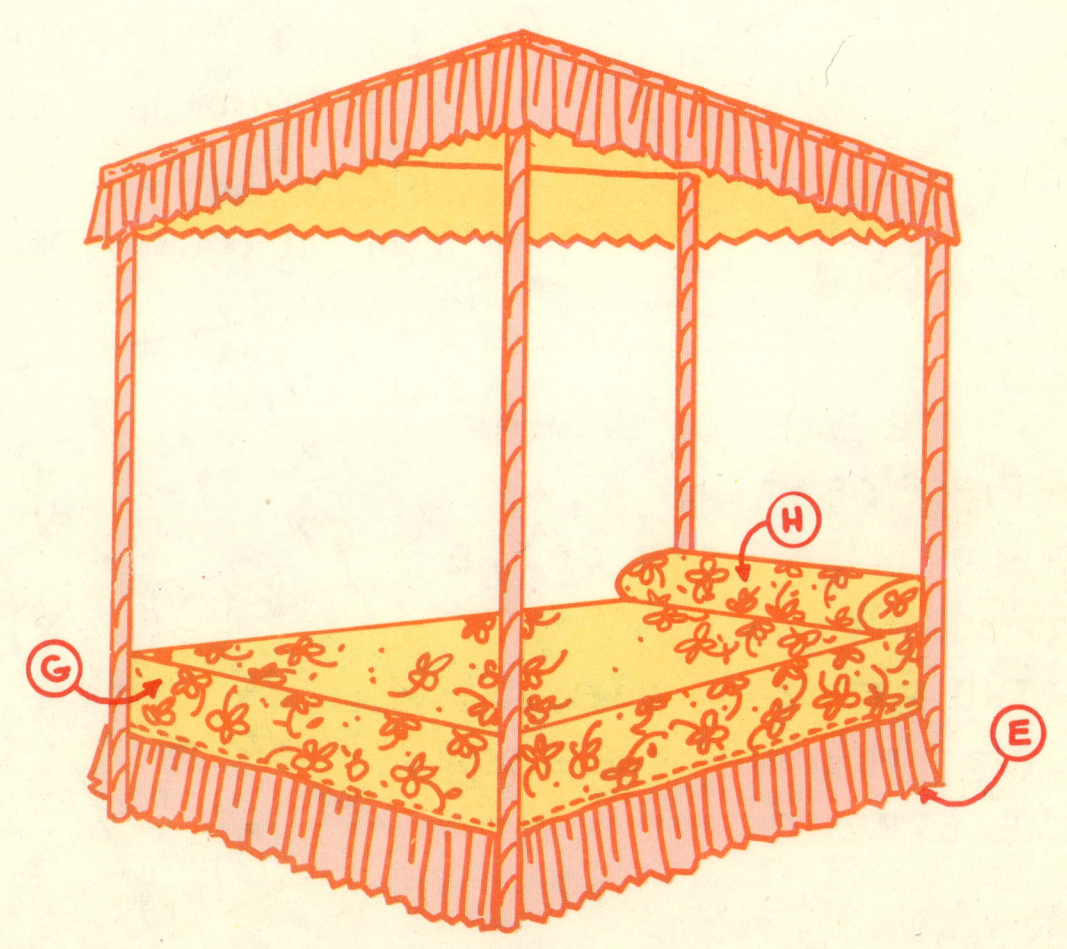

TWIN BEDS

① ASK THE FLORIST TO CUT 4 PIECES STYROFOAM THE SIZE OF "TWIN BEDS" 2¼"W x 4½"L x ¾"H.
2 PIECES WILL BE MATTRESSES Ⓐ
2 PIECES WILL BE BOX SPRINGS Ⓑ

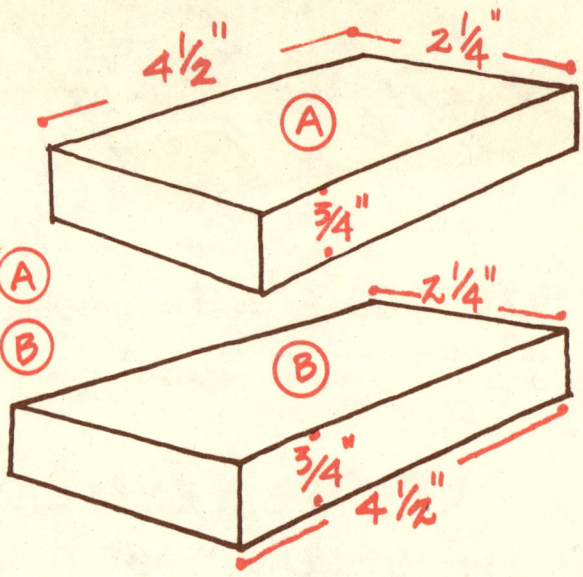

② TAKE 2 HAIR COMBS Ⓒ 2" OR 2¼" WIDE (ONE FOR EACH BED) - AND STICK INTO EACH MATTRESS ABOUT ¼" IN FROM THE BACK - FOR THE "HEADBOARDS".

③ FOR EACH TOP SPREAD CUT A PIECE OF FABRIC 4¾"W x 5¾"L TUCK-IN ON ALL 3 SIDES OF THE MATTRESS Ⓐ.
TURN THE MATTRESS OVER AND GLUE (OR TAPE DOWN) THE ENDS OF THE SPREAD.

④ FOR EACH BOLSTER CUT ANOTHER PIECE OF THE SAME FABRIC 3"W × 2"L AND MAKE AND COVER BOLSTERS (AS SHOWN ON PAGE 106).

⑤ FOR DUST RUFFLES CUT 9" STRIPS OF RUFFLED SHELF EDGING (ONE STRIP FOR EACH BED) PASTE TO TOP OF BOX SPRING Ⓑ.
(IF EDGING IS TOO LONG CUT THE RUFFLE SO THAT IT WILL BE EVEN WITH THE BOTTOM OF THE BED).

⑥ PLACE THE MATTRESS (WITH THE SPREAD AND HEADBOARD IN PLACE) ON THE TOP OF BOXSPRING. TO SECURE BOTH, STICK LONG PINS, UNDER THE BED, THRU THE BOXSPRING AND INTO THE MATTRESS. THEN PUT THE BOLSTER IN PLACE.

BUNK-BEDS

① USE THE INSIDE BOX Ⓐ OF AN EMPTY BOX OF KITCHEN MATCHES.

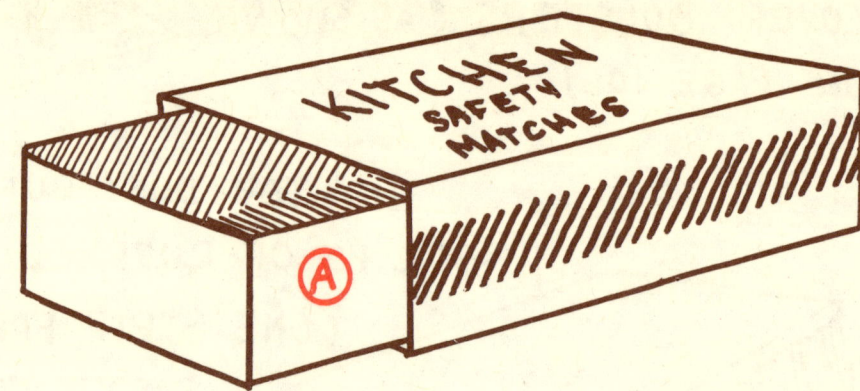

② CUT A PIECE OF WHITE CONTACT PAPER 5¼"W × 7¾"L Ⓑ AT EACH CORNER CUT OUT A SQUARE 1½" × 1½".

③ COVER BOX Ⓐ BY PASTING THE CONTACT PAPER FIRMLY ON BOTTOM AND ALL 4 SIDES OF BOX.

④ WITH A FLOW PEN DRAW 2 DRAWERS Ⓒ ¼" UP FROM BOTTOM OF "BED" AND ¼" IN FROM THE SIDES. EACH DRAWER ⅜"H × 1⅞"L.

⑤ CUT A STRIP OF DARK BLUE OR DARK BROWN PAPER 15" LONG X ½" WIDE. PASTE THE STRIP TO THE TOP OF THE "BED" AS SHOWN.

⑥ MEASURE OFF 1" FROM EACH CORNER AT THE FRONT OF THE BED. CUT OUT A STRIP ¼" X 2½" AT THE TOP BETWEEN THE TWO 1" MARKS. SO YOU WILL HAVE A CUT OUT SHAPE LIKE THIS.

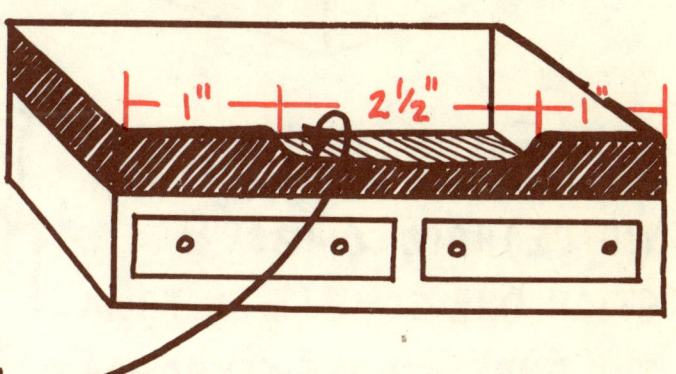

⑦ CUT A PIECE OF STYROFOAM 4½"L X 2¼"W 1½"H. COVER THE TOP AND SIDES IN A PIECE OF WHITE FABRIC (OR TURKISH TOWELING) 3¼"W X 5½"L.

⑧ SLIP THE COVERED MATTRESS Ⓓ INTO THE BED ADD TWO BOLSTERS (SEE PAGE 106) COVERED IN THE SAME FABRIC AS Ⓓ AND SOME COLORFUL PILLOWS.

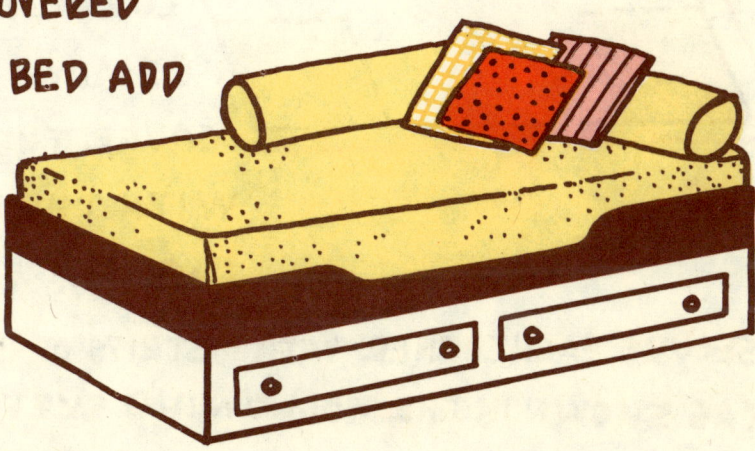

89

CRIB

① CUT A PIECE OF STYROFOAM 2"W x 3¾" x 1"H.

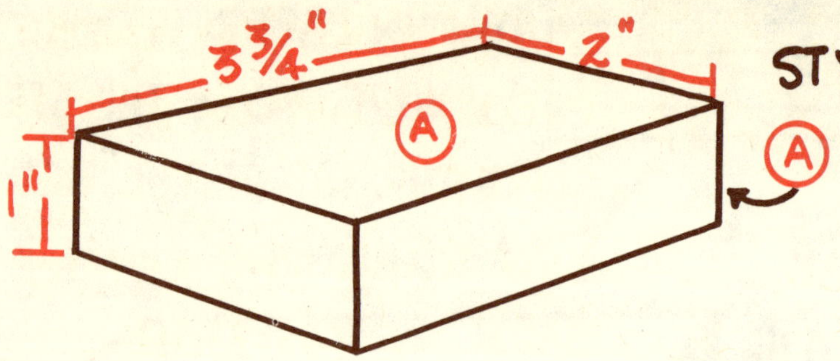

② USE 2 - 2" GREY (OR WHITE) HAIR COMBS Ⓑ. STICK ONE COMB (⅛" IN FROM THE END) INTO THE STYROFOAM PIECE Ⓐ. AS IN THE SKETCH THEN STICK THE OTHER COMB INTO OPPOSITE END. (⅛" IN FROM THAT END).

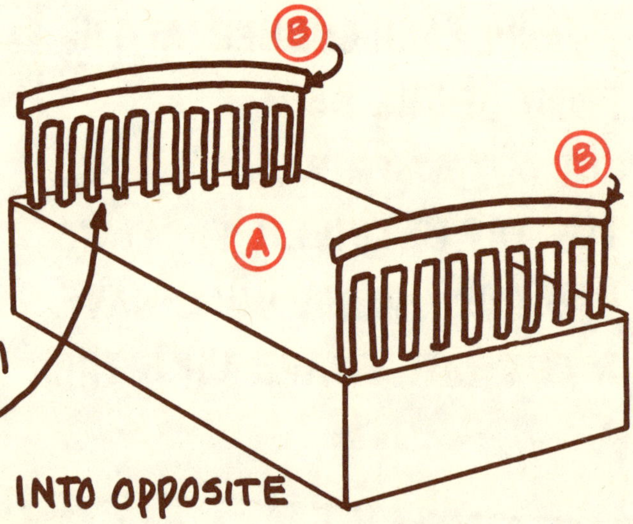

③ CUT A PIECE OF FABRIC (OR PRINT CONTACT PAPER) 3"W x 5½"L Ⓒ. CUT OUT 1"x 1" SQUARES FROM EACH CORNER.

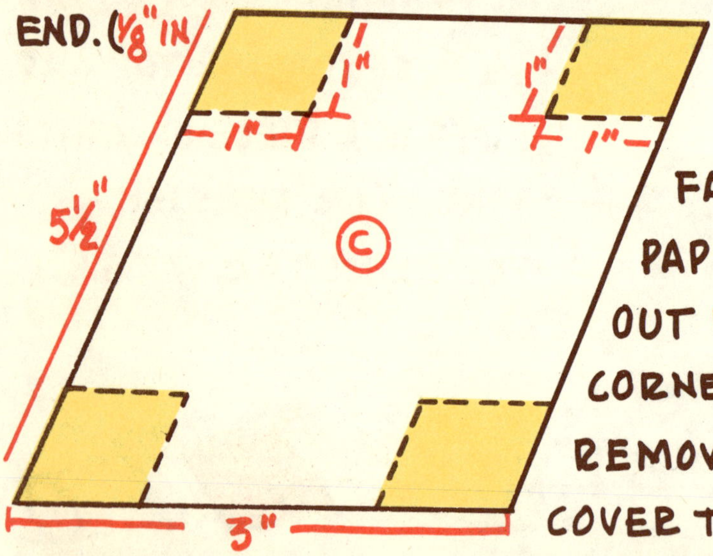

REMOVE THE COMBS Ⓑ

COVER THE STYROFOAM PIECE Ⓐ WITH THE FABRIC (OR CONTACT PAPER).

SECURE EACH CORNER WITH 1" STRIPS OF SCOTCH MENDING TAPE. (AS SHOWN IN THE FOLLOWING SKETCH) →

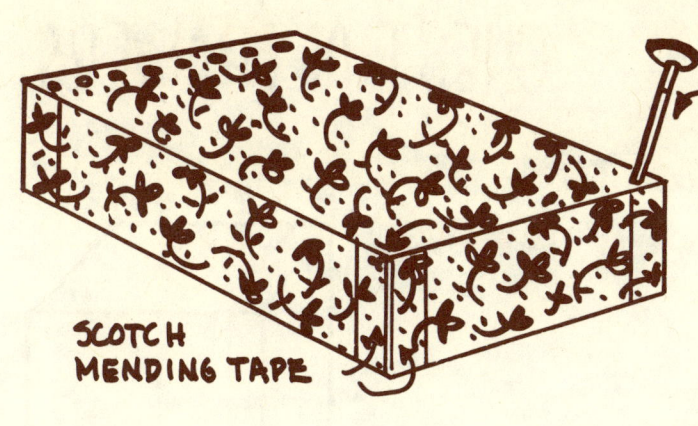
SCOTCH MENDING TAPE

④ USE A NAIL... AND PIERCE THROUGH THE FABRIC DIRECTLY INTO THE HOLES MADE BY THE COMBS.
NOW STICK THE COMBS BACK IN POSITION.

⑤ CUT 2 STRIPS (OF THE SAME FABRIC YOU USED FOR THE COVER Ⓒ.) EACH STRIP SHOULD BE ½" X 8½" L Ⓓ.

⑥ LACE 1 STRIP Ⓓ THROUGH THE FIRST TEETH OF THE COMBS AT EACH END OF THE CRIB. PULL THE STRIP TAUT, THEN GLUE THE ENDS OF THE STRIP TOGETHER.

REPEAT WITH SECOND STRIP Ⓓ ON THE OTHER SIDE OF CRIB.

⑦ USE 4 (WHITE RUBBER HEAD) ¾" TACK BUMPERS STICK ONE IN EACH CORNER AS LEGS FOR THE CRIB.

CHEST OF DRAWERS

① USE THE TOP OR BOTTOM OF A GIFT BOX ABOUT 2"W × 1¼"D × 3½"H Ⓐ

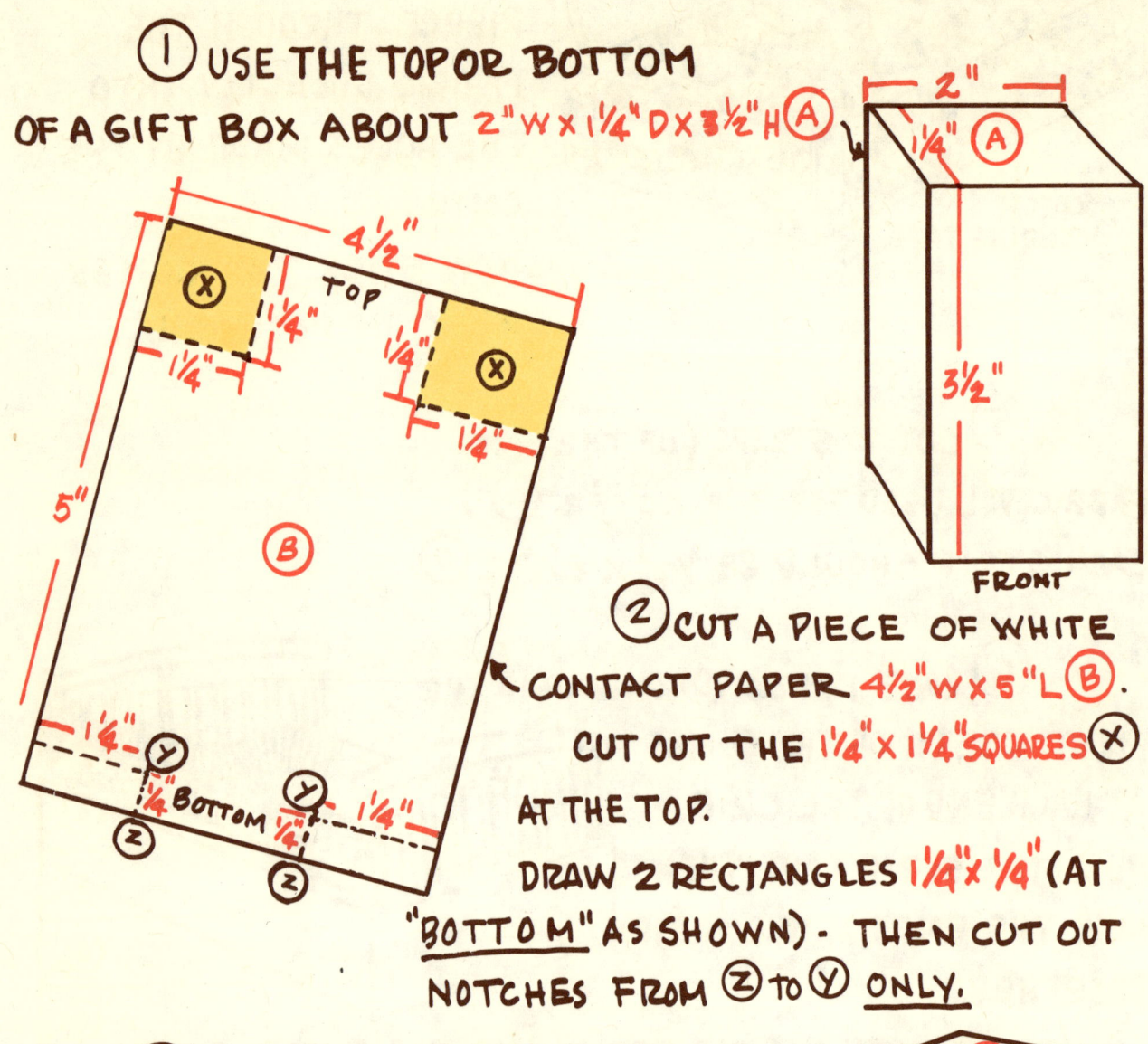

② CUT A PIECE OF WHITE CONTACT PAPER 4½"W × 5"L Ⓑ. CUT OUT THE 1¼" × 1¼" SQUARES Ⓧ AT THE TOP.

DRAW 2 RECTANGLES 1¼" × ¼" (AT "BOTTOM" AS SHOWN) - THEN CUT OUT NOTCHES FROM Ⓩ TO Ⓨ ONLY.

③ COVER THE BOX Ⓐ WITH THE CONTACT PAPER Ⓑ - ALLOWING THE ¼" (CUT FROM Ⓨ) TO FOLD AROUND, SO YOU CAN PASTE IT ON THE INSIDE OF THE BOX, LIKE THIS.

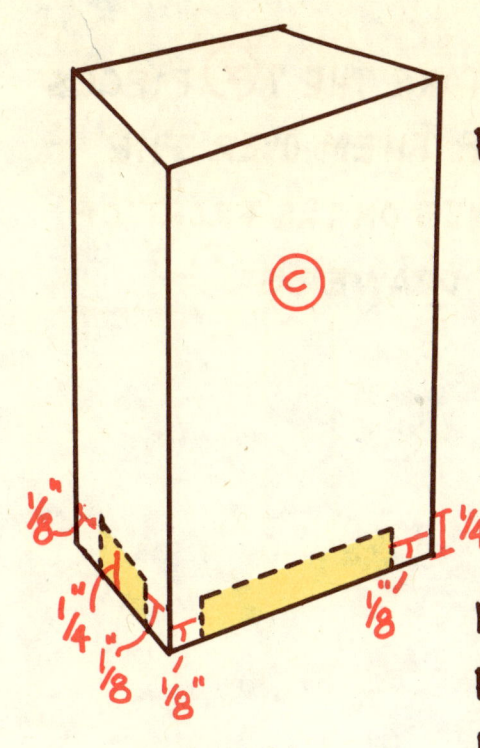

④ TO MAKE THE LEGS - TURN THE BOX AROUND AND WITH A RULER MARK OFF THE MEASUREMENTS SHOWN ON THE SKETCH IN EACH CORNER.

NOW CUT ALONG THE (DOTTED) LINES YOU HAVE DRAWN.

⑤ CUT A PIECE OF BRIGHT COLOR PAPER (STRONG YELLOW, SHOCKING PINK) OR WOOD GRAIN CONTACT PAPER 1¾" X 2⅝" Ⓓ.

⑥ USE THE MEASUREMENTS SHOWN IN THE SKETCH AND DRAW THE 6 LINES ACROSS FROM ⓐ TO ⓐ ALL THE WAY DOWN.

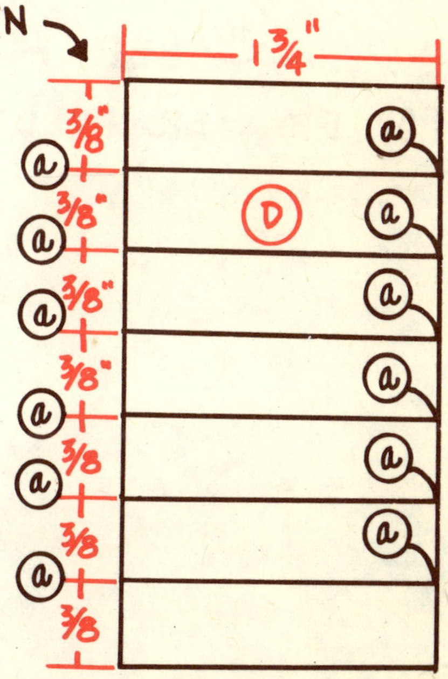

⑦ NOW CUT ALONG THE LINES YOU HAVE DRAWN, YOU WILL HAVE 7 PIECES ⅜" X 1¾" L. Ⓧ

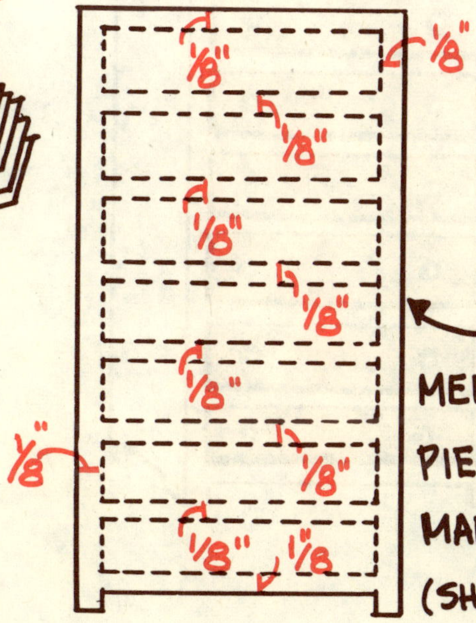

⑧ USE THE MEASUREMENTS SHOWN IN THE SKETCH PIECE Ⓓ. THEN LIGHTLY MARK OFF THE GUIDE LINES (SHOWN IN DOTTED LINES).

93

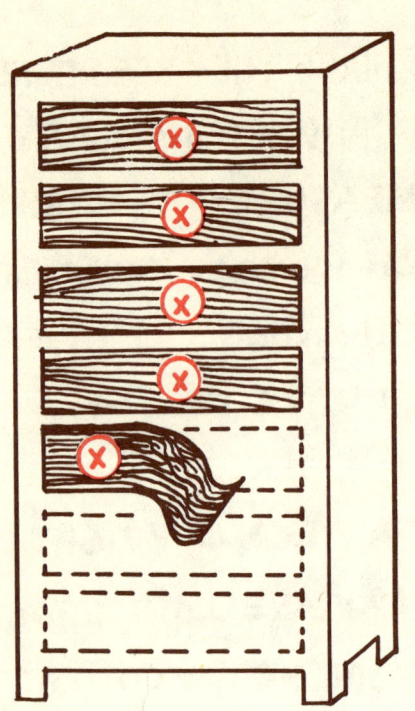

⑨ TAKE THE 7 Ⓧ PIECES AND PASTE THEM OVER THE GUIDE LINES ON THE FRONT OF CHEST OF DRAWERS Ⓒ.

⑩ USE 14 WHITE MAP PINS (2 ON EACH DRAWER) FOR DRAWER PULLS.

DRESSER

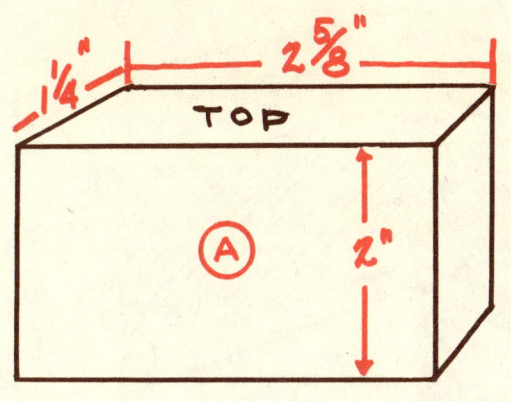

① USE THE TOP OR BOTTOM OF A GIFT BOX Ⓐ ABOUT 2⅝" L X 1¼" D X 2" H -

OR

USE THE INSIDE BOX Ⓑ OF KITCHEN MATCHES (SEE PAGE 88) AND CUT IT TO 2" HIGH (THE LENGTH & WIDTH OF THIS BOX IS CORRECT AS IS).

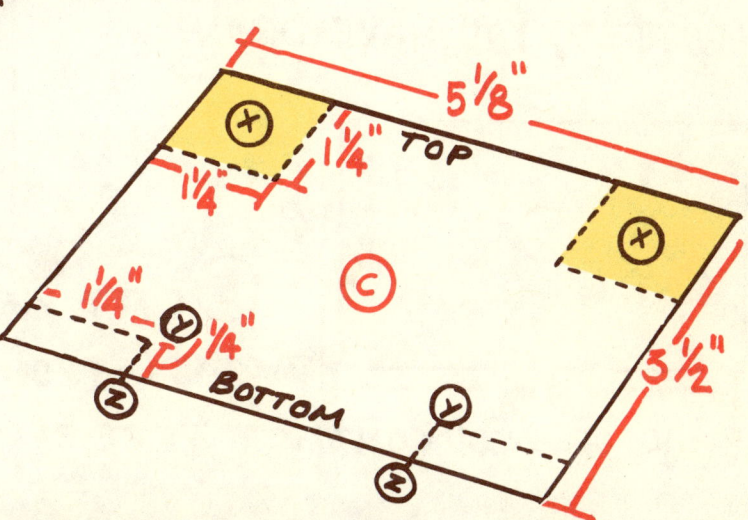

② CUT A PIECE OF WHITE CONTACT PAPER 5⅛" X 3½". CUT OUT 1¼" X 1¼" SQUARES Ⓧ AT TOP.

DRAW 2 RECTANGLES 1¼" X ¼" (AT "BOTTOM" AS SHOWN) - THEN CUT OUT NOTCHES FROM Ⓩ TO Ⓨ ONLY.

③ COVER EITHER BOX Ⓐ OR Ⓑ WITH THE CONTACT PAPER Ⓒ ALLOWING THE ¼" (CUT OUT FROM Ⓨ)

TO FOLD AROUND, SO YOU CAN PASTE IT ON THE INSIDE OF THE BOX - LIKE THIS

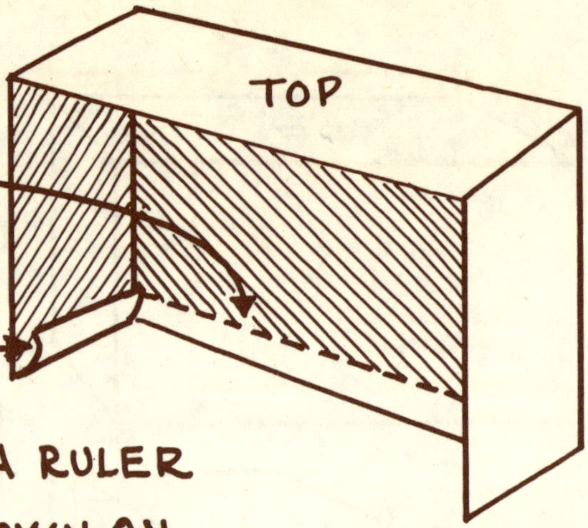

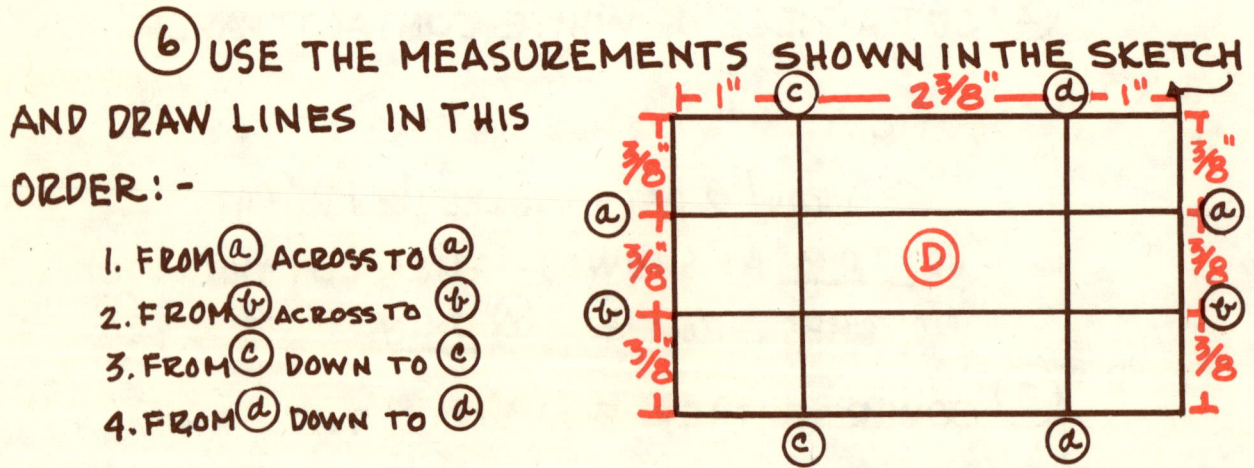

④ TO MAKE THE LEGS, TURN THE BOX AROUND, AND WITH A RULER MARK OFF THE MEASUREMENTS SHOWN ON THE SKETCH IN EACH CORNER.

NOW CUT ALONG THE LINES (DOTTED) YOU HAVE DRAWN.

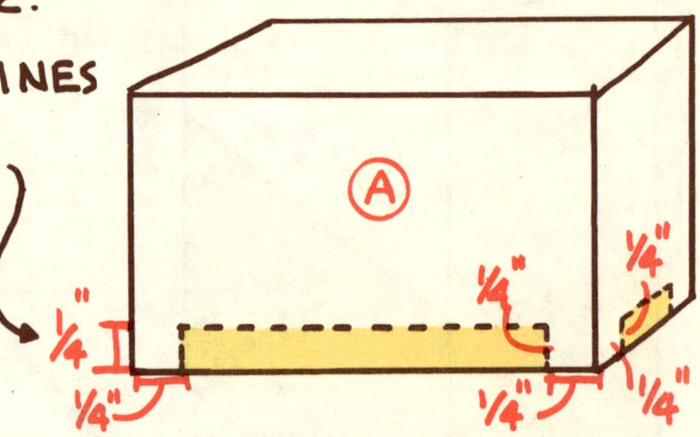

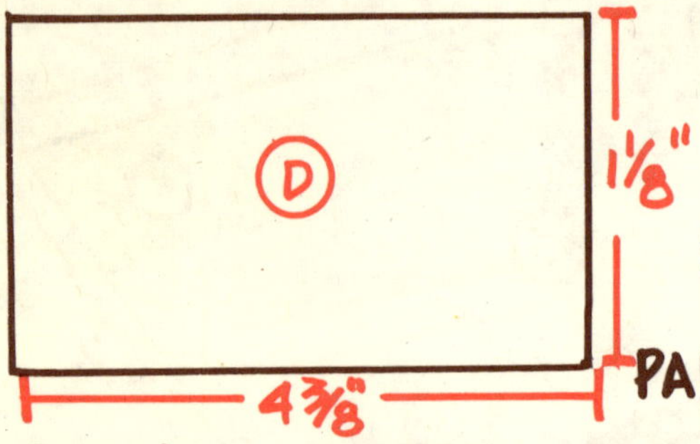

⑤ CUT A PIECE OF BRIGHT COLOR PAPER (STRONG YELLOW, SHOCKING PINK) OR WOOD CONTACT PAPER 4⅜" × 1⅛".

⑥ USE THE MEASUREMENTS SHOWN IN THE SKETCH AND DRAW LINES IN THIS ORDER:-

1. FROM ⓐ ACROSS TO ⓐ
2. FROM ⓑ ACROSS TO ⓑ
3. FROM ⓒ DOWN TO ⓒ
4. FROM ⓓ DOWN TO ⓓ

⑦ NOW CUT ALONG ALL THE LINES YOU HAVE DRAWN. YOU WILL HAVE 6 PIECES 1" X 3/8" Ⓧ AND 3 PIECES 2 3/8" X 3/8" Ⓨ

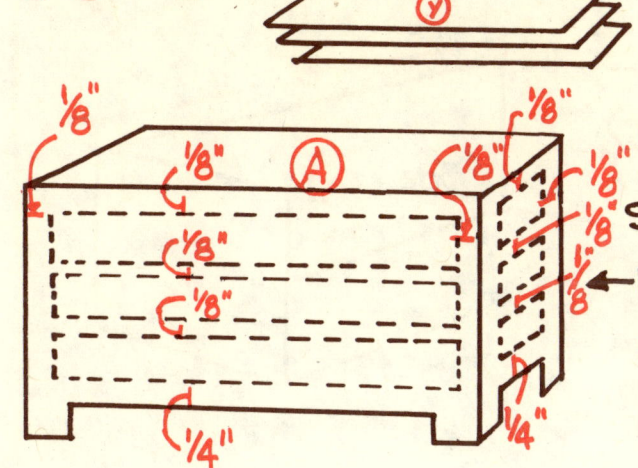

⑧ USE THE MEASUREMENTS SHOWN IN THE SKETCH ON PIECE Ⓐ, THEN LIGHTLY MARK OFF THE GUIDE LINES (SHOWN IN DOTTED LINES)

⑨ TAKE THE 3 Ⓨ PIECES AND PASTE THEM OVER THE GUIDE LINES ON THE FRONT OF THE DRESSER Ⓐ

AND TAKE THE 6 PIECES Ⓧ PASTE 3 OVER THE GUIDE LINES ON EACH SIDE.

⑩ USE 6 WHITE MAP PINS (2 ON EACH DRAWER) FOR DRAWER-PULLS.

LOVESEAT

① USE A BOX (OR BOX TOP) 3"L × 2"D × 1 3/8"H OR CUT ONE TO THIS SIZE.

② THEN CUT A PIECE OF CARDBOARD Ⓑ 4"L × 3"W.

③ USING THE MEASUREMENTS SHOWN, AND WITH A RULER DRAW YOUR LINES:

FROM ⓐ TO ⓐ
FROM ⓑ TO ⓑ
FROM ⓒ TO ⓒ
FROM ⓓ TO ⓓ

④ NOW FOLD ALONG THE LINES YOU HAVE DRAWN AND PIECE Ⓑ WILL HAVE A SHAPE LIKE THIS.

⑤ CUT 2 PIECES OF CARDBOARD Ⓒ TO FILL IN THE ENDS OF PIECE Ⓑ.

FASTEN IN PLACE WITH SCOTCH TAPE.

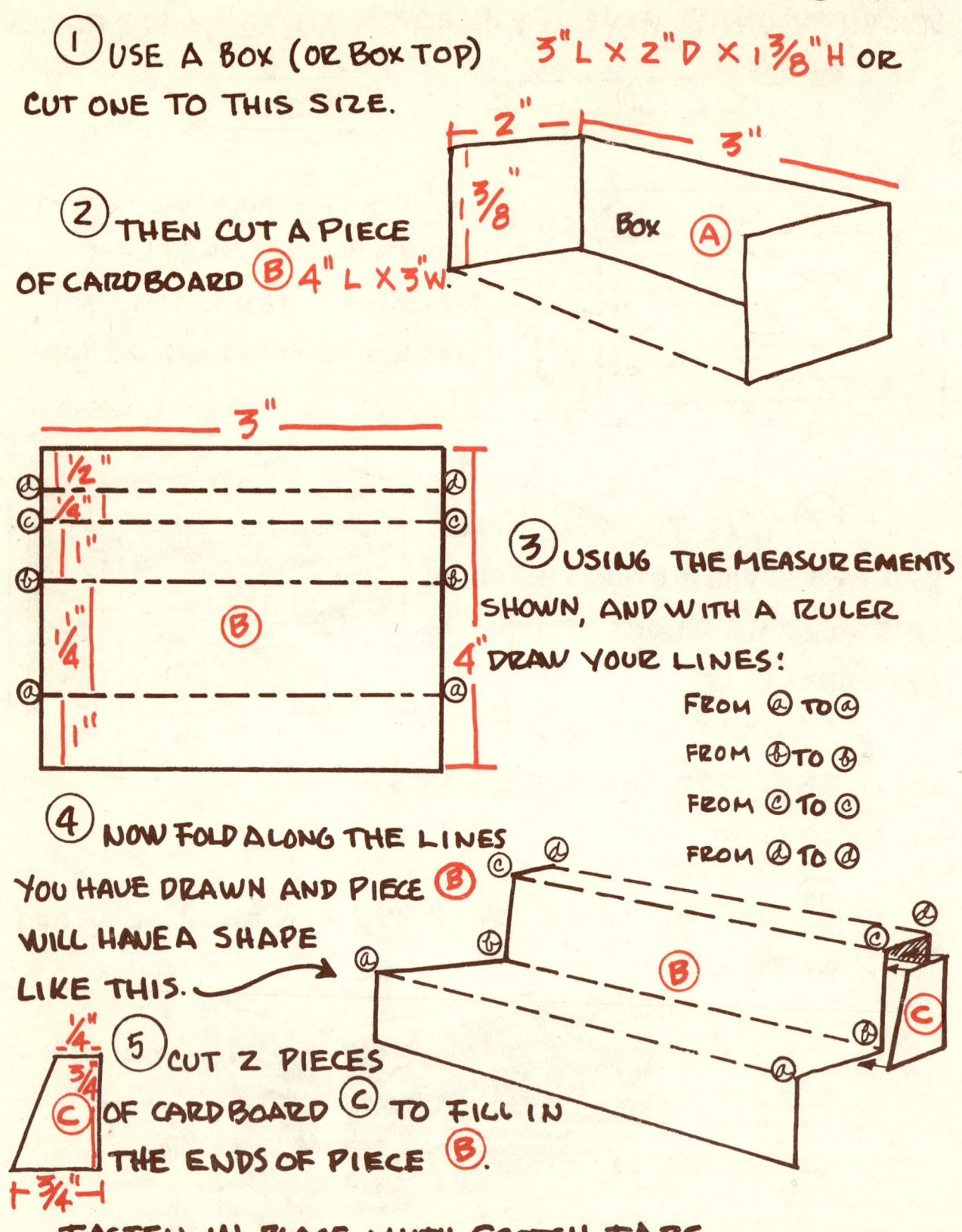

⑥ CUT PIECES OF FABRIC OR CONTACT PAPER THE SAME SIZES AS ② AND ⑤ AND PASTE OVER PIECE Ⓑ AS SHOWN

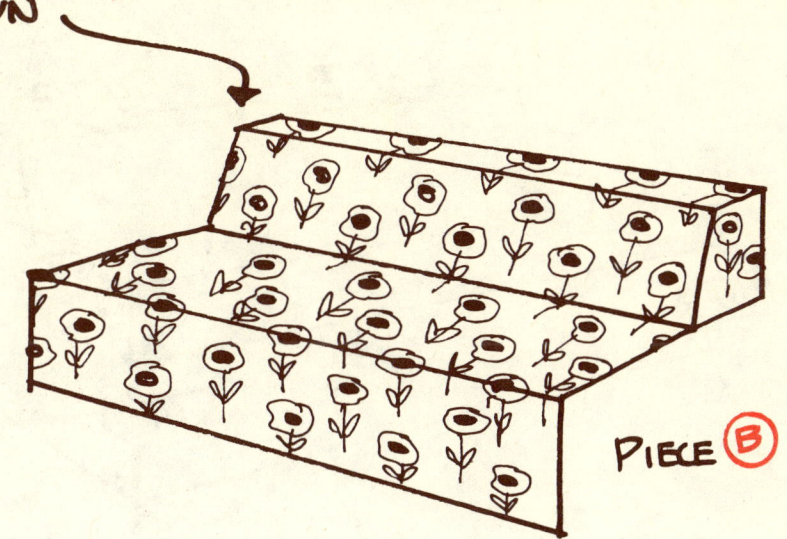

PIECE Ⓑ

⑦ NOW CUT THE SAME FABRIC OR PAPER IN A STRIP 11"L × 1 3/8"W AND PASTE IT ON BOX Ⓐ ON THE <u>INSIDE</u> AND <u>OUTSIDE</u> OF BOTH ENDS, AND ON THE <u>OUTSIDE BACK</u> ONLY

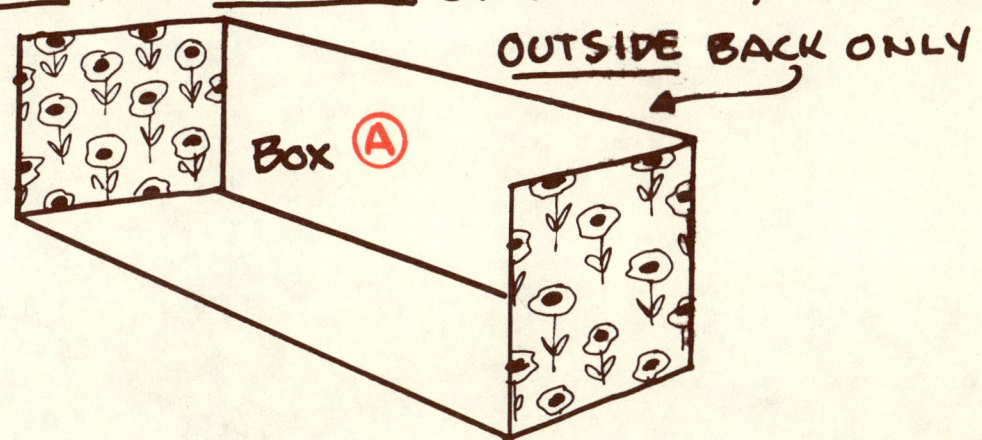

BOX Ⓐ

⑧ CAREFULLY SLIP PIECE Ⓑ INTO BOX Ⓐ

9. FASTEN PIECE B AND BOX A TOGETHER WITH STRIPS OF CLEAR MENDING TAPE AT POINTS H, I, J, K, L, M.

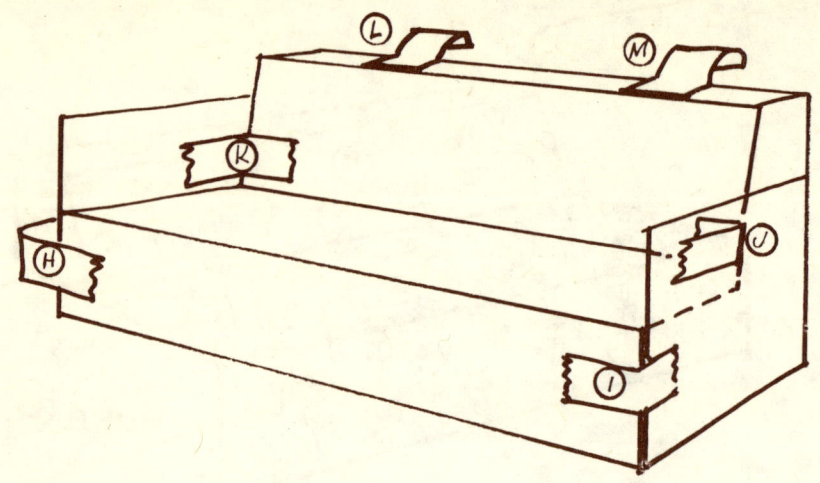

ADD CONTRASTING PILLOWS. (SEE PAGE 122).

BLANKET CHEST

① USE A SMALL GIFT BOX ABOUT 2½" L x 1¼" W x 1¼" H.

② CUT OUT A PIECE OF FABRIC (TO MATCH THE BEDSPREAD), OR A PIECE OF CONTACT PAPER (TO MATCH THE "WALLPAPER") 3" LONG x 2" WIDE ⒟. CUT OUT ¼" SQUARES TO MAKE THE CORNERS FIT. PASTE ON THE TOP AND ALL 4 SIDES OF THE BOX COVER Ⓑ.

③ FROM THE SAME FABRIC (OR CONTACT PAPER) CUT A PIECE 4" LONG x 3¾" WIDE Ⓔ AND CUT OUT 1¼" SQUARES TO MAKE THE CORNERS FIT. PASTE ON THE BOTTOM AND ALL 4 SIDES OF BOX Ⓒ.

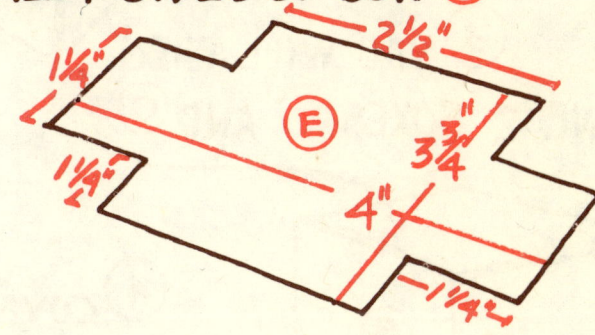

④ PUT THE COVER BACK ON THE BOX. TAKE 4 SMALL BRASS UPHOLSTERY TACKS PUSH ONE UNDER EACH CORNER — FOR "LEGS".

NIGHT TABLES

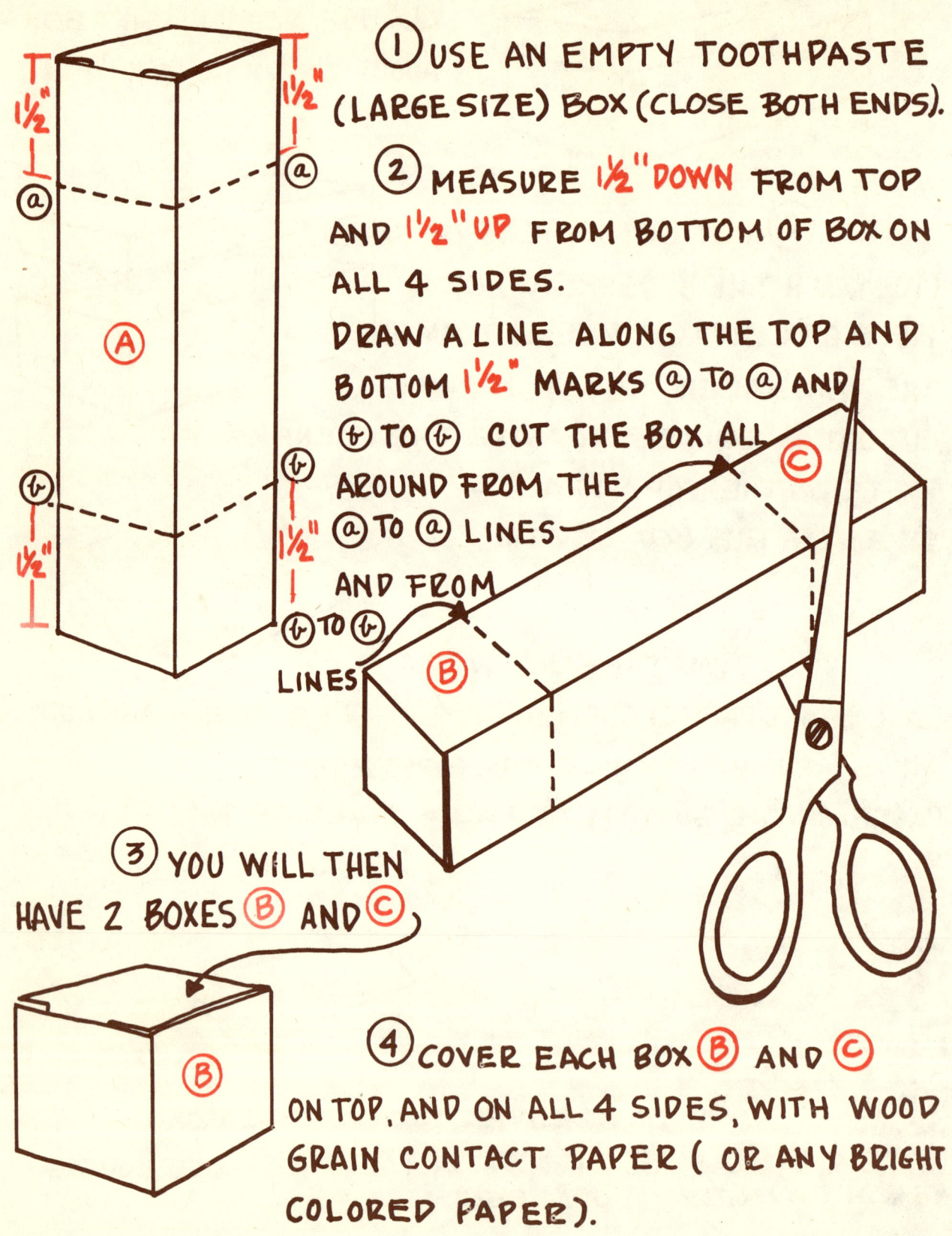

① USE AN EMPTY TOOTHPASTE (LARGE SIZE) BOX (CLOSE BOTH ENDS).

② MEASURE 1½" DOWN FROM TOP AND 1½" UP FROM BOTTOM OF BOX ON ALL 4 SIDES.

DRAW A LINE ALONG THE TOP AND BOTTOM 1½" MARKS ⓐ TO ⓐ AND ⓑ TO ⓑ CUT THE BOX ALL AROUND FROM THE ⓐ TO ⓐ LINES AND FROM ⓑ TO ⓑ LINES

③ YOU WILL THEN HAVE 2 BOXES Ⓑ AND Ⓒ

④ COVER EACH BOX Ⓑ AND Ⓒ ON TOP, AND ON ALL 4 SIDES, WITH WOOD GRAIN CONTACT PAPER (OR ANY BRIGHT COLORED PAPER).

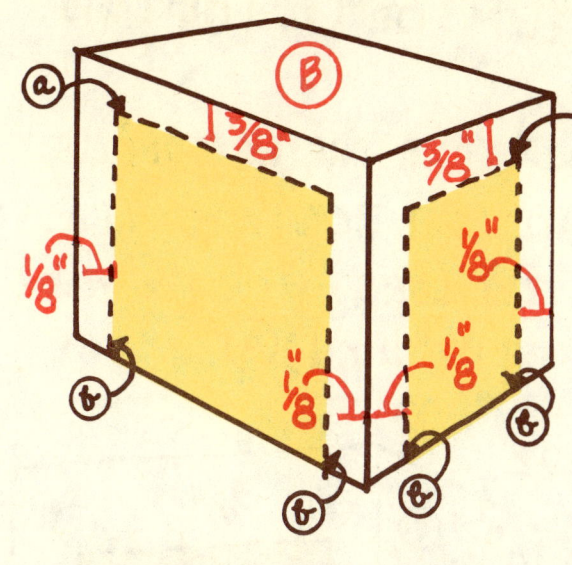

⑤ DRAW A LINE ⓐ AROUND ALL SIDES OF Ⓑ 3/8" DOWN FROM THE TOP. THEN DRAW A LINE ⓑ 1/8" IN FROM THE BOTTOM OF EACH CORNER OF THE BOX TO MEET ⓐ.

⑥ CUT ALONG LINES YOU HAVE DRAWN.

⑦ REPEAT THE SAME ⑤ AND ⑥ STEPS FOR BOX Ⓒ — AND YOU WILL HAVE A PAIR OF NIGHT TABLES LIKE THIS.

BENCH OR OTTOMAN

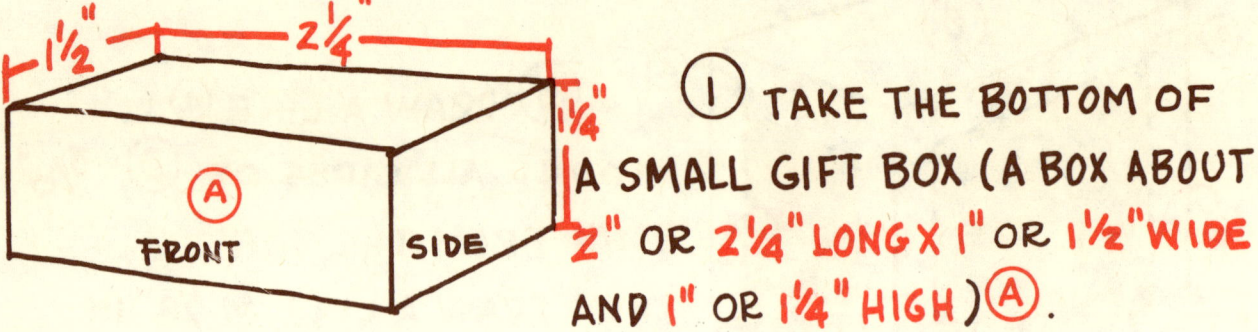

① TAKE THE BOTTOM OF A SMALL GIFT BOX (A BOX ABOUT 2" OR 2¼" LONG X 1" OR 1½" WIDE AND 1" OR 1¼" HIGH) Ⓐ.

② TURN THE BOX Ⓐ UPSIDE DOWN.

③ DRAW A LINE @ AROUND ALL 4 SIDES OF Ⓐ ¾" DOWN FROM THE TOP.
THEN DRAW A LINE & ¼" IN FROM THE BOTTOM OF EACH CORNER OF THE BOX TO MEET @.

④ CUT OUT THE 4 LEGS OF THE BENCH BY CUTTING ALONG ALL THE LINES YOU HAVE DRAWN.

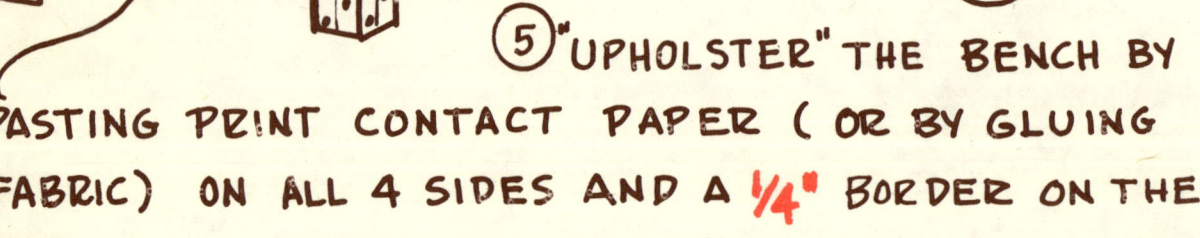

⑤ "UPHOLSTER" THE BENCH BY PASTING PRINT CONTACT PAPER (OR BY GLUING FABRIC) ON ALL 4 SIDES AND A ¼" BORDER ON THE TOP.

⑥ CUT A PIECE OF A "CELLULOSE" KITCHEN SPONGE (OR A PIECE OF STYROFOAM) 2"X1"X¼"THICK (OR A LITTLE THINNER IF YOU CAN) FOR THE TOP CUSHION Ⓑ OF THE BENCH.

⑦ "UPHOLSTER" THE CUSHION Ⓑ IN THE SAME PRINT CONTACT PAPER (OR THE FABRIC) BY PASTING IT ON THE TOP, ON ALL 4 SIDES AND ¼" BORDER ON THE BOTTOM.

⑧ TURN THE CUSHION Ⓑ RIGHT SIDE UP AND GLUE IT TO THE TOP OF BENCH Ⓐ.

BOLSTER FOR BED

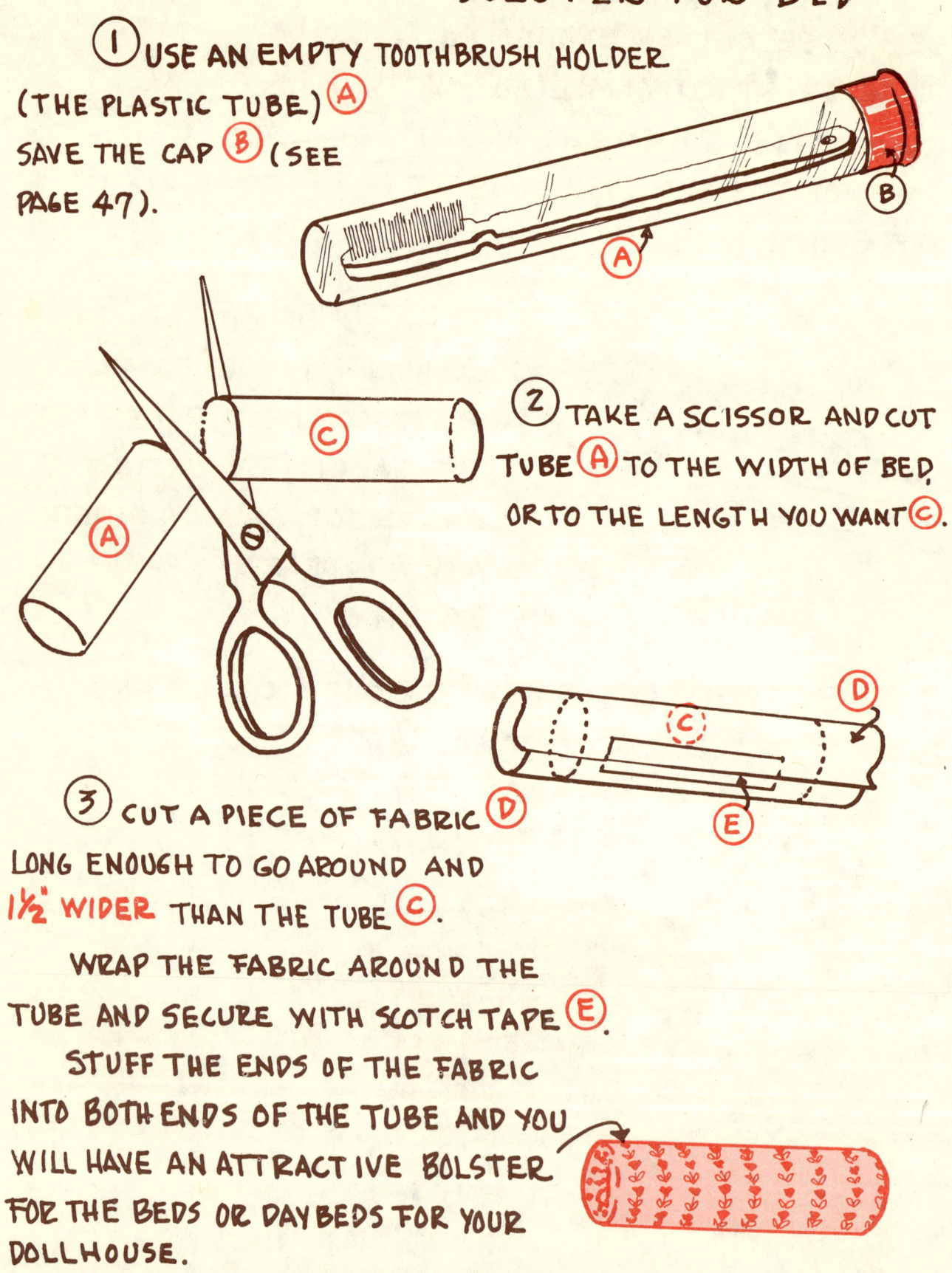

① USE AN EMPTY TOOTHBRUSH HOLDER (THE PLASTIC TUBE) Ⓐ SAVE THE CAP Ⓑ (SEE PAGE 47).

② TAKE A SCISSOR AND CUT TUBE Ⓐ TO THE WIDTH OF BED OR TO THE LENGTH YOU WANT Ⓒ.

③ CUT A PIECE OF FABRIC Ⓓ LONG ENOUGH TO GO AROUND AND 1½" WIDER THAN THE TUBE Ⓒ.

WRAP THE FABRIC AROUND THE TUBE AND SECURE WITH SCOTCH TAPE Ⓔ.

STUFF THE ENDS OF THE FABRIC INTO BOTH ENDS OF THE TUBE AND YOU WILL HAVE AN ATTRACTIVE BOLSTER FOR THE BEDS OR DAYBEDS FOR YOUR DOLLHOUSE.

TABLE CLOCK

① FIND A LARGE BRASS OR WHITE UPHOLSTERY TACK.

② BEND THE "TACK" PART DOWN FAR ENOUGH, AT AN ANGLE, SO THE UPHOLSTERY TACK WILL STAND ALONE.

③ WITH A FLOW PEN, DRAW IN THE 12 DOTS, FOR THE HOURS AS SHOWN ON A CLOCK.

④ DRAW IN THE HOUR HAND, DRAW IN THE MINUTE HAND.

PLACE CLOCK ON A NIGHT TABLE DESK OR DRESSER.

The Guest Room

TODAY THE GUEST ROOM means: a room that can take care of overnight guests a few times a year, but is in reality a den or study all the rest of the year. In fact most of the time.

It was the guest room that really became the first "double purpose" room of the house. It could possibly have worked the other way around, with the den first having to double as a guest room. But one thing is certain—no one wants to keep a room unused most of the time. This is wasteful.

It was the sofa bed that made it possible for the guest room to become a den because the sofa bed was designed to be used as a sofa during the day and as a bed during the night. This double purpose piece made the double purpose room possible.

Let's decide first what the room (no matter what it's called) will need to work well for both: for a guest room and for a den. Of course the sofa bed is still most important to the success of the room—it should be comfortable for sleeping. The best way to get both is to use a good mattress and box spring (exactly as for a narrow bed) so your dolls will have the same comfort for sleeping they would have in any other bed. But with such a bed, the seating can present a problem, because even a narrow bed is too wide to sit on, and it is never pleasant to sit with your back against the wall and your feet straight out. To solve this problem, use long bolsters (see page 106) along the length of the mattress unit against the wall and lots of pillows (see page 122) against the bolsters. This way your dolls can sit against the bolsters and pillows as they would in a club chair, or as they would on a real sofa. At night you remove the bolsters, pillows and top spread and the "sofa" becomes the "bed."

Besides the sofa bed or (daybed) you must think of what the room still needs. Naturally it should have a night table. Here again the large corner table (see page 118) that we used in the "children's room" would work well and would do the same job. It would serve as a headboard and it would hold a lamp, a radio and magazines or books. A small chest of drawers (see page 92) would do for the other end of the sofa bed and serve a double purpose too—as a night table and as a place for the visiting dolls to keep their clothes.

If there is no room at the end of the sofa bed for the chest, you must find another place for it, because this piece is important for the guest's comfort. If there is no other place, use an unpainted chest of drawers built into part of the "closet" to solve the problem.

The rest of the furniture in the room can be for the room's other purpose: for the den or study for the family. A desk (see page 18) is always good for this kind of room; every one of your dolls needs a desk, for homework, for writing thank-you notes, and sometimes for games—especially for a big jigsaw puzzle. The drawers are handy, too. Be sure the desk has a good lamp on it because good lighting is important when you are reading or writing.

Books should also be a part of the den. I love books and I believe they should be in almost every room, but especially in the den. So bookcases would do splendidly here and would serve their double purpose, too. The shelves of course would be for the books, and the bottom storage space is great for games, for cameras and films and even for the TV.

Add to all this some nice comfy chairs, a desk chair, tables and good reading lamps, and the room is set with the basic pieces it needs to do double duty—to work as a guest room and as a den for the family.

If you wish, the walls in this room can be quite different from those in all the other rooms in your doll house—they can be wood, instead of paint or paper. Wood on the walls of a room is called "paneling." And paneling is the most charming thing you can do, with lots of bookcases, for a den.

Wood or paneling on the walls will make a room look a little dark, therefore it is important to use bright and cheerful patterns (such as printed chintz or printed linen) on some of the upholstered pieces and also for curtains at the windows. Add a gay solid color or a bright plaid (that has the same colors as the printed material) for the daybed spread. If you choose plaid for the top spread, then the bolsters and the "skirt" can be in a matching solid color—or the other way around (as on page 119), or the "skirt" and bolsters can be one pattern and the top spread another pattern.

The bright, gay colors you add to a room or to a color scheme are called "accent colors." In this room the accent colors can be used for the pillows and sometimes for the lamp shades, if you like a lot of color.

If the room is small and you would like it to look larger, then use shutters at the windows instead of draperies. To make the room look still larger, then finish or make the shutters in the same "wood" as the walls.

A small patterned rug or wall to wall carpeting in a gay color will give the whole room a lift. But the real lift a room always needs is books, pictures, flowers and plants. Don't forget them in this room. Your dolls and their guests will love it.

BOOKCASES AND BOOKS

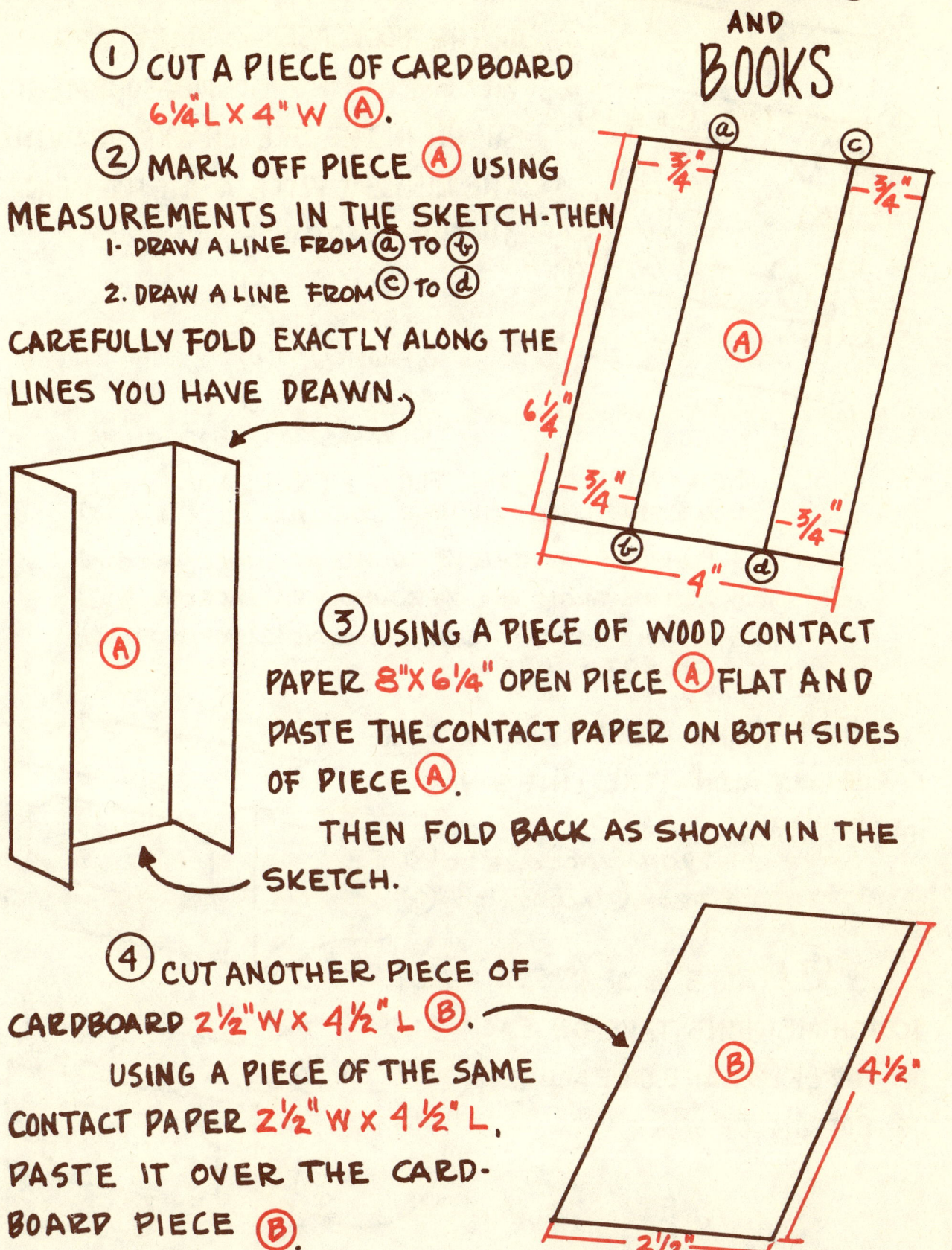

① CUT A PIECE OF CARDBOARD 6¼" L × 4" W Ⓐ.

② MARK OFF PIECE Ⓐ USING MEASUREMENTS IN THE SKETCH — THEN
  1. DRAW A LINE FROM ⓐ TO ⓑ
  2. DRAW A LINE FROM ⓒ TO ⓓ

CAREFULLY FOLD EXACTLY ALONG THE LINES YOU HAVE DRAWN.

③ USING A PIECE OF WOOD CONTACT PAPER 8" × 6¼" OPEN PIECE Ⓐ FLAT AND PASTE THE CONTACT PAPER ON BOTH SIDES OF PIECE Ⓐ.

THEN FOLD BACK AS SHOWN IN THE SKETCH.

④ CUT ANOTHER PIECE OF CARDBOARD 2½" W × 4½" L Ⓑ.

USING A PIECE OF THE SAME CONTACT PAPER 2½" W × 4½" L, PASTE IT OVER THE CARDBOARD PIECE Ⓑ.

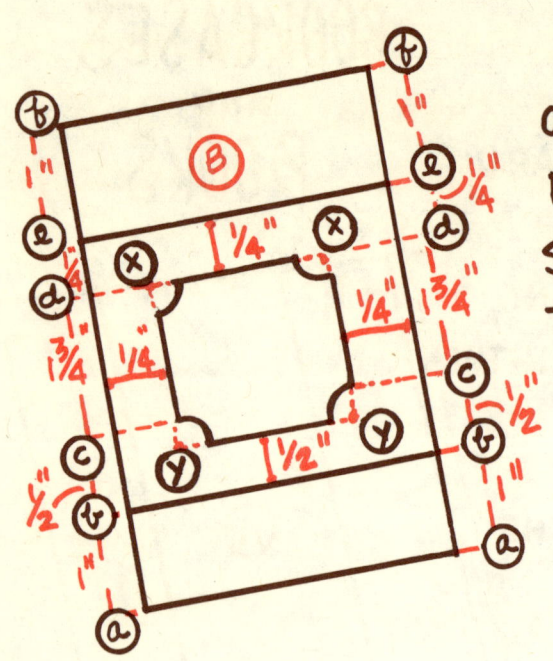

⑤ TO MAKE CABINET BASE OF THE BOOKCASE — MARK OFF PIECE Ⓑ, USING THE MEASUREMENTS SHOWN IN THE SKETCH AND DRAWING THE LINES (WITH A LIGHT PENCIL) IN THIS ORDER:—

1. FROM ⓑ TO ⓑ
2. FROM ⓒ TO ⓒ
3. FROM ⓓ TO ⓓ
4. FROM ⓔ TO ⓔ
5. FROM ⓧ TO Ⓨ BOTH SIDES.

NOW, WITH A BLACK FLOW PEN DRAW —
1. ¼ ROUND LINES IN EACH CORNER AT Ⓧ AND Ⓨ
2. A LINE FROM THE ¼ ROUND AT Ⓧ ACROSS TO Ⓧ
3. A LINE FROM THE ¼ ROUND AT Ⓨ ACROSS TO Ⓨ
4. A LINE FROM THE ¼ ROUND AT Ⓧ DOWN TO Ⓨ ON BOTH SIDES.

⑥ TAKE PIECE Ⓑ AND <u>FOLD</u> CAREFULLY ALONG THE LINES YOU HAVE DRAWN:—
1. FROM ⓔ ACROSS TO ⓔ
2. FROM ⓑ ACROSS TO ⓑ

⑦ PASTE ½ OF 1" STRIPS OF SCOTCH MENDING TAPE ON EACH END OF TOP OF Ⓑ — AND ON EACH END OF BOTTOM OF Ⓑ.

⑧ INSERT PIECE Ⓑ AS SHOWN - AND FASTEN THE OTHER HALF OF EACH OF THE SCOTCH TAPE STRIPS. IN THIS ORDER

1. PASTE THE STRIPS ON THE <u>BOTTOM</u> OF Ⓑ TO THE <u>OUTSIDE</u> OF THE SIDES OF BOOKCASE Ⓐ

2. PASTE THE STRIPS ON THE <u>TOP</u> OF Ⓑ TO THE <u>INSIDE</u> OF THE SIDES OF BOOKCASE Ⓐ

⑨ TO MAKE THE SHELVES. TAKE A PIECE OF CARDBOARD 2½" X 3¾". MARK OFF 5 SECTIONS. EACH 2½" X ¾" THEN CUT EACH SECTION Ⓒ ALONG THE LINES YOU HAVE DRAWN.

⑩ CUT <u>5 PIECES</u> OF CONTACT PAPER - EACH PIECE 2½" X 1½" W. FOLD EACH PIECE OF CONTACT PAPER IN HALF (FOLD IN THE WIDTH). AND PASTE 1 FOLDED PIECE OVER BOTH SIDES OF EACH SHELF Ⓒ.

⑪ PASTE ½ OF 1" STRIPS <u>TOP</u> AND <u>BOTTOM</u> AT <u>BOTH</u> ENDS OF EACH OF THE 5 SHELVES Ⓒ.

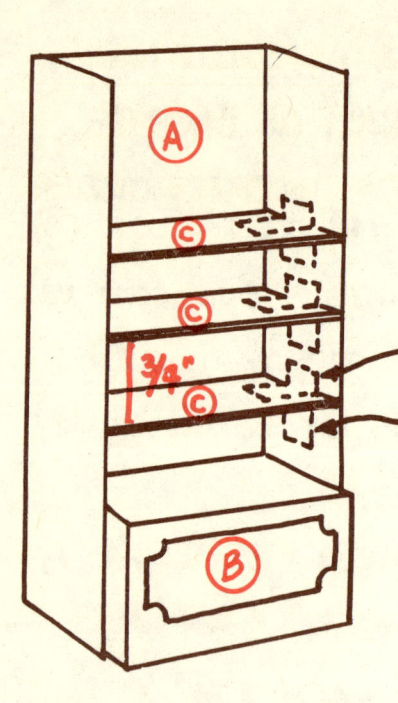

⑫ INSERT ALL 5 SHELVES ¾" APART IN BOOKCASE Ⓐ. FASTEN EACH SHELF, ON BOTH ENDS WITH THE ½ OF THE SCOTCH TAPE STRIPS ABOVE AND BELOW EACH SHELF - AS SHOWN IN THE SKETCH.

⑬ CUT A STRIP OF ¾" BROWN MYSTIK CLOTH TAPE 7" LONG. SPLIT THE STRIP Ⓓ DOWN THE CENTER SO YOU HAVE 2 STRIPS Ⓓ EACH 7"L × ⅜"W

USE 1 STRIP Ⓓ AND WRAP IT AROUND THE TOP OF THE BOOKCASE

USE THE OTHER STRIP AND WRAP IT AROUND THE BOTTOM OF THE BOOKCASE LIKE THIS.

⑭ CUT 6 STRIPS OF CORRUGATED PAPER Ⓔ IN THE FOLLOWING SIZES:
1. 2 STRIPS - 2¾"L × 5/8"H.
2. 3 STRIPS - 2¾"L × ½"H.
3. 1 STRIP - 2¾"L × ¾"H.

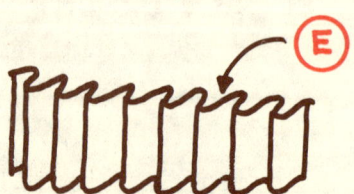

⑮ WITH A SOFT (4B) PENCIL DRAW LABELS ON EACH FOLD. BUT NOT AT THE SAME HEIGHT. AS IN THE SKETCH.

PAINT GROUPS OF "BOOKS" IN DIFFERENT COLORS. AND PAINT THE LABELS WHITE OR BLACK. INSERT A STRIP OF BOOKS ON EACH SHELF.

DAYBEDS

① USE THE INSIDE BOX Ⓐ OF AN EMPTY BOX OF KITCHEN SAFETY MATCHES.

② TURN BOX Ⓐ UPSIDE DOWN.

③ CUT 4 PIECES OF FABRIC 1½"H × 2"W Ⓑ PASTE ONE PIECE OF FABRIC AROUND EACH CORNER OF BOX Ⓐ.

④ CUT A PIECE OF FABRIC 5½" × 7¾" Ⓒ CUT 1½" SQUARES FROM EACH CORNER.

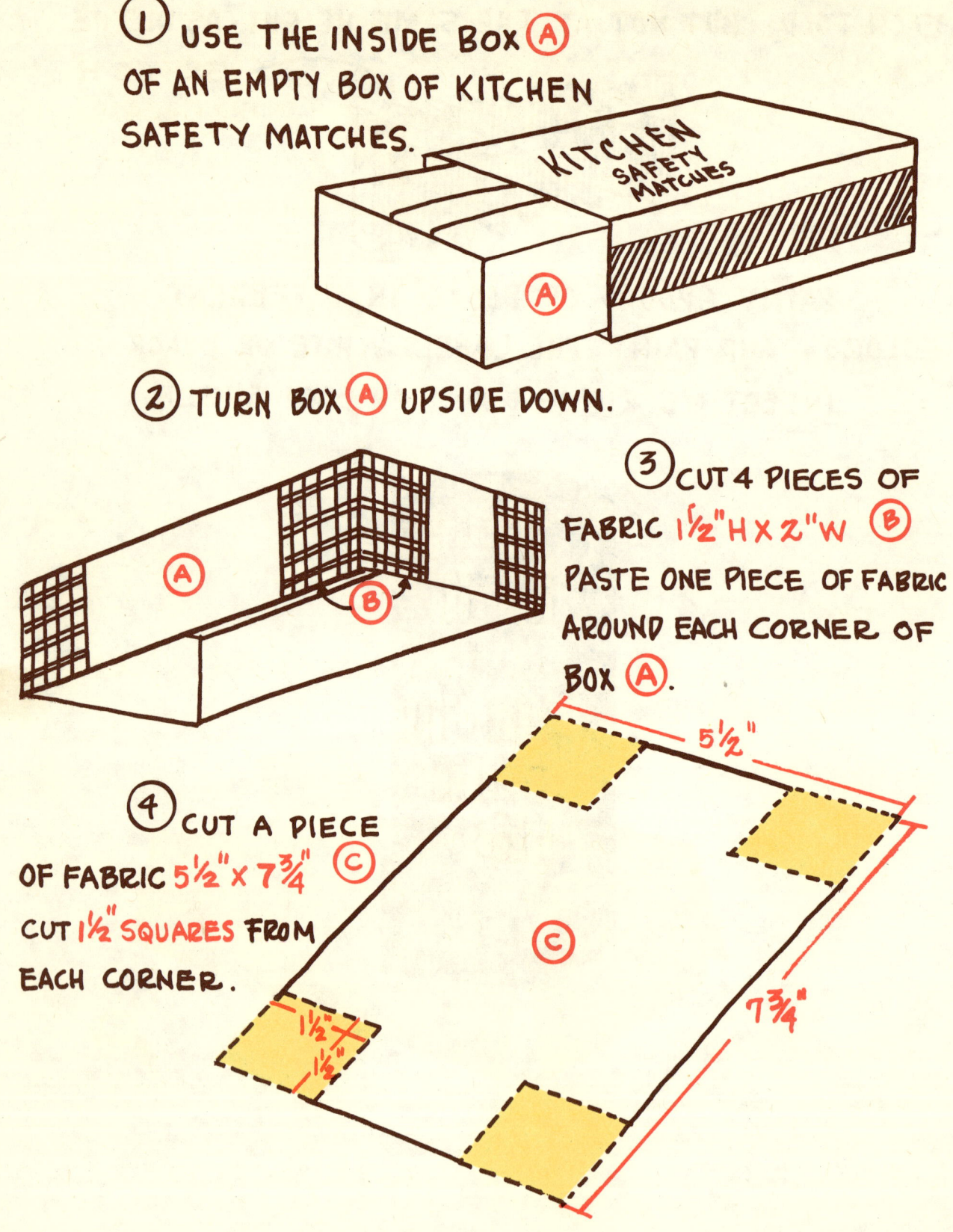

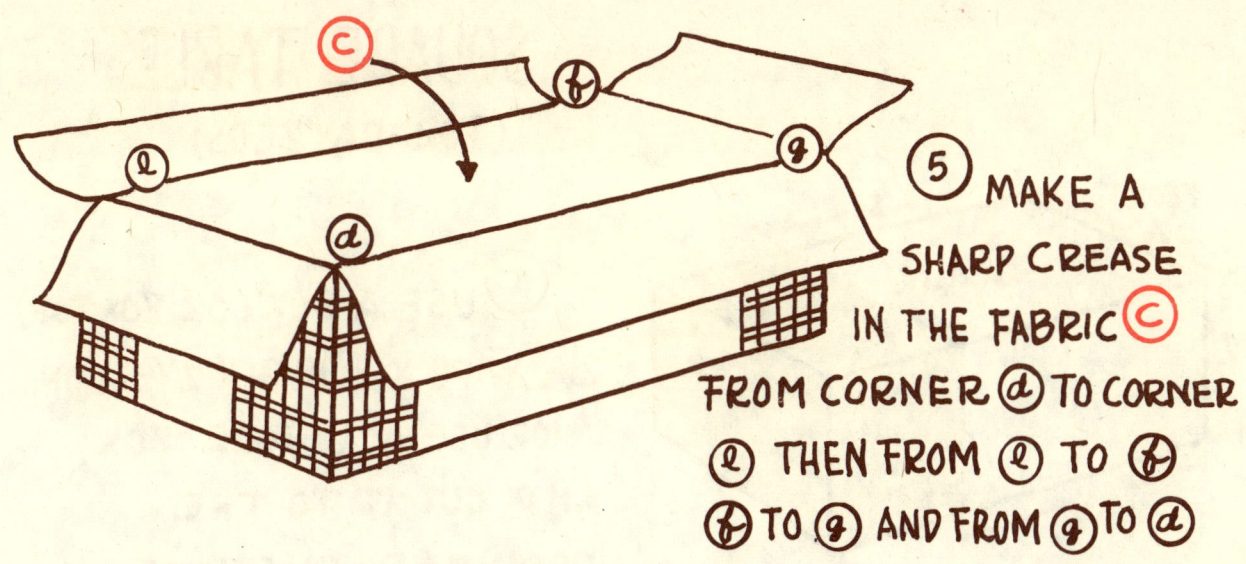

⑤ MAKE A SHARP CREASE IN THE FABRIC Ⓒ FROM CORNER Ⓐ TO CORNER ⓑ THEN FROM ⓑ TO ⓕ ⓕ TO ⓖ AND FROM ⓖ TO Ⓐ DRAPE THE CREASED FABRIC TO FIT OVER BOX.

⑥ MAKE 2 BOLSTERS (ONE 2½" LONG AND ONE 3") CUT 2 PIECES OF THE SAME FABRIC USED FOR THE CORNERS OF BOX Ⓐ MAKE AND COVER BOLSTERS (AS SHOWN ON PAGE 106).

ADD 2 "WILD COLORED" PILLOWS FOR ACCENT (SEE PAGE 122).

SQUARE TABLE
(FOR DAY BEDS)

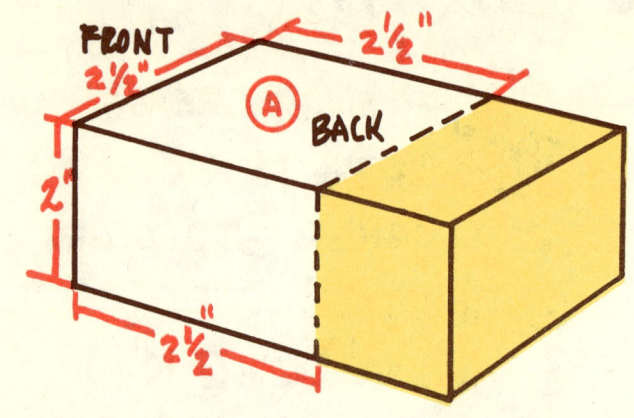

① USE A BOX (OR BOX TOP) 2½" WIDE × 2" HIGH × 2½" LONG Ⓐ OR USE A LONGER BOX AND CUT IT TO THE REQUIRED LENGTH OF 2½".

② CUT A PIECE OF WOOD GRAIN CONTACT PAPER 6½" LONG × 4½" WIDE Ⓑ. CUT OUT TWO 2" × 2" SQUARES FROM THE FRONT CORNERS AS SHOWN HERE.

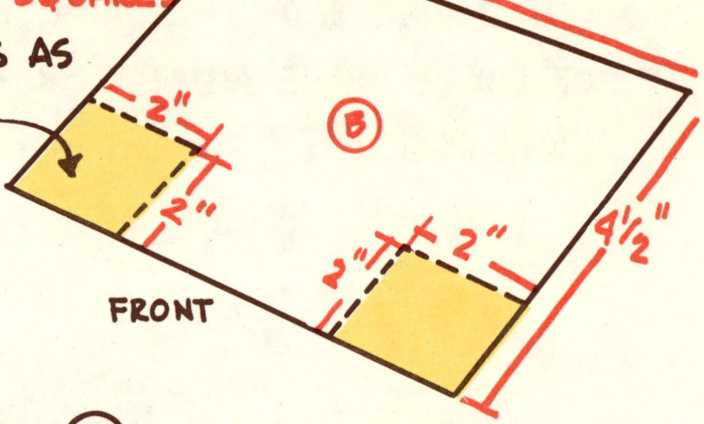

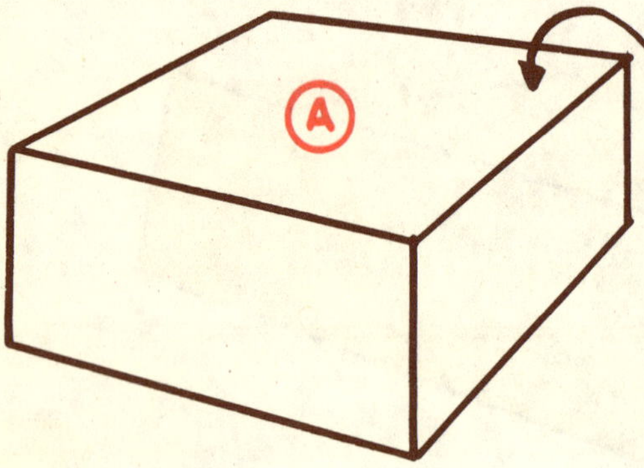

③ PASTE CONTACT PAPER TO TOP, SIDES AND FRONT OF Ⓐ. THE BACK CAN BE LEFT OPEN.

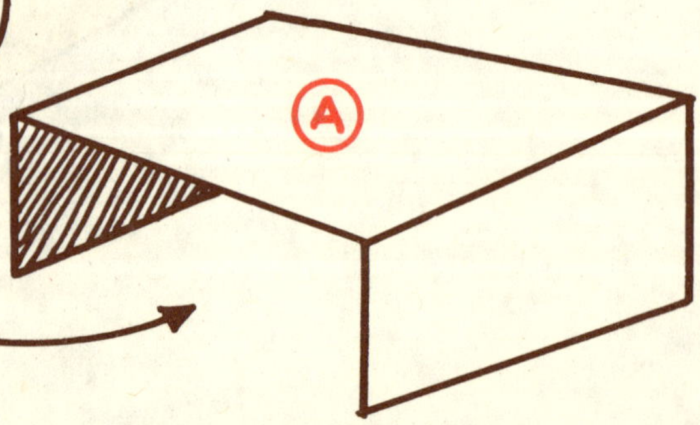

④ PLACE THE TABLE IN THE CORNER OF YOUR DOLL'S ROOM AND PUT ONE DAYBED (PAGE 116) AGAINST ONE SIDE OF THE TABLE.

AND THE OTHER DAYBED AT RIGHT ANGLE TO THE FIRST (AGAINST THE OTHER SIDE OF THE TABLE)

SHUTTERS

① TAKE A WHITE GIFT BOX COVER AND CUT OUT A PIECE 2¾" X 6" Ⓐ THIS PIECE WILL MAKE 2 PAIRS OR 4 SINGLE SHUTTERS.

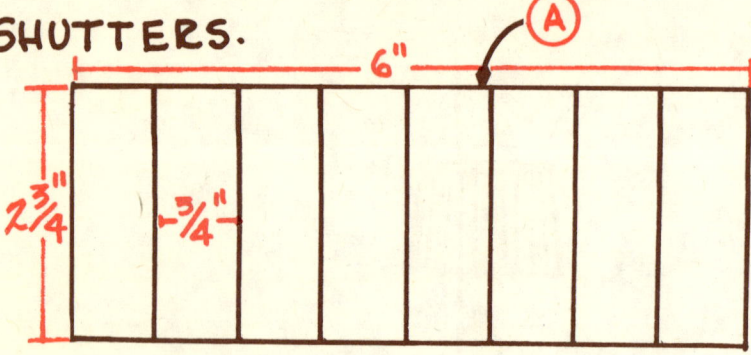

② WITH A RULER MARK OFF 8 SECTIONS, EACH ¾" WIDE AND CUT THEM APART. Ⓐ

③ ON ONE OF THE PIECES Ⓐ MARK OUT A RECTANGLE ⅛" IN FROM BOTH SIDES. ⅛" DOWN FROM THE TOP, AND 1⅛" UP FROM THE BOTTOM. THE RECTANGLE Ⓑ WILL BE ½" WIDE AND 1½" LONG.

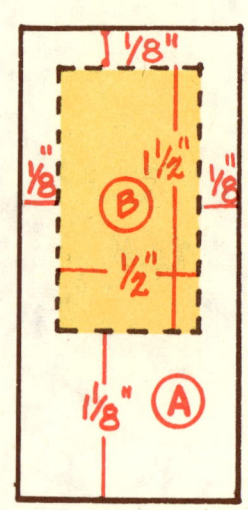

④ CUT OUT RECTANGLE Ⓑ WITH A SHARP X-ACTO KNIFE. TRY TO LEAVE CLEAN STRAIGHT EDGES.

⑤ USE THE CUT OUT PIECE Ⓑ AS A PATTERN TO MARK OFF THE SAME RECTANGLE ON EACH OF THE OTHER PIECES. CUT ALL OF THEM OUT CAREFULLY.

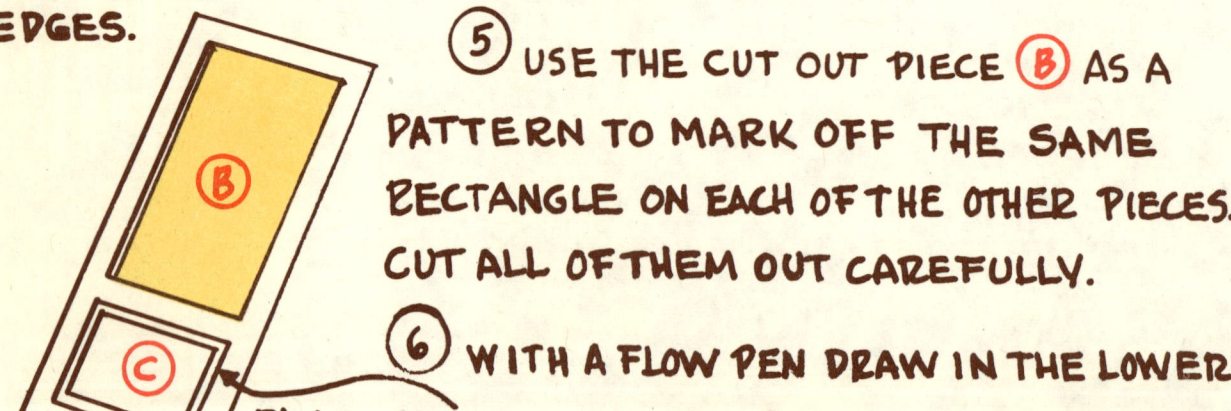

⑥ WITH A FLOW PEN DRAW IN THE LOWER PANEL ON EACH CUT OUT PIECE. NOW YOU HAVE 8 SHUTTER "FRAMES"! Ⓒ

⑦ GLUE 4 TOOTHPICKS EVENLY SPACED, OVER THE CUT OUT ⒷPART OF ONE FRAME. REINFORCE WITH SCOTCH TAPE, TOP AND BOTTOM OVER EDGES OF TOOTHPICKS Ⓓ.
DO THE SAME WITH 3 MORE FRAMES.

⑧ PASTE A PLAIN CUT OUT FRAME Ⓒ SECURELY OVER EACH OF THE FRAMES WITH TOOTHPICKS Ⓔ.

⑨ "INSTALL" THE SHUTTERS BY CAREFULLY PASTING THE BACK OF A SHUTTER TO EACH SIDE OF THE WINDOW.

PILLOWS

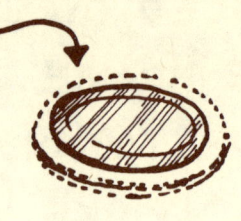

① TAKE 2 LITTLE (1½" DIAMETER) COMPACT POWDER PUFFS, AND CUT ONE INTO A 1"X 1" SQUARE Ⓐ CUT THE OTHER INTO A PIECE ¾"W X 1"L Ⓑ.

② USING FABRIC, CONTACT, OR GIFT WRAP PAPER, CUT THESE PIECES IN SIZES:-
   Ⓒ 1 PIECE 3"X 3" SQUARE.
   Ⓓ 1 PIECE 2¾"W X 3" L.

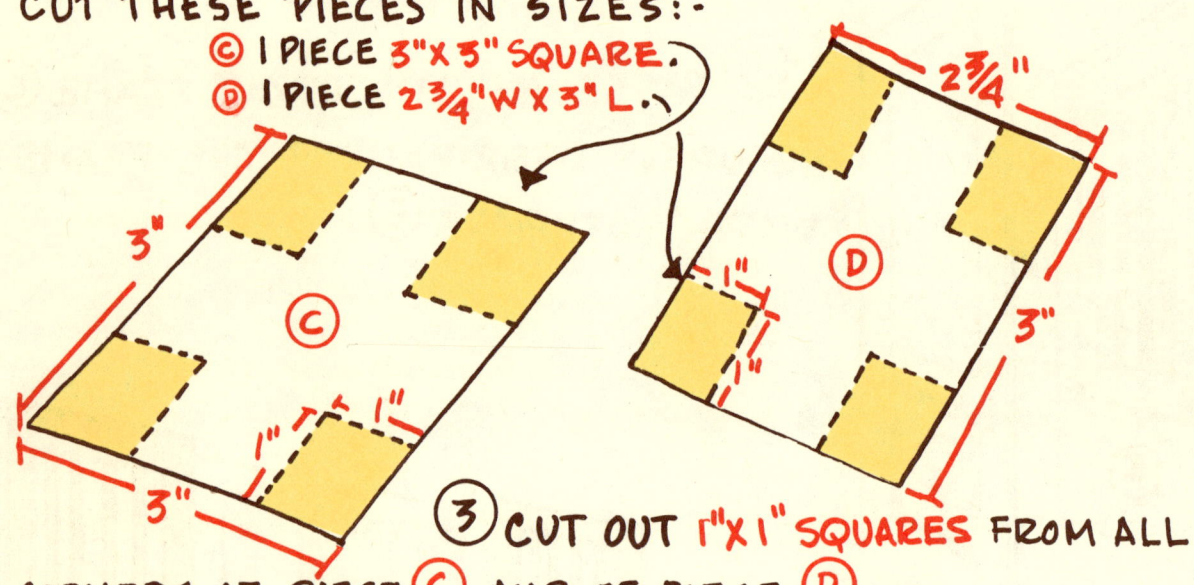

③ CUT OUT 1"X 1" SQUARES FROM ALL 4 CORNERS OF PIECE Ⓒ AND OF PIECE Ⓓ.

④ NOW PASTE PIECE Ⓒ ON "PUFF" Ⓐ. AND PASTE PIECE Ⓓ ON "PUFF" Ⓑ.

YOU WILL NEED LOTS OF PILLOWS. SO REPEAT STEPS ①, ② ③ AND ④ FOR ALL OF THEM.

The Kitchen

THE KITCHEN IS ONE room that has to work. But that doesn't mean that it can't be fun to do. If the kitchen is well planned in the beginning, it can work like a charm and it can be easy as pie to decorate.

Do you know how to cook? If you know something about cooking, it is easier to plan a kitchen because there is always a "cooking-reason" for everything in a kitchen, and for everything a kitchen must do.

For instance, a kitchen must have cupboards to store dishes, glasses, groceries and supplies.

It must have a refrigerator to keep the milk, butter, eggs and all the perishable foods fresh and good.

It must have a stove to cook and bake the food.

It must have a sink to wash the fresh vegetables and fruits before eating —and of course to wash all the pots and pans and all the dishes *after* eating. But then a dishwasher is really better for that job, and a good kitchen should have one.

The kitchen must also have lots of counter space to work on to prepare the food. The counter space is always the top of the base cabinets. These base cabinets, or lower cabinets are for the storage of pots and pans. Some have drawers that are used for table silver, for cooking knives and mixing spoons, for dish towels, for paper napkins and doilies, and one drawer is great for string, hammer, nails and tools. There is also a cabinet that does not have a counter top because it is very high. It has to be! It has to be high enough to hold the big brooms and mops that you need to keep the kitchen clean all the time. There is still a third kind of a cabinet: it is known as a wall or hung cabinet because it is fastened to the wall well above the counters. These cabinets are very useful for the storage of dishes, glasses and canned goods or for dry groceries.

There are three basic and quite different ways to arrange all these things in a kitchen. Which of these three you use, depends on the shape and size of your kitchen.

But before you begin to plan you must consider the housekeeping reasons for placing some of the important units in special places in any kitchen. Ideally the place to prepare food and to clean up should be in one area—this, of course, is where you put the sink and must provide counter space. The dishwasher has to be next to the sink, because it uses the same water supply to do its job. Cooking and baking should be in another area, with a range for cooking and an oven for baking or roasting. If the oven is the kind that is built into a wall, there should be a counter right next to it, so you have a place to put down a very hot baking pan (full of brownies, I hope), the moment you take it from the oven. If it is the other kind, the stove that has the burners on the top and baking oven underneath, one needs counter space too and for the same reason. The refrigerator should always be handy to both the stove and the sink.

Now here are the three typical arrangements for kitchens of different shapes and sizes:

1. If the kitchen is small, with only two good walls to work with then the "L" shape plan is good.

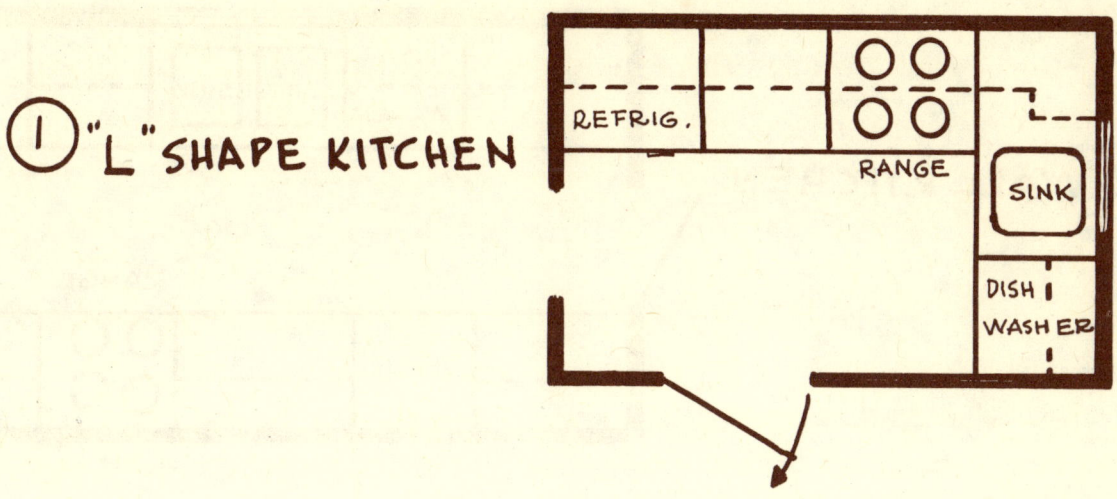

① "L" SHAPE KITCHEN

2. If the kitchen is large and almost square then this plan is the best of all plans and is called the "U" shape.

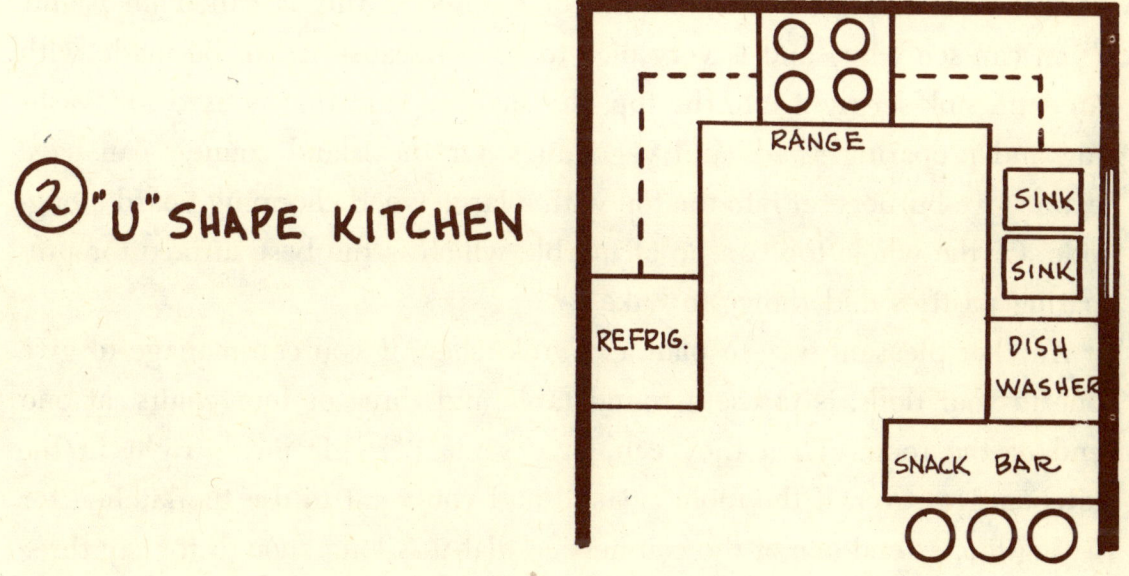

② "U" SHAPE KITCHEN

3. If the kitchen is long and narrow it is called a "two-wall kitchen" and the layout explains why.

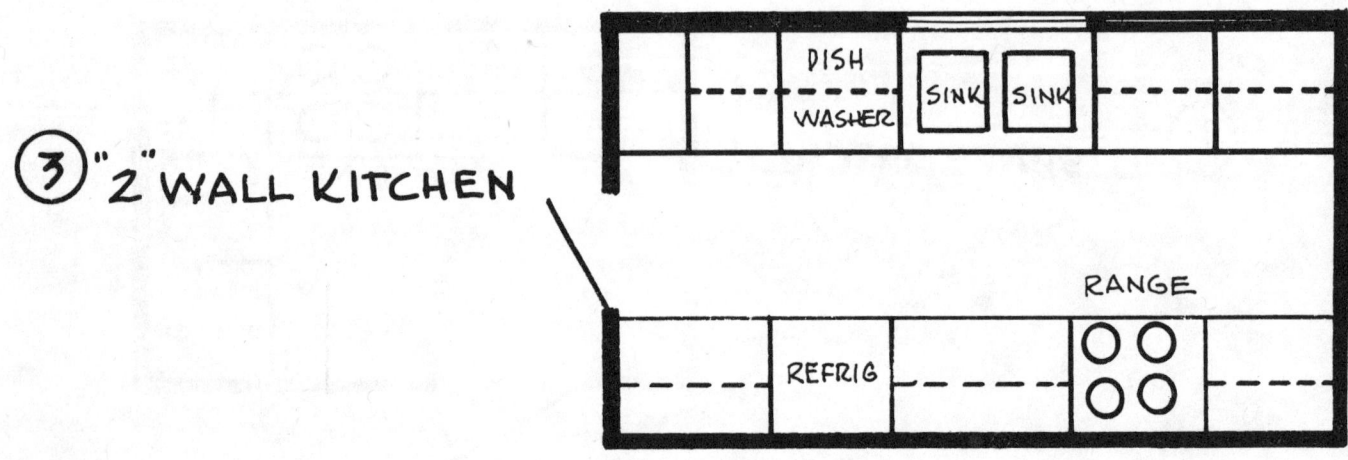

You can choose whichever of these kitchens fits your doll house—but you are especially lucky if your doll house has a kitchen that is really good and large. Then it can have many wonderful, extra things. Such as a big square counter right in the middle of the room; this is called an island (you can see why) and is very nice to have because it can be made with an extra sink set right into the top, the shallow kind that is used for washing and preparing salads and vegetables. Or the island counter can have extra stove burners set into the top with a large wood chopping board alongside. Or the whole top can be of marble which is the best surface for preparing pastries and things to bake.

Another pleasant way to plan a large kitchen, if you can manage to give one to your dolls, is to use a round table and three or four chairs, at one end of the room. Then they can have some of their meals right in the kitchen. However, if the room is small and you want to use the kitchen for eating too, extend one of the counters so that it is long enough for say three places. Use three high stools or bar chairs against the counter, and your dolls have a charming place for breakfast and snacks. This is called a snack bar.

Once the planning (or the layout) is completed and all the equipment, that is the stove, sink, etc., is set for your dolls' kitchen, you are ready for the creative part—decorating it.

Remember that the kitchen is a room, too, and it deserves exactly the same "decorating thinking" as other rooms in the house. The only difference is that in a kitchen you don't have the freedom of colors and materials that you have in other rooms.

The wall covering should be vinyl (or contact paper) so it can easily be washed down. The curtains should be made of fabric that will survive endless trips to the washing machine. The floors must be of serviceable vinyl tile, or if you are going to have an elegant kitchen then glazed ceramic tile, or brick floors, but in any case, the floors must be easy to keep clean.

Just because you are limited in materials and colors does not mean you will be limited in ideas, because this is the sort of thing in decorating that makes you think harder, try harder and always come up with your best ideas.

In decorating your kitchen you must, as in every room, decide on your color scheme. But in the kitchen you must begin with the stove, the sink and dishwasher, and the refrigerator, in other words what I have referred to as "equipment." The standard "equipment" for all kitchens comes in five or six colors from most manufacturers. These colors are white, pink, yellow, copper (a kind of soft glowing brown), avocado (pronounced a-vo-kā-doe, a soft dark gray green exactly like a real avocado when you remove the peel), and aqua. Since these are the colors available, any color scheme for a kitchen must begin with the equipment. From there it must go to cabinets and counters.

Cabinets are available in almost any wood—birch, walnut, oak, pine and fruitwood are the most popular. Any wood cabinet can be painted any color, and of course there are many cabinets made of laminates too. Laminate is a plastic material that comes in a zillion colors as well as imitation wood finishes and won't break or stain. It is almost always used for counter tops too, unless you want to be very grand and use stainless steel or Dutch tiles for your counter tops. If you look hard and think hard you will find things you can use in your doll house that will look like any of these.

A great deal of the color in a kitchen can be found on the floors. Today there are many exciting colors and designs in vinyl flooring—the colors are endless, and the designs are patterns made to look like real brick, French clay tile, pegged wood planks, patterned Dutch tiles and flagstones or slate. All of these are "color" and must be part of your scheme. Many of these can be made with contact or colored papers.

Your kitchen can have its own style too—it doesn't have to be just a kitchen, it can be an "Early American Kitchen." Pine cabinets, red brick floors, copper equipment, painted shutters at the window instead of curtains, a painted tole (tin) chandelier, a calico cloth for the table and matching calico wallpaper for the walls, maple or pine chairs and spice racks and the kitchen is "Early American."

To create a "modern" kitchen use white cabinets with dark walnut doors, the equipment in white, vinyl floors that look like small mosaic white tiles, a stainless steel hood over the stove, paint the ceiling a bright strong yellow, upholster the stools or chairs in yellow, black and white stripe vinyl material and use the same material for a window shade. Hang a good-looking modern painting or print on one wall and a shelf (below the print) with large glass jars on it for flour, sugar, etc.

If you want a "French Provincial Kitchen," the cabinets should be in fruitwood with white porcelain door knobs. The equipment in yellow or white, the floors in vinyl that looks like French red clay tiles, the counter tops in laminate that looks like fruitwood or in white; a real butcher's block for a worktable; one wall in "brick" painted white and fake "old beams" nailed to the ceiling; an old French Provincial grandfather's clock; a copper hood for the stove and lots of beautiful copper pots or molds hanging on a wall.

Add to any of these kitchens the charm of shelves for cookbooks and spices, bulletin boards for shopping lists, wall phones for color and convenience, pictures to please the eye, a colorful jug to hold gobs of wooden mixing spoons, an indoor window box to grow herbs, a "mobile" made of light kitchen utensils, a striped awning *inside* the windows, or bamboo shades and no curtains—these are the touches that add to kitchen decorating flavor and help make a kitchen a wonderful place to work and to live in.

KITCHEN BASE CABINETS

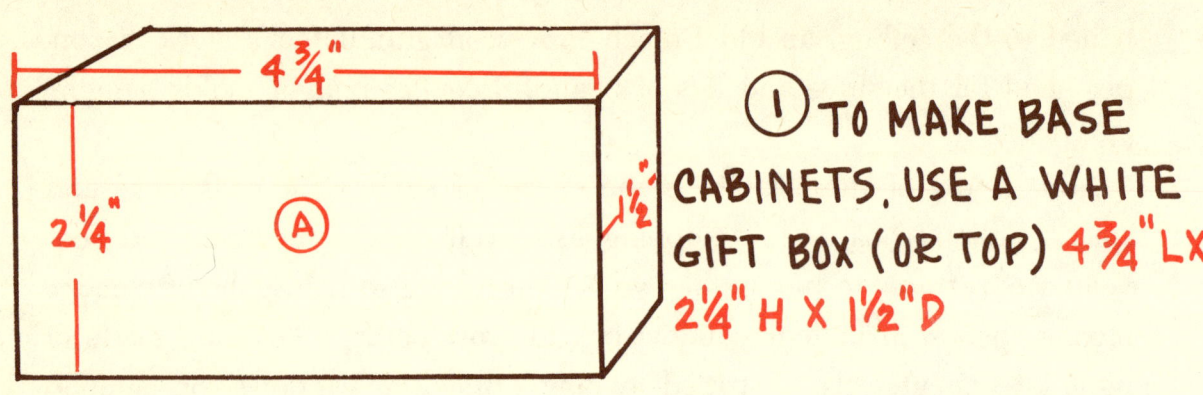

① TO MAKE BASE CABINETS, USE A WHITE GIFT BOX (OR TOP) 4¾" L X 2¼" H X 1½" D

② FOR THE DRAWERS AND DOORS ON THE CABINETS, USE A BLACK FLOW PEN TO MARK OFF PIECE Ⓐ FOLLOWING THE MEASUREMENTS IN THE SKETCH.

DRAW YOUR LINES IN THIS ORDER:-

1.) FROM ⓣ ACROSS TO ⓣ
2.) FROM ⓓ UP TO ⓓ - (BOTH)
3.) FROM ⓧ UP TO ⓧ - (BOTH)
4.) FROM ⓨ UP TO ⓨ

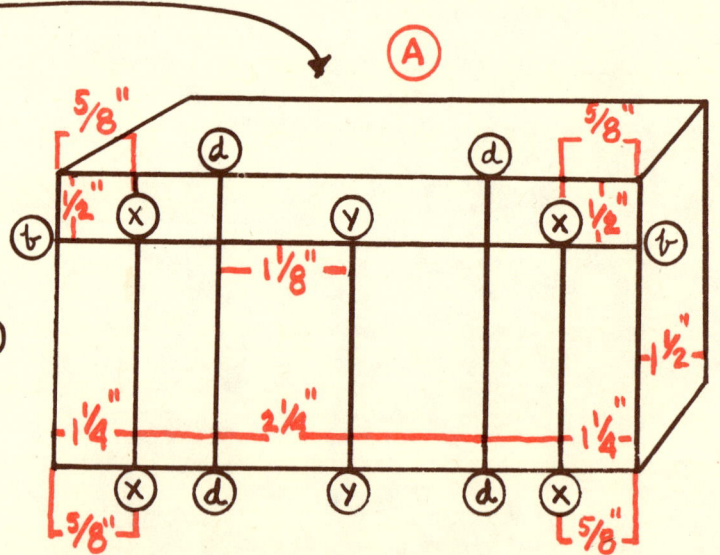

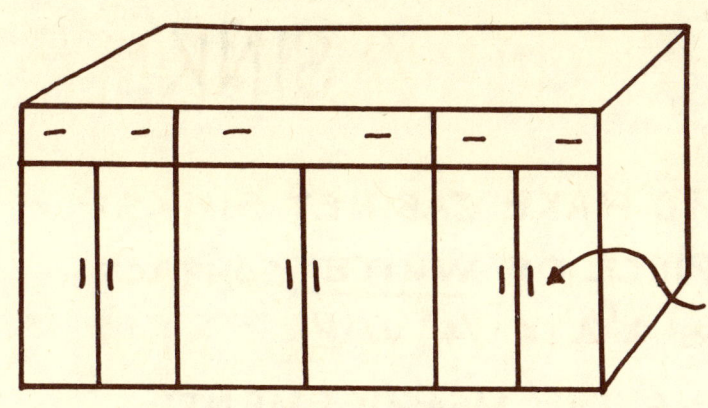

③ NOW DRAW IN THE HANDLES ON THE DOORS AND DRAWERS AS SHOWN HERE.

④ FOR THE KICK PLATE Ⓑ CUT A PIECE OF BLACK MYSTIK TAPE 7¾" L X ¼" W AND PASTE ALONG BOTTOM (FRONT AND SIDES)

ONCE YOU HAVE THIS BASIC CABINET, YOU MAY USE IT FOR ANY OF A NUMBER OF PURPOSES, DEPENDING ON WHAT YOUR KITCHEN NEEDS.

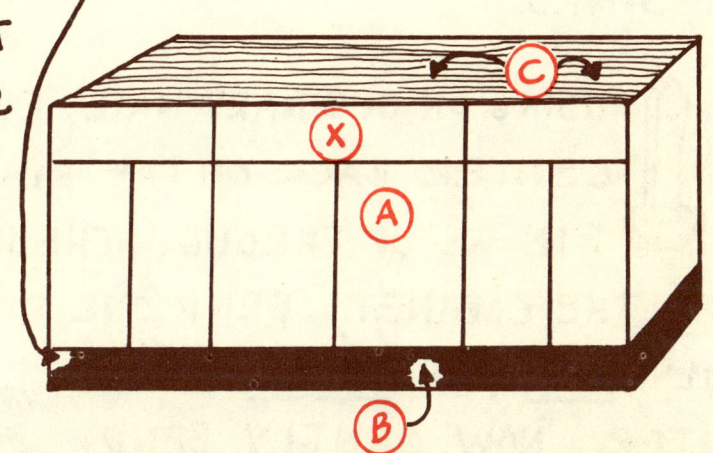

⑤ FOR "BUTCHER BLOCK" COUNTER TOP CUT A PIECE OF LIGHT WOOD CONTACT PAPER 4¾" L X 1½" W AND PASTE TO TOP OF CABINETS Ⓒ.

OR FOR A STANDARD COUNTER TOP CUT A PIECE OF CONTRASTING COLOR PAPER, THE SAME SIZE AND PASTE TO THE TOP OF CABINETS Ⓒ.

SINK

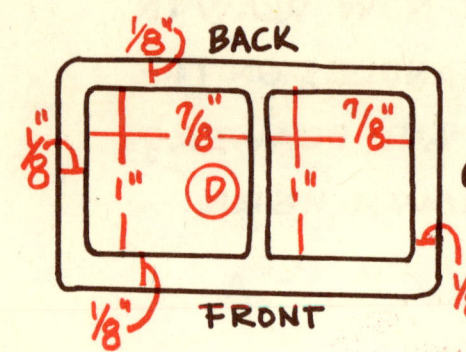

⑥ TO MAKE CABINET SINKS CUT A PIECE OF <u>WHITE</u> CONTACT PAPER 2¼"L X 1¼"W Ⓓ USING THE MEASUREMENTS SHOWN IN THE SKETCH - DRAW IN THE DOUBLE SINKS.

NOW PASTE THE SINKS Ⓓ ON THE COUNTER Ⓒ, DIRECTLY IN THE CENTER, OVER CABINET Ⓧ.

⑦ USE A FOLDER PIN Ⓔ FOR THE FAUCET OF THE SINKS.

USING AN ORDINARY NAIL, PUNCH A HOLE IN THE CENTER BACK OF THE SINKS AND PUSH THE PIN Ⓔ UP THROUGH THE HOLE (FROM <u>UNDERNEATH</u> THE CABINET.) BEND ONE PRONG @ OF THE PIN FIRMLY <u>BACK</u> AND <u>UNDER</u> THE COUNTER. NOW GENTLY BEND THE OTHER PRONG ⓣ <u>FORWARD</u> IN THE SHAPE SHOWN.

DISHWASHER

USE EITHER THE <u>RIGHT</u> OR <u>LEFT</u> UNIT OF THE SINK CABINET FOR YOUR DISHWASHER:

① CUT A PIECE OF WHITE GIFT BOX OR TOP 2" X 1⅛" Ⓐ

② AT THE CENTER OF PIECE Ⓐ AND ¼" DOWN, PUT A LIGHT PENCIL MARK +.

③ NOW, WITH A BLACK FLOW PEN, DRAW A <u>DOUBLE</u> CIRCLE ¼" DIAMETER USING YOUR MARK + AS THE CENTER.

THEN DRAW A "CROSS" IN THE <u>INSIDE</u> OF THE DOUBLE CIRCLE, AND SHADE OR COLOR THE 2 SECTIONS AS SHOWN.

④ PASTE PIECE Ⓐ ON SINK CABINET

RANGE

⑧ FOR THE RANGE AND OVEN MAKE ANOTHER UNIT OF BASE CABINETS BY REPEATING STEPS ①②③④ AND ⑤.

⑨ TO MAKE A RANGE, CUT A PIECE OF THIN CARDBOARD 2½"L X 1½"W Ⓕ

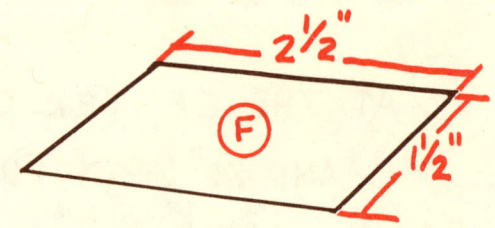

THEN CUT A PIECE OF SILVER PAPER (OR FOIL) 3"L X 2"W AND COVER THE CARDBOARD Ⓕ — ALLOWING ¼" TO FOLD UNDER (ON ALL FOUR SIDES)

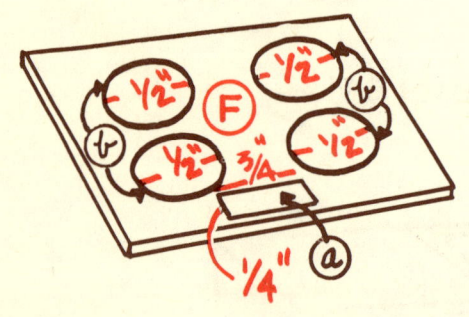

⑩ WITH PEN AND INK, DRAW IN THE SWITCH PANEL ⓐ ¼"W X ¾"L AT THE FRONT (CENTER) OF RANGE.

NOW DRAW 4 CIRCLES ½" DIAMETER FOR HEATING UNITS ⓑ

⑪ PASTE RANGE Ⓕ ON THE COUNTER TOP DIRECTLY IN THE CENTER OVER CABINETS Ⓧ.

TAKE 4 SMALL MAP PINS AND STICK THEM THRU THE SWITCH PANEL ⓐ FOR CONTROL KNOBS.

⑫ TO ADD THE OVEN — COVER A THIN PIECE OF CARDBOARD 2"L X 1½"W Ⓖ WITH SILVER PAPER (OR FOIL) PASTE OVER CENTER AREA.   DRAW IN OVEN DOOR HANDLE, AS SHOWN.

NOTE: THE SIZE AND LAYOUT OF YOUR KITCHEN WILL DETERMINE HOW MANY "BASE" CABINETS YOU WILL NEED. TO INSTALL THEM AND THE STOVE, SINK AND DISHWASHER, SEE PAGE 163.

REFRIGERATOR

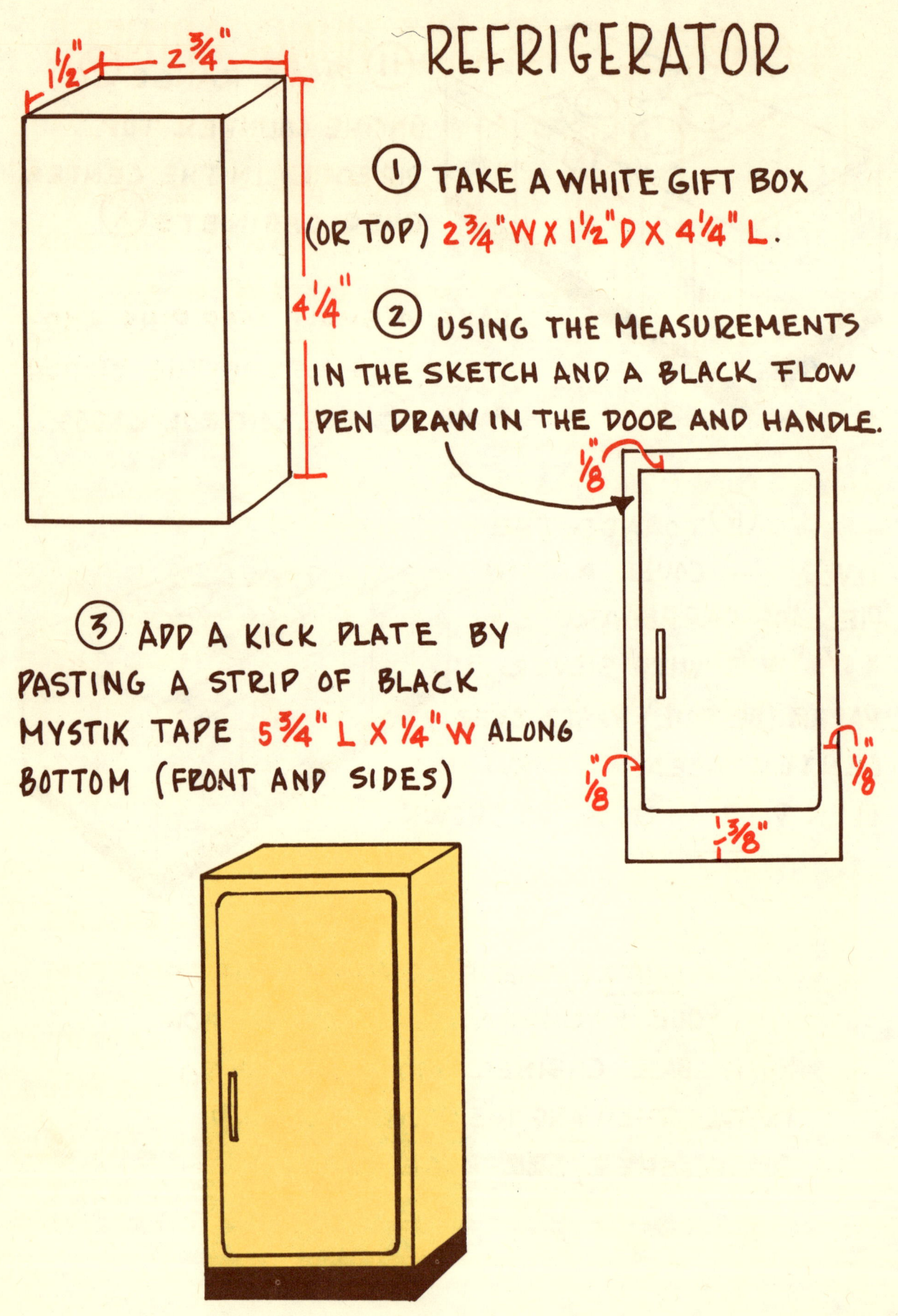

① TAKE A WHITE GIFT BOX (OR TOP) 2¾"W X 1½"D X 4¼"L.

② USING THE MEASUREMENTS IN THE SKETCH AND A BLACK FLOW PEN DRAW IN THE DOOR AND HANDLE.

③ ADD A KICK PLATE BY PASTING A STRIP OF BLACK MYSTIK TAPE 5¾"L X ¼"W ALONG BOTTOM (FRONT AND SIDES)

DOUBLE-HUNG CABINETS

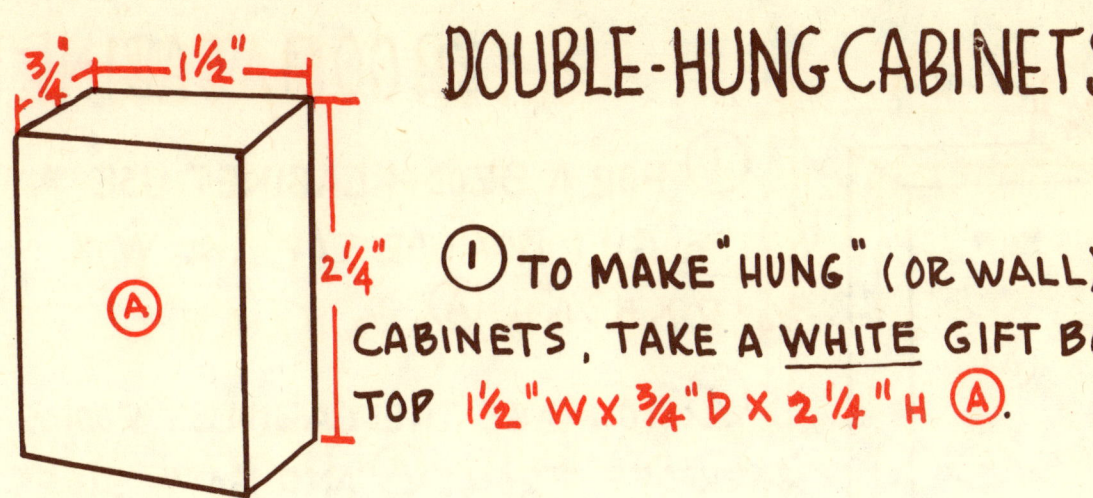

① TO MAKE "HUNG" (OR WALL) CABINETS, TAKE A <u>WHITE</u> GIFT BOX TOP 1½"W x ¾"D x 2¼"H Ⓐ.

② FOR THE CABINET DOORS, USE A BLACK FLOW PEN TO MARK OFF PIECE Ⓐ, USING THE MEASUREMENTS IN THE SKETCH

DRAW YOUR LINES IN THIS ORDER:
1. FROM ⓐ TO ⓑ
2. TWO LINES FROM ⓒ TO ⓓ AND FROM ⓓ TO ⓔ (ON BOTH SIDES)

③ NOW DRAW IN THE HANDLES FOR THE DOORS, TOP AND BOTTOM

<u>NOTE</u>: THE SIZE AND LAYOUT OF YOUR KITCHEN WILL DETERMINE HOW MANY "HUNG" CABINETS YOU WILL NEED. TO INSTALL CABINETS SEE PAGE #163.

BROOM-CABINETS

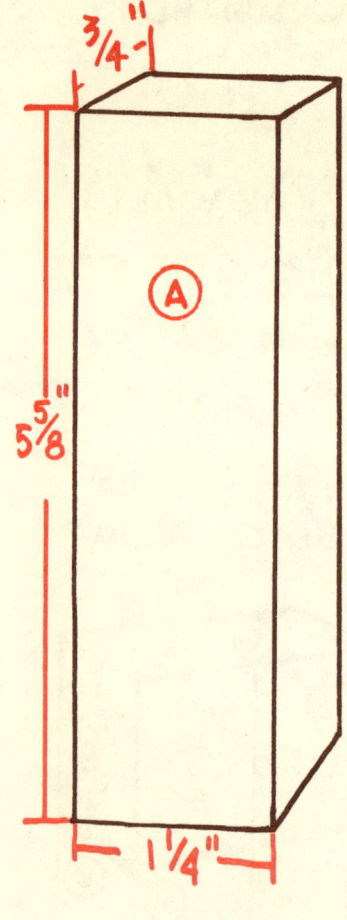

① FOR A BROOM CABINET USE A WHITE GIFT BOX (OR TOP) 1¼" W X ¾" D X 5⅝" L Ⓐ.

② TO MAKE THE CABINET DOORS MARK OFF FRONT Ⓐ AND BOTH SIDES USING THE MEASUREMENTS IN THE SKETCH. USING A BLACK FLOW PEN, DRAW YOUR LINES IN THIS ORDER:-

1. ONE LINE ⓐ UP TO ⓑ
2. TWO LINES FROM ⓒ TO ⓐ AND FROM ⓓ TO ⓑ (ON BOTH SIDES.)

③ NOW DRAW IN THE DOOR HANDLES, TOP AND BOTTOM.

④ ADD A KICK PLATE BY PASTING A STRIP OF BLACK MYSTIK TAPE 1¾" L X ¼" W ALONG BOTTOM (FRONT AND SIDES) OF CABINET.

CAFE CURTAINS

APPLY PLASTIC SHELF EDGING TO TOP OF WINDOW TO MAKE CORNICE.

PLASTIC SHELF EDGING

APPLY DOUBLE ROWS OF PLASTIC SHELF EDGING TO MAKE CAFE CURTAINS.

TOWEL RACK
(OR TIE RACK)

① TAKE PAPER CLIP Ⓐ

② CUT OFF A PIECE OF SCOTCH MENDING TAPE ABOUT 1" LONG Ⓑ SLIP ¼" OF THE TAPE Ⓑ THRU TOP PART Ⓧ OF PAPER CLIP, AND SEAL IT TO THE LONGER PIECE OF TAPE. TAKE THE LONGER PIECE OF TAPE AND PASTE IT TO THE WALL.

KITCHEN TOWEL RACK

BEDROOM TIE OR BELT RACK

BATH TOWEL RACK

WALL CLOCK

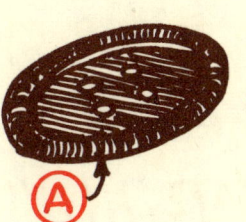

① USE A BUTTON (ABOUT THE SIZE OF A QUARTER) WITH A RIM Ⓐ

② FROM A PIECE OF WHITE PAPER Ⓑ CUT A CIRCLE TO FIT INSIDE RIM OF BUTTON.

③ WITH A BLACK INK FLOW PEN DRAW IN DOTS OR NUMBERS FOR THE HOURS ON THE CLOCK.
DRAW IN HOUR HAND
DRAW IN MINUTE HAND.

④ PASTE CLOCK FACE Ⓑ ON TOP OF BUTTON Ⓐ. THE RIM WILL THEN BECOME THE FRAME OF YOUR CLOCK.

⑤ GLUE THE CLOCK IN PLACE ON THE WALL IN THE KITCHEN, DEN, HALL, OR LIVING ROOM.

How to "Build" a Doll House

IF YOU OR YOUR MOTHER were to go to a store to buy a broom—that's exactly what you would ask for—a broom! The storekeeper wouldn't dream of asking you: "What size or what style please?" Because brooms are just brooms. But if you want to buy a dress or a coat, probably the very first thing the salesperson would ask is: "What size and what style please?"—because clothes are very personal, and they must fit different people and must be suitable for any age group. Houses are much more like clothes than they are like brooms! Because houses are personal, too, they come in styles and in many sizes to fit different families. They even come in different colors.

One way to find a nice house is to go shopping and look and look until you find just what you want. Now when people go looking for a house, they come upon many that they are sure they couldn't enjoy. Some are quite lovely, but they are too grand. Some are very charming, but they are too old. Some are rather quaint, but they are too hard to take care of. Some are too big, and some are just too small. It is for reasons like these that many people decide to build their own home. Then they can be sure to have a house that is just right.

You too can build your very own house just to fit your doll family. This is the kind of house I am going to tell you about. This is the house I am going to tell you how to build—a doll dream house!

Let's plan your dream house to have all the things you could ever dream of. Pretend it will have all the modern things it could possibly have for the kitchen and need for all the plumbing and heating. It will have the newest lighting, the prettiest hardware and the best fireplace ever. If the plan of the house is done wisely, it will have the kitchen facing east to fill the room with the best of the morning sun. The terrace should be shaded so it is nice and cool during the hot summer months. The bathrooms should be large, at least large enough for the family needs and convenient to all the bedrooms. The front door should open onto a hall, or a passageway, that takes you to the bedrooms or to the kitchen without traipsing through the living room or dining room. The back door should be where a back door belongs—in the back—so muddy feet or delivery boys won't have to walk through the whole house.

What is also important is that the house itself, every corner of it, can be all yours—with all your best ideas for living. Some of the other dividends you can have if you build your own house is a kitchen just the size you want, with the stove, the sink and the refrigerator where they should be. You can have a laundry either as part of the kitchen or right next to it, not in the basement. This way your dolls won't have to run up and down stairs, instead they can go on with many of their kitchen duties while the clothes are whirling around like mad in *that* machine.

You can plan for every room to be exactly the size you want and need. For instance, if you feel that the living room is too big, that practically no one really uses it, that the den is too small and practically everyone in the family *lives* in the den—then the den should be the *larger* room and the living room should be the *smaller* one.

This same principle holds for all the other rooms as well. In other words in building, just as in decorating, you must always first decide what you and your doll family need.

Then resolve how you and your dolls prefer to live with and use the things they need.

Now let's begin building our doll house. Of course you knew all along it wasn't going to have plumbing or heating or lighting and all those things that real houses must have—but I thought it was such fun to talk about as a lark. Also remember not all doll houses are alike. Some may be complete with a bathroom or a powder room, others may not.

In my plans for a doll house I have included the rooms that are the most creative and interesting to decorate. Generally I tried to keep it simple—with most of the rooms big enough and high enough so you can reach into them easily to place or to rearrange the furniture.

On the second floor I suggested a "hall" by setting the second floor 2" back from the first floor and pretending that the "doors" to each room opened from the "hall." That is why no doors are shown on the plans of the second floor. (Of course in a real house there would be a "hall" leading from the top of the stairs to the front "hall" but I did not put it in our house so you could have larger bedrooms to work in.)

Of course you can place the doors leading from one room to another anywhere you wish—or just place them to suit your furniture arrangements. You can also eliminate some of the windows or, if you want to, you can add some. But in building the doll house itself (for the first try at least) I suggest you follow carefully all the construction plans as the instructions and the illustrations show. If you do, then this is what your doll house should look like when it's finished. (Sketch #1)

Sketch #1

Now, in the actual building there is a great deal that I'm sure you can do by yourself. But let's face it, building is man's work and you will have to have some help—so why don't you have your father stand by—just in case!

MATERIALS NEEDED:

Be sure you have a good size cutting board or a large piece of Masonite, so that when you are using a sharp knife, you will not cut through to your worktable.

The other materials you will need are special but simple:

1. A heavy duty stapler
2. A ruler
3. A metal-edge ruler

4. Lots of pencils
5. Sturdy scissors
6. Glue
7. An X-Acto knife
8. Masking tape
9. Mystik cloth tape
10. Scotch tape
11. Flow pens
12. Colored or white map pins
13. Upholstery nails (the little brass kind)
14. Poster paints
15. Paint brushes
16. Sponge
17. 3 or 4 big clean cardboard boxes.
18. Contact Paper in:
    a. Solid colors (for the rooms you want to "paint")
    b. Tiny stripes (for the rooms you want to paper—such as the hall or the dining room)
    c. Tiny floral (for bedrooms you want to paper)
    d. Wood paper (for rooms you want to "wood panel," such as the den. You will also need lots of it for floors)
    e. Tiny checks or polka dots (for the nursery or the parts of the kitchen you want to paper)
    f. Marble (this is great for some of the floors, as in the entrance hall or the dining room)
19. Gift-wrap tape (This should be the very narrowest you can get or about ¼" wide. Try to find the ones that are printed in stripes or in tiny designs. These are great for "borders" around windows or doors or to create panels on "painted" walls for a very elegant look.)

PLANS:

Here are the plans for the doll house to use as a model. The model is a "scale model" (the scale is ¾" = 1 foot), which means that your doll's new home will be built by using measurements used in building a real house. There are 5 big separate operations in building this house:

I. Making the Ground Floor.
II. Making the Second Floor.
III. Painting, Papering and General Installation.
IV. Putting the two floors together.
V. Making the Roof and Attic.

All the furniture in this book is the same scale as the doll house—which also means that all the furniture you make will fit correctly in your doll's new house.

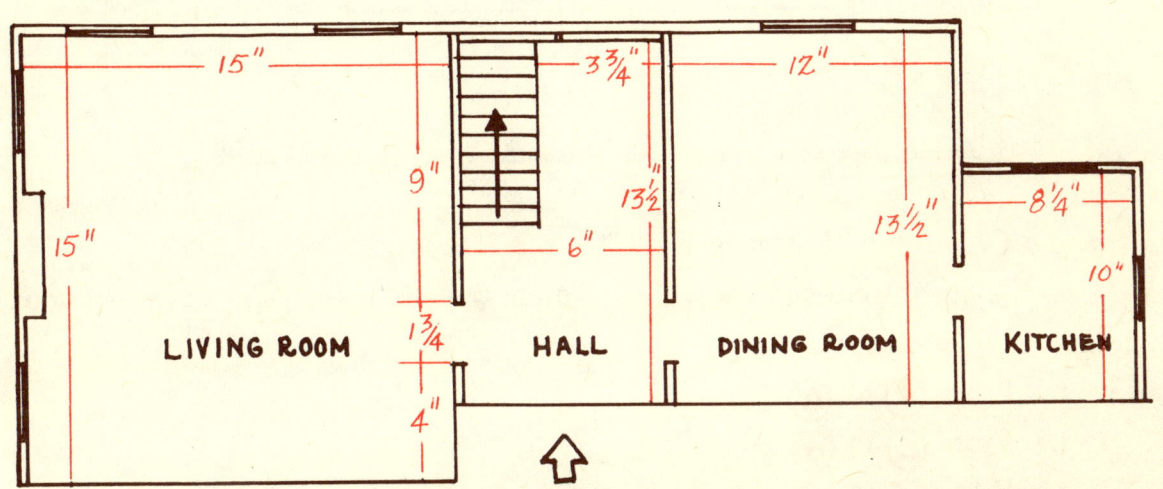

FIRST FLOOR PLAN

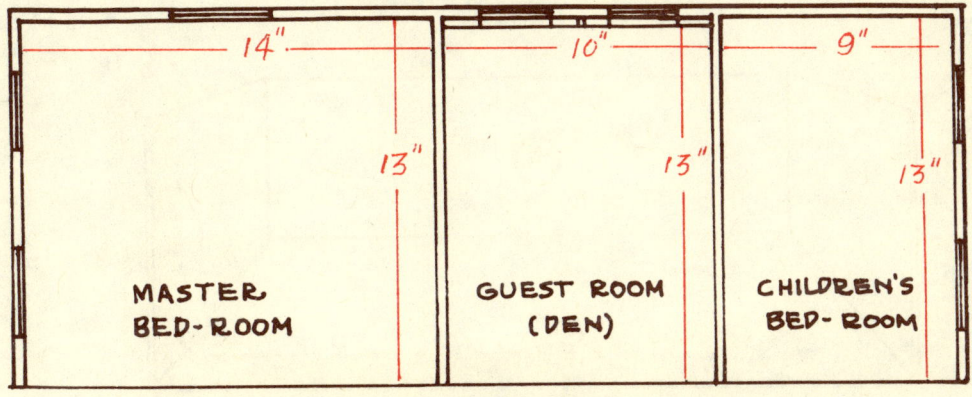

SECOND FLOOR PLAN

Sketch #2

I Making the Ground Floor (First Floor)

1. *To Begin the House*

Find a fresh, strong cardboard carton (A), 33″ long X 15″ wide X about 7″ high, (if you don't have any around your home, supermarkets and department stores are good places to go for cartons that are in good condition), and cut it down so that it is 6¾″ high all the way around. Then cut off one of the 33″ long sides of the carton (as in sketch #3), leaving one whole side of the box open. This will be the *front* of your doll house.

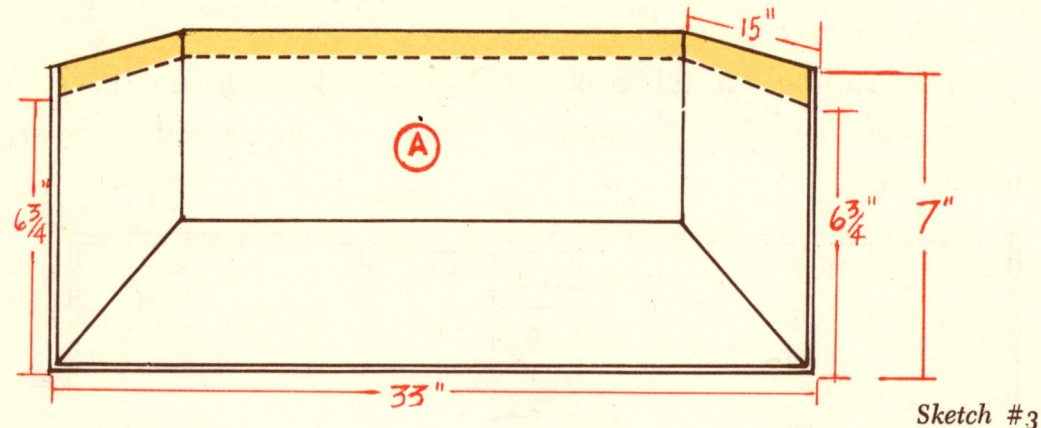

Sketch #3

2. *To Create the "Entrance Walk" to the House*

Use the measurements shown in sketch #4 on piece (A) and draw your lines in this order

  1.) From (a) to (c)
  2.) From (c) to (d)
  3.) From (d) to (e)

Use a heavy scissors and cut away the piece shaded in yellow.

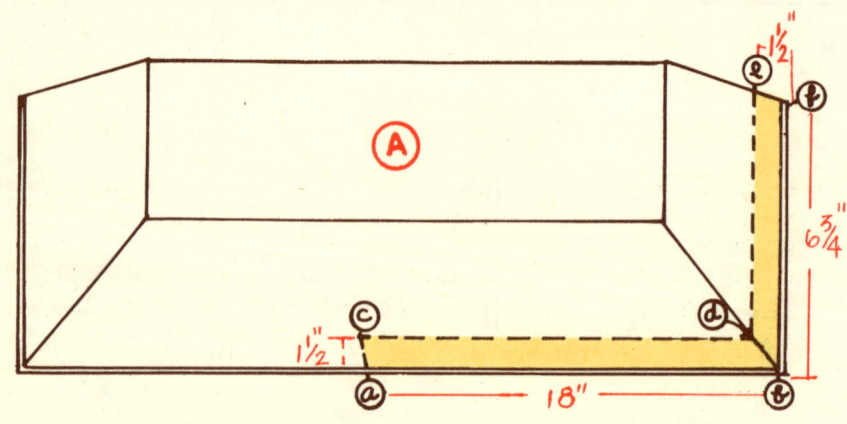

Sketch #4

Now mark off the rooms which will be on the ground floor of your doll house Ⓐ. There will be three rooms to begin with—the Living Room, Hall, and Dining Room. To create these areas follow the measurements on sketch #5 and with a ruler draw your lines this way:

1.) From ⓐ to ⓑ (Living Room and Hall)
2.) From ⓒ to ⓓ (Hall and Dining Room)

On the back wall draw lines:

3.) From ⓑ up to ⓔ
4.) From ⓓ up to ⓕ

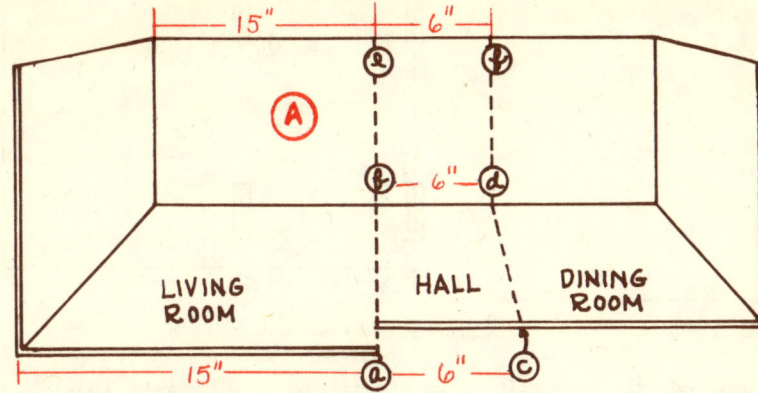

Sketch #5

3. To Make Partitions and Door Openings

You will have to have partitions (walls) between the rooms, of course. Before making the partitions, however, you will need a way to fasten them firmly to the floor of the house. To prepare for the partition between the living room and the hall, use sketch #6, which is a *plan only* of the first floor. By this I mean you do not see the sides or back walls in this sketch. Now using the measurements in sketch #6, mark off lines for the "slots" in this order along the ⓐ to ⓑ line:

1.) From ⓑ to ⓜ
2.) From ⓜ to ⓝ draw double lines
3.) From ⓝ to ⓞ
4.) From ⓞ to ⓟ draw double lines

5.) Repeat steps 1.) through 4.) along the ⓒ to ⓓ line.

Now using an X-Acto knife and a metal ruler as a guide, cut out *all* four "slots" by drawing the knife firmly *through* the double lines:

1.) From ⓜ to ⓝ
2.) From ⓞ to ⓟ

The "slot" must be about ¼" wide—so you will have to repeat this cut out process one or two times until you have the correct width for the "slot."

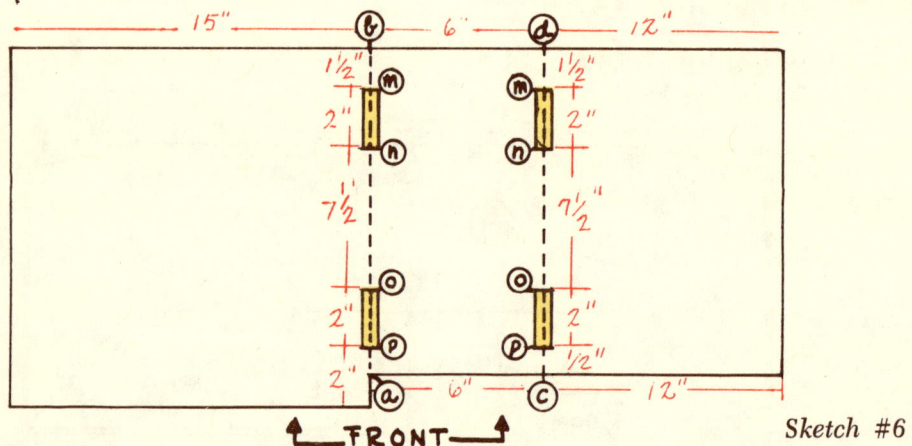

Sketch #6

Now you are ready to make the partition walls and the door openings between the three rooms on the ground floor of your doll house. You will need two partitions. See sketches #7 and #8.

Take two strips of cardboard, one 18¼" long [A] and the other 16¾" long [B] . Both should be 7" wide. Here's how to make them:

Measure ¼" from ⓑ to ⓐ on both ends of [A] . (Sketch #7)

Draw a *light* line from ⓐ across to ⓐ.

Now using the other measurements in the sketch, draw *heavy* lines in this order:

1.) From ⓧ down to ⓒ
2.) From ⓧ down to ⓓ
3.) From ⓜ down to ⓔ
4.) From ⓝ down to ⓕ

5.) From ⓜ across to ⓝ
6.) From ⓨ down to ⓟ
7.) From ⓨ down to ⓗ

With a sharp scissors cut along all the *heavy* lines you have drawn (as shaded in yellow in the sketch), and throw these pieces away.

8.) Repeat steps 1.) through 7.) for piece B . (Sketch #8)

9.) *Lightly* draw a line from ⓚ down to ⓘ on both pieces A and B .

On piece A fold along the line ⓚ to ⓘ . Holding the part marked "front" towards you, fold the flap A-1 to the right.

On piece B fold along the line ⓚ to ⓘ . Again hold the "front" towards you, but now fold the flap B-1 in the opposite way, to the left.

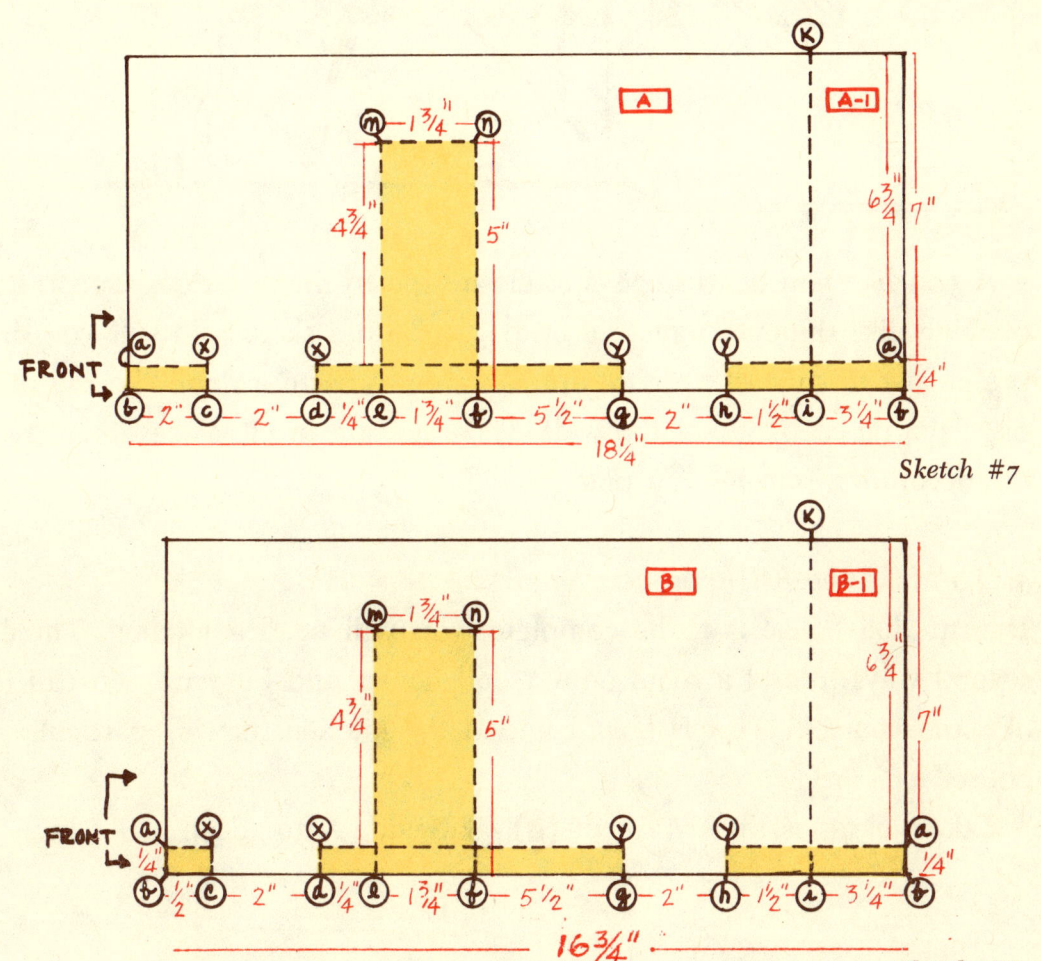

Sketch #7

Sketch #8

4. *To Install Partitions*

Now take partition B and firmly insert both tabs Y into floor slots Y. To further secure the partition B, staple (or tape) the folded section "flap" B-1 to the back wall. Four staples, (marked +), one in each corner of section B-1 should do. (Sketch #9)

Repeat these steps with partition A and its "flap" A-1.

You now have three rooms on the first floor with a door opening leading from the Hall into the Living Room and another door opening from the Hall into the Dining Room.

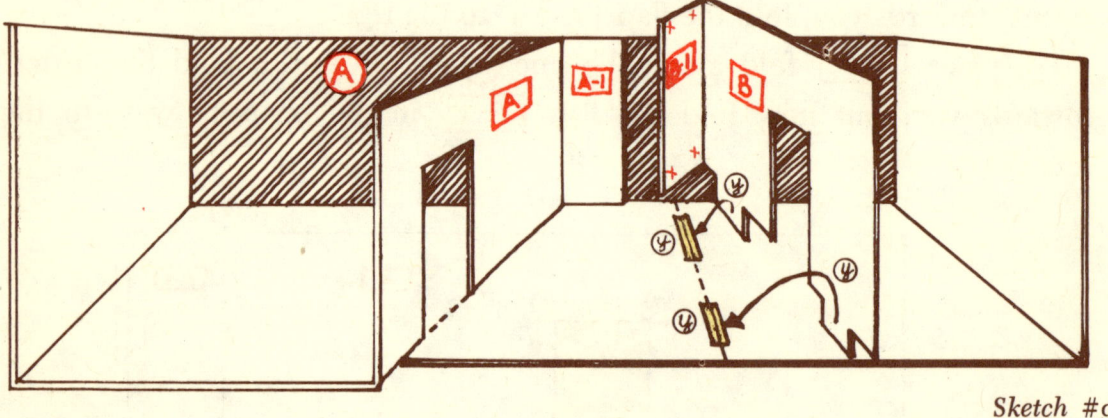

Sketch #9

If you like you can use Mystik cloth tape to hinge a door, cut to fit the opening, like the one suggested on page 160 and sketch #16. If you should prefer just to suggest a door, you can simply paste a door like the one on page 174 on each side of the wall. Make a door, in either case, that will fit the decorating scheme you plan.

5. *To Make the Kitchen*

If your doll house is to be complete, you will need a kitchen. There are several ways to add a room onto a doll house, and I'm sure you can think of some yourself. This is how I added the kitchen for this particular doll house.

Take a clean cardboard carton B, 8¼" wide X 10" deep X 6¾" high. Cut out one of the 8¼" wide ends as shown in sketch #10 (page 154), so that the box is open on one side.

Using the measurements for carton (B) in sketch #10 (page 154),

Draw your lines:
1.) From (a) up to (b)
2.) From (d) up to (c)
3.) From (b) across to (c)
4.) From (a) across to (d)

With an X-Acto knife carefully cut out the opening along the lines you have drawn, and discard the piece shaded in yellow.

Using the measurements shown on the Dining Room wall of carton (A) in sketch #10 (page 154),

Draw your lines:
1.) From (m) up to (n)
2.) From (p) up to (o)
3.) From (n) across to (o)
4.) From (m) across to (p)

Again, carefully cut out the opening along the lines you have drawn and throw away the piece shaded in yellow.

With a heavy duty stapler, fasten the two portions (the *right* wall of the Dining Room and the *left* wall of the Kitchen) together at the places marked ✢.

To do this—be sure the floors of both rooms are even, then
1.) Hold (a) and (p) together and place a staple ✢ ¼" from the opening.
2.) Hold (m) and (d) together and place a staple ✢ ¼" from the opening.
3.) Hold (b) and (o) together, and
4.) Hold (c) and (n) together and place a staple ✢ just above the openings at those two points.
5.) Hold the *front* edges of both walls together and place a staple ✢ at the top and bottom ⅛" from the front edge of the *right* wall on the

Dining Room *through* the *left* wall of the Kitchen.

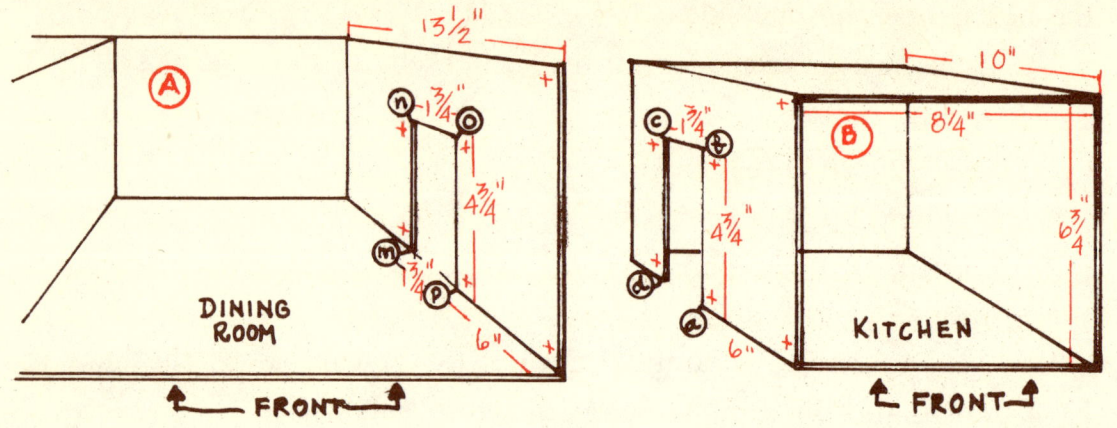

Sketch #10

This completes the first floor, and now you are ready to build the second floor of your doll house.

II MAKING THE SECOND FLOOR

1. *To Begin the Second Floor*

Find a firm, clean cardboard carton ⓒ 33″ long X 15″ deep and at least 15″ high. With a sharp scissors cut out one of the long 33″ sides. The cut out part becomes the "front" of the second floor. Then using the measurements shown in sketch #11 draw your lines in this order on both the *left* and the *right* walls of ⓒ

    1.) From ⓐ across to ⓑ
    2.) From ⓑ up to ⓒ
    3.) From ⓓ across to ⓔ
    4.) From ⓔ up to ⓕ
    5.) From ⓕ across to ⓖ
    6.) From ⓖ down to ⓗ
    7.) From ⓗ across to ⓘ

On the *back* wall of carton ⓒ

    Draw your lines:

1.) From ⓘ angled up to Ⓜ

2.) From Ⓜ angled down to ⓘ

On the *front* of carton Ⓒ

Draw a line:

1.) From Ⓑ across to Ⓑ

Using an X-Acto knife and a metal ruler as a guide, carefully cut *through* the lines you have drawn and throw away the pieces you have cut out.

The front section (from Ⓑ across to Ⓑ) that you have cut away becomes the "upstairs hall," which gives you access to each of the bedrooms.

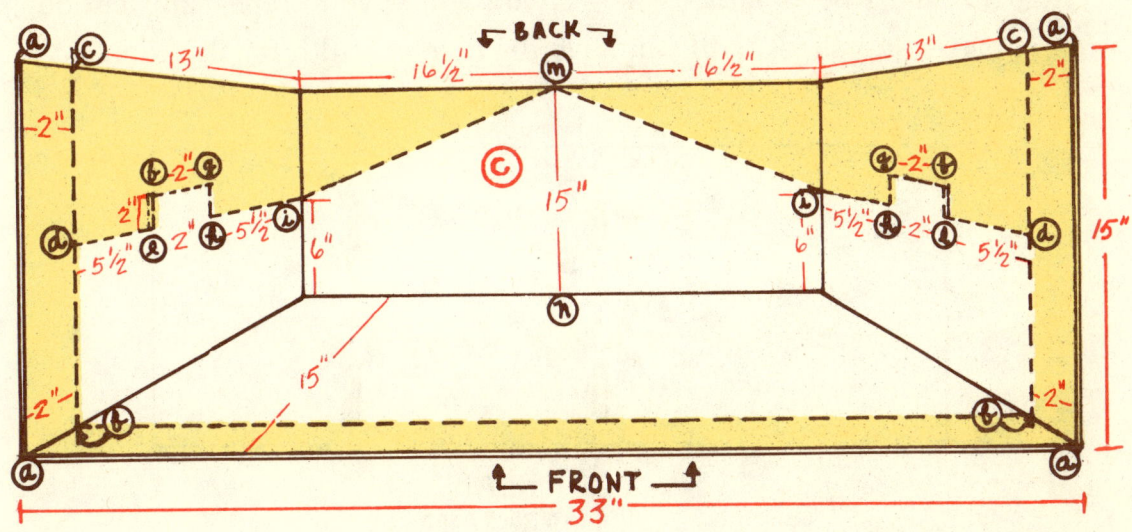

Sketch #11

2. *To Lay Out the Second Floor Partitions for the Bedrooms*

The rest of your second story is easy to build. You need partitions between the three upstairs rooms—one between the Master Bedroom and the Guest Room, and one between the Guest Room and the Children's Room. You can make these just like the partitions separating the rooms on the ground floor.

Use sketch #12 (page 156), which is a *plan* only of the second floor.

Now using the measurements in this sketch, mark off lines for the "slots" in this order along the ⓐ to Ⓑ line:

155

1.) From ⓑ to ⓜ
2.) From ⓜ to ⓝ draw double lines
3.) From ⓝ to ⓞ
4.) From ⓞ to ⓟ draw double lines
5.) Repeat steps 1.) through 4.) along the ⓒ to ⓓ line

Now using an X-Acto knife and a metal ruler, cut out *all* four "slots" by drawing the knife firmly *through* the double lines:

1.) From ⓜ to ⓝ
2.) From ⓞ to ⓟ

The "slot" must be about ¼" wide—so you will have to repeat this cut out process *one* or *two* times until you have the correct width for the "slot."

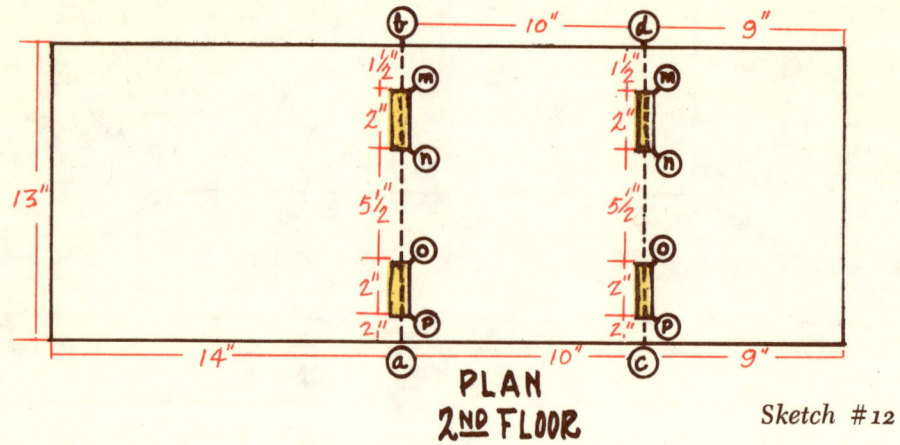

Sketch #12

3. *To Make the Second Floor Partitions*

The two upstairs partitions will be identical. So, take two strips of cardboard ☐ D and ☐ E , each 18" long and 6½" wide. See sketch #13. Follow the same directions for both:

Measure ¼" from ⓑ to ⓐ on both ends of piece ☐ D . Draw a *light* line from ⓐ across to ⓐ.

Now using the other measurements in sketch #13, draw your *heavy* lines in this order:

1.) From ⓐ across to ⓧ

2.) From Ⓧ down to ⓒ
3.) From Ⓧ down to ⓓ
4.) From Ⓧ across to Ⓨ
5.) From Ⓨ down to ⓔ
6.) From Ⓨ down to ⓕ
7.) From Ⓨ across to ⓐ

With a sharp scissors cut along the *heavy* lines you have drawn (the yellow areas in the sketch will be cut and thrown away).

8.) Repeat steps 1.) through 7.) for piece E .

9.) Draw a *light* line from Ⓗ down to Ⓖ on pieces D and E .

Holding piece D with the "front" towards you:

Fold the "flap" D-1 along the line Ⓖ and Ⓗ , to the right.

Holding piece E with the "front" towards you:

Fold the "flap" E-1 along the line Ⓖ and Ⓗ , but now fold the "flap" in the opposite way, to the left.

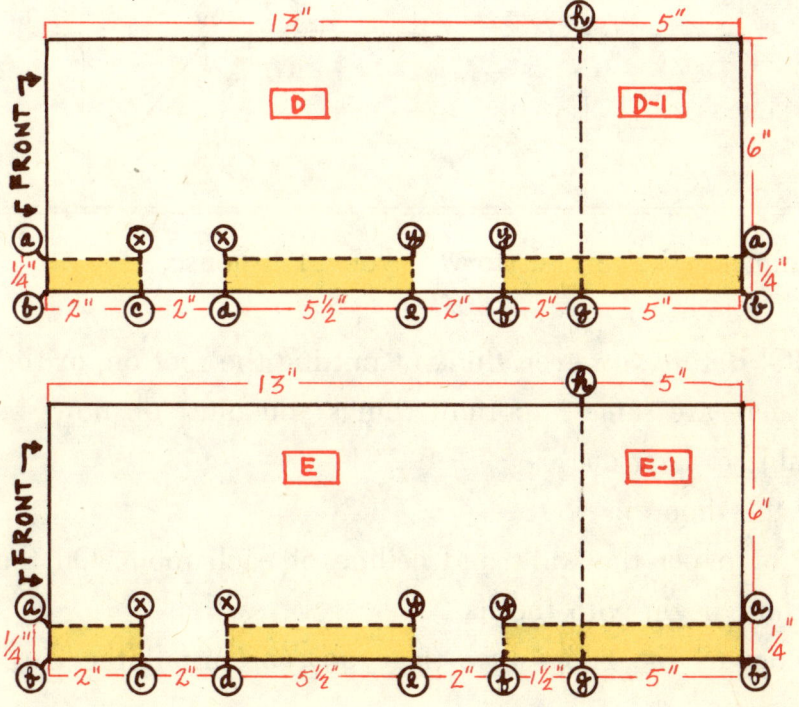

Sketch #13

4. *To Install the Second Floor Partitions*

Take the partition [E] in sketch #14 and firmly insert "tabs" (Y) into floor slots (Y), marked on carton (C).

To further secure the partitions, staple (or tape) the folded "flap" [E-1], to the back wall (as shown). Four staples, one in each corner of "flap" [E-1] (marked +) should do.

Repeat these steps with partition [D] and its "flap" [D-1].

You now have three rooms on the second floor; the Master Bedroom, the Guestroom—Den and the Children's Room.

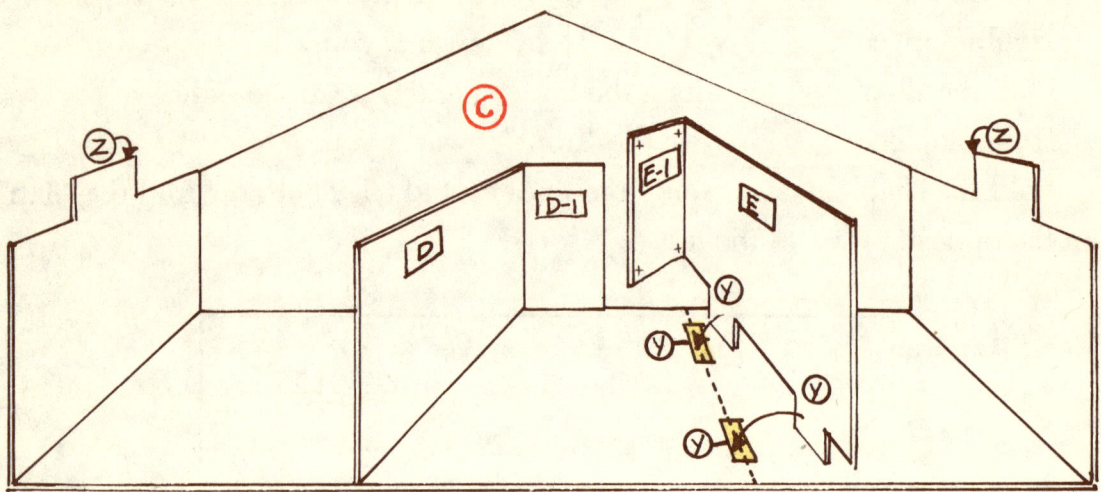

This completes the second story of your doll house.

Sketch #14

WARNING! Before you even think of putting the roof on, or the two floors together, there are some important things you must do now—because you won't be able to later on.

So now is the time to:

1. Paint or paper the walls and ceiling of each room. On the first floor you must begin with the hall.
2. "Put down" the floors (see page 40), or install the carpeting (see pages 38-39).

158

3. Install the staircase (see page 159).
4. Install windows (see page 161) and hang doors (see page 160) and shutters (see page 161).
5. Install handrails for stairs (see page 171) and the carpet for the stairs (see page 172).
6. Hang draperies, poles, curtains, etc. (see pages 42-43).

III PAINTING, PAPERING AND GENERAL INSTALLATION

Now is the time to decorate the doll house. If you haven't already begun, you'll want to start by painting the outside walls, setting in the windows, papering the walls, covering the floors, and adding the doors, the stairs, the shutters, the fireplace, and installing the cabinets and equipment in the Kitchen. For color schemes see page 8.

1. *Papering and Flooring*

Before you fasten the upper (second) floor to the first floor it is much simpler to paper each room first and "finish" the floors and ceilings except for the Living Room (see *"Installing the Staircase"*). To correctly paper a room always do the back wall *first* and *then* the side walls. Then you paper the ceiling. If you chose to paint the ceiling—you must do this *before* papering.

Next paint or use appropriate contact paper and "set in" your floors.

2. *Installing the Staircase*

After the walls of the hall have been papered and the ceiling is painted, and *before* the Living Room is papered:

Take the stairs (page 168), and with the bottom stair facing you, gently force the top stair to the back of the hall, and the left side of the stairs against the *left* wall of the hall.

Holding it in this position take a heavy duty stapler and from the *Living*

Room side staple through the Living Room wall and through the *left* wall of the stairs. Staple at the 4 places marked " + " (as in sketch #15).

Now take 5 strips (each about 2" long) of transparent mending tape and use 2 strips to paste the top steps to the hall wall.

Use 3 strips to paste the right wall of the stairs to the hall floor. With the staircase in place you should now carpet the stairs as suggested on page 172. And now you can paper the walls in the Living Room.

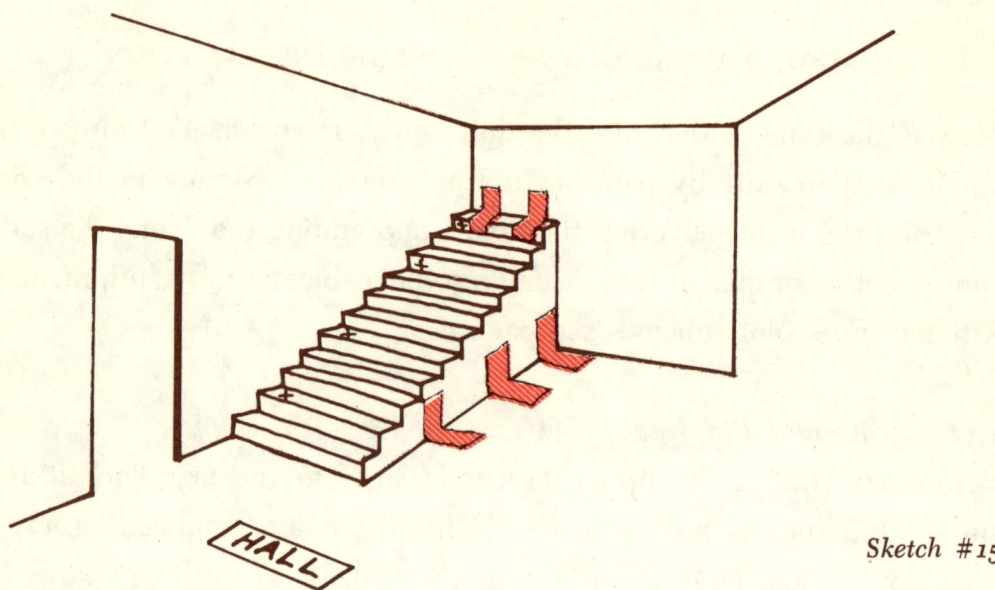

Sketch #15

3. Installing or Hanging the Doors

Make the doors (see page 173). You will need 3 doors, finished on both sides. To "hang" them so they will "hinge" take 2 strips of Mystik white cloth tape 4½" long X ¾" wide (see sketch #16).

1.) Draw a line from *b* down to *a* on both pieces of tape.
2.) Paste the *d* part of the strip on the wall next to the door opening.
3.) Paste the *c* part of the strip on *one* side of the door.
4.) Paste the *c* part of the second strip on the *other* side of the door.
5.) Paste the *d* part of the second strip on the wall *behind* the door opening.

Sketch #16

4. Installing Windows and Shutters

Decide where you want to place the windows in your doll house. For this doll house the plans (page 147) show 11 windows, therefore you must make 22 windows (see page 175). You can then measure and mark off the placement of each window location, then glue one on the *inside* wall of the *room,* and another on the exact location on the *outside* of the *house.*

Most houses look very attractive if the windows have shutters on the outside of the house. Traditionally they are used on the front and sides and rarely on the rear windows. It is also correct to use them on the lower floor only. So if you want to follow this convention you will only need *4 pairs* of shutters (see page 120).

It is a *must,* however, to paint them a different color from the house itself.

5. Installing the Fireplace

There is one rule for this installation, and that is that a fireplace must be placed in the room on the wall that is directly under the chimney. To make

161

the fireplace see page 176. Usually the fireplace is painted either white, or to match the woodwork. The marble trim and the hearth can be any realistic marble color.

6. *Installing the Kitchen Equipment*

Using the "U plan" for the Kitchen set the pieces in (as shown in sketch #17) in this order:

1.) Left wall
   a.) Broom closet (see page 138).
   b.) Refrigerator (see page 136).
   c). Base cabinet (see page 130).
      Note: To fit this kitchen layout, base cabinet ⓒ must be only 3½" long.
   d.) Door to Dining Room.
2.) Back wall
   e.) Base cabinet (see page 130).
      Note: To fit this kitchen layout, base cabinet ⓔ must be only 2" long.
   f.) Range and oven in base cabinet (see page 134).
3.) Right wall
   g.) Base cabinet (see page 130).
      Note: To fit this kitchen layout, base cabinet ⓖ must be 3" long and only one half (the right hand half) should have doors or drawers; the other half is hidden in the corner by the range cabinet.
   h.) **Sink and Dishwasher** (see pages 132-133).
   i.) Base Cabinet (see page 130).
   j.) All the wall hung cabinets (see page 137).

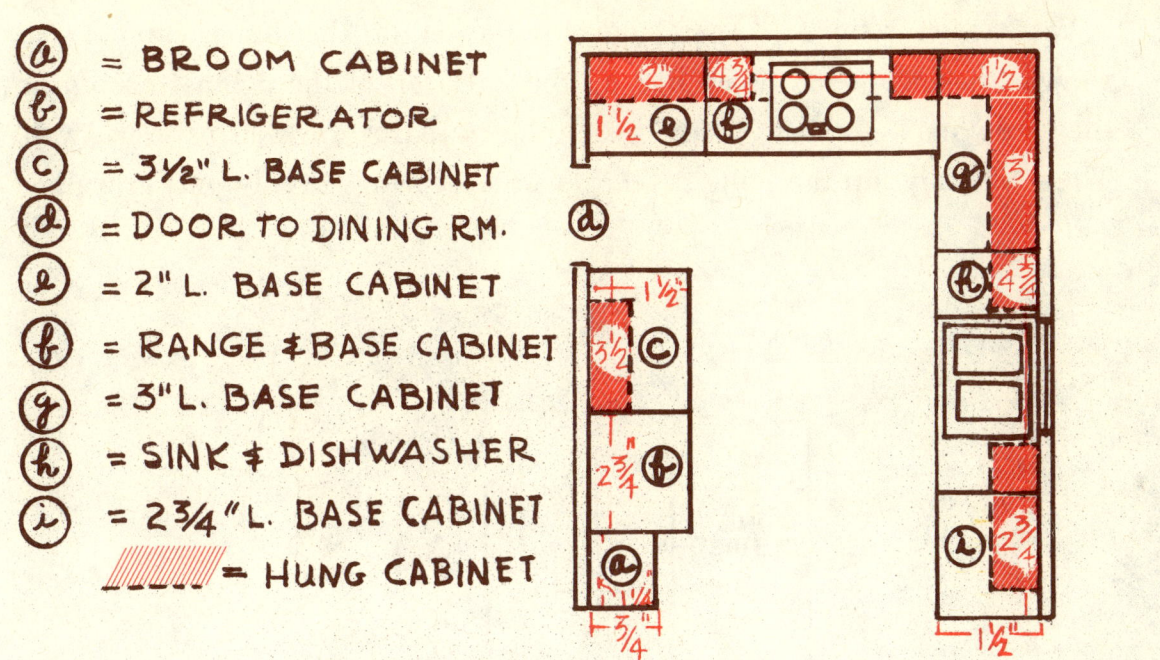

- ⓐ = BROOM CABINET
- ⓑ = REFRIGERATOR
- ⓒ = 3½" L. BASE CABINET
- ⓓ = DOOR TO DINING RM.
- ⓔ = 2" L. BASE CABINET
- ⓕ = RANGE & BASE CABINET
- ⓖ = 3" L. BASE CABINET
- ⓗ = SINK & DISHWASHER
- ⓘ = 2¾" L. BASE CABINET
- ▨ = HUNG CABINET

Sketch #17

7. Installing the Base Cabinets and Hung Cabinets

To install all the base cabinets use the measurements shown in sketch #17 and *lightly* draw a guide line from ⓑ to ⓑ along all walls of the kitchen.

For each cabinet take 2 strips of Scotch tape 5" long. The ⓔ part of the strip should be about 3" long and the ⓓ part about 2" long. Paste each strip (ⓔ part) on the *inside* of the cabinet (as shown in sketch #18), then line up the back-top of the cabinet *evenly* on your guide line (ⓑ to ⓑ) and use the ⓓ part of the strips to fasten them to the wall. Then gently flip the cabinet over so it rests on the floor.

To install the hung cabinets, again use the measurements in sketch #17 but now draw a line from ⓒ to ⓒ along all walls that will receive a hung cabinet. Remember, none will go over the sink, refrigerator, range, or broom closet.

Cut 2 more 5" long strips of Scotch tape for each hung cabinet (the ⓕ part of the strips should be about 3" long and the ⓖ part 2" long).

Paste each strip (ⓕ part) on the *inside* of the hung cabinet (as shown in sketch #18). Now line up the back-top of the cabinet *evenly* on the guide line (ⓒ to ⓒ) and fasten the ⓖ parts of the strips to the wall. Then carefully flip the hung cabinet over so it hangs evenly on the wall.

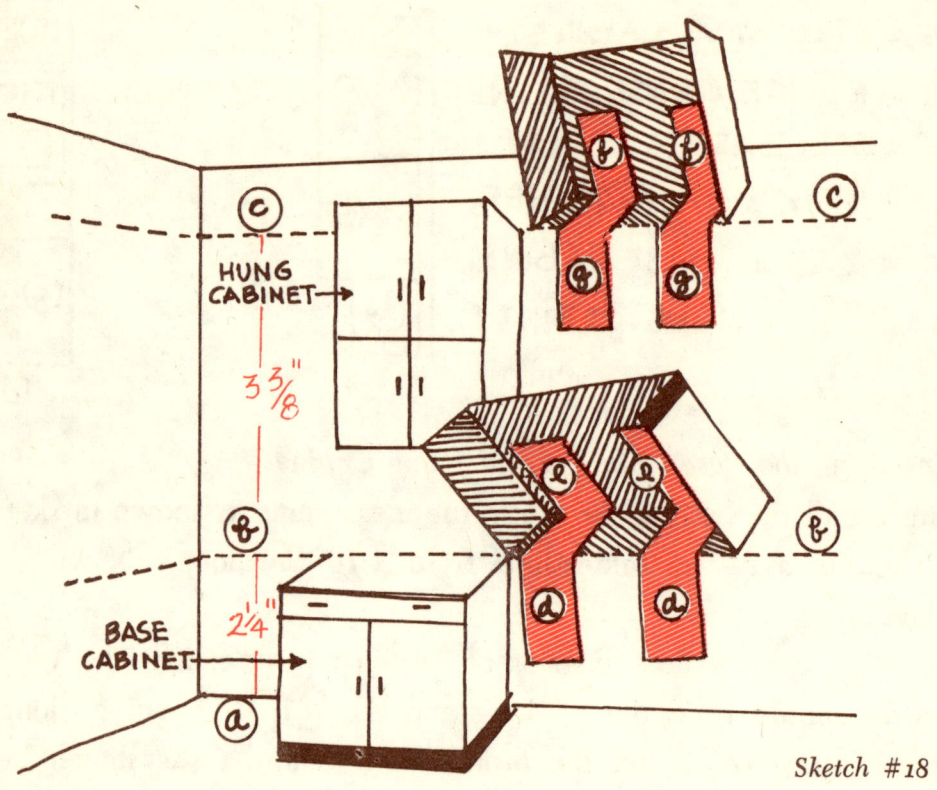

Sketch #18

IV Putting the Two Floors Together

To put the 1st floor and the 2nd floor together, you may try any one of three different suggestions:

1.) Simply pick up the carton that is your "second story" and set it on the tops of the outer walls and room partitions of your "ground floor". This way you can remove the upper floor easily to decorate and furnish the ground floor, and then put it back. However, this arrangement is a bit shaky.

2.) Another idea is to take a flat strip of cardboard 13″ wide and 33¼″

long and rest it (unfastened) on the walls and partitions of the ground floor. Then place the second story (unfastened) on top of the strip. This way it's possible to take the two stories apart and put them together again easily, so that you can work and play with the whole house at once, or with parts of it. The flat strip must be about 33¼" long so that it will sit firmly on the downstairs partitions and provide a sturdy base for the second story section, but try not to allow it to stick out too far beyond the outside walls.

3.) Of course, if you want to fasten the second floor of your house to the ground floor, you may use strong, double-faced tape along the tops of the ground floor walls and the floor of the second story.

V Making the Roof and Attic

1. *To Begin the Roof*

Use a stiff piece of clean cardboard (D) 40½" long and 16" wide. If such a sheet is not available, two identical sheets, (D) and (E), each measuring 20¼" long X 16" wide will do just as well, as in sketch #19.

In either case the left side of the roof will be (D) and the right side (E).

If you use *one* piece of cardboard (40½" long X 16" wide), then:

Using the measurements in sketch #19 draw your line

1.) From (a) down to (b) (on both sides of (D) (E)).
2.) With a metal-edged ruler as a guide, *lightly* draw a knife over (*not through*) line (a) to (b) on both sides of piece (D) (E).
3.) This will permit you to make a *sharp* fold along line (a) to (b).

If you use *two* pieces of cardboard (D) and (E) (each 20¼" long X 16" wide), then:

Take *two* 16" long strips of Mystik linen tape (1" wide). Take *one* strip and paste (D) and (E) together along the (a) to (b) line. Then reinforce this joint by pasting the other strip of tape on the other side of (D) and (E) along the ⓐ to ⓑ line.

2. To Make the Roof "Slots" for the Chimneys

Using the measurements shown on sketch #19, *lightly* draw your lines:

1.) From ⓒ down to ⓓ on Ⓓ
2.) From ⓒ down to ⓓ on Ⓔ

Draw two *heavy* lines:

3.) From ⓜ to ⓝ on Ⓓ
4.) From ⓜ to ⓝ on Ⓔ

Now using an X-Acto knife and a metal-edged ruler as a guide, cut out *both* "slots" by drawing the knife firmly *through* both lines.

5.) From ⓜ to ⓝ on Ⓓ
6.) From ⓜ to ⓝ on Ⓔ

The "slots" must be about ¼" wide, so you may have to repeat this cut out process one or two times until you have the correct width for the "slots."

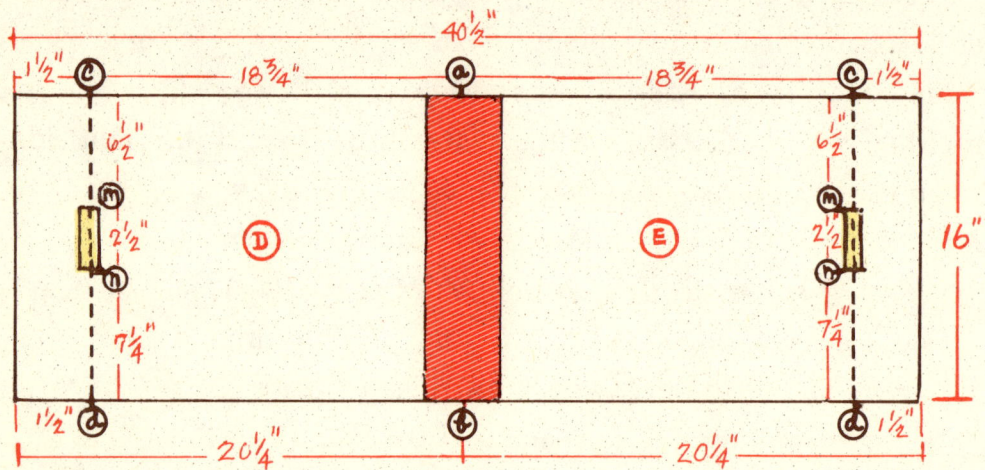

Sketch #19

3. Installing the Roof

Now you are ready to place the roof on the second story of your doll house. Gently lift the roof onto the second story and slip the chimney tabs Ⓩ on the walls through the "slots" cut into the roof as shown in sketch #20.

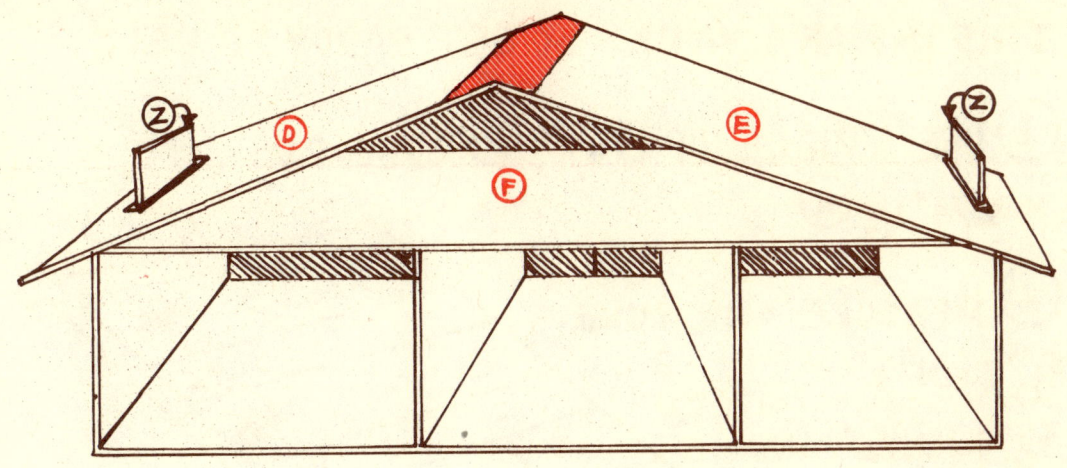

Sketch #20

The next step is very important. Check the peak of the roof to make sure it is secure—if not, re-tape it both outside and in. Another way to make the house sturdy is to fasten the side and back walls to the underside of the roof with heavy tape. If tape is needed to secure the edges of the roof where they meet the tops of the second story walls, don't hesitate to use it.

4. *To Make the Attic*

Every homeowner—even a doll family—needs a place to store old clothes and old furniture. The doll house must have an attic. To make one, simply cut out a piece of cardboard 13" wide X 33" long Ⓕ . Wedge it in under the roof (see sketch #20), resting it on the tops of the second story partitions. Now you have not only an attic, but a ceiling for your bedrooms and den.

If you have already painted the outside of the house you will probably have to touch it up again—especially if you have taped the roof to the sides of the doll house.

Now paint the roof. Use any color that will contrast pleasantly with the color you used for the house itself.

Now isn't it pretty? *Your* own doll house and *you* built it!

HOW TO MAKE STAIRS

THIS IS MAN'S WORK - SO GET DADDY TO HELP!

① USE A PIECE OF LIGHT CARDBOARD 14"L X 2¼"W Ⓐ

② MEASURE AND RULE OFF ⅝" THEN ½" ⅝" THEN ½" AND SO ON TO THE END OF PIECE Ⓐ

③ ALONG THE LINES YOU HAVE DRAWN ON PIECE Ⓐ
1. FOLD ONE WAY - ½"
2. FOLD OPPOSITE WAY ⅝"
3. FOLD FIRST WAY ½"
4. FOLD SECOND WAY ⅝"
5. FOLD FIRST WAY - ½"

AND SO ON

YOU WILL THEN HAVE YOUR FOLDED CARDBOARD STAIRS Ⓑ

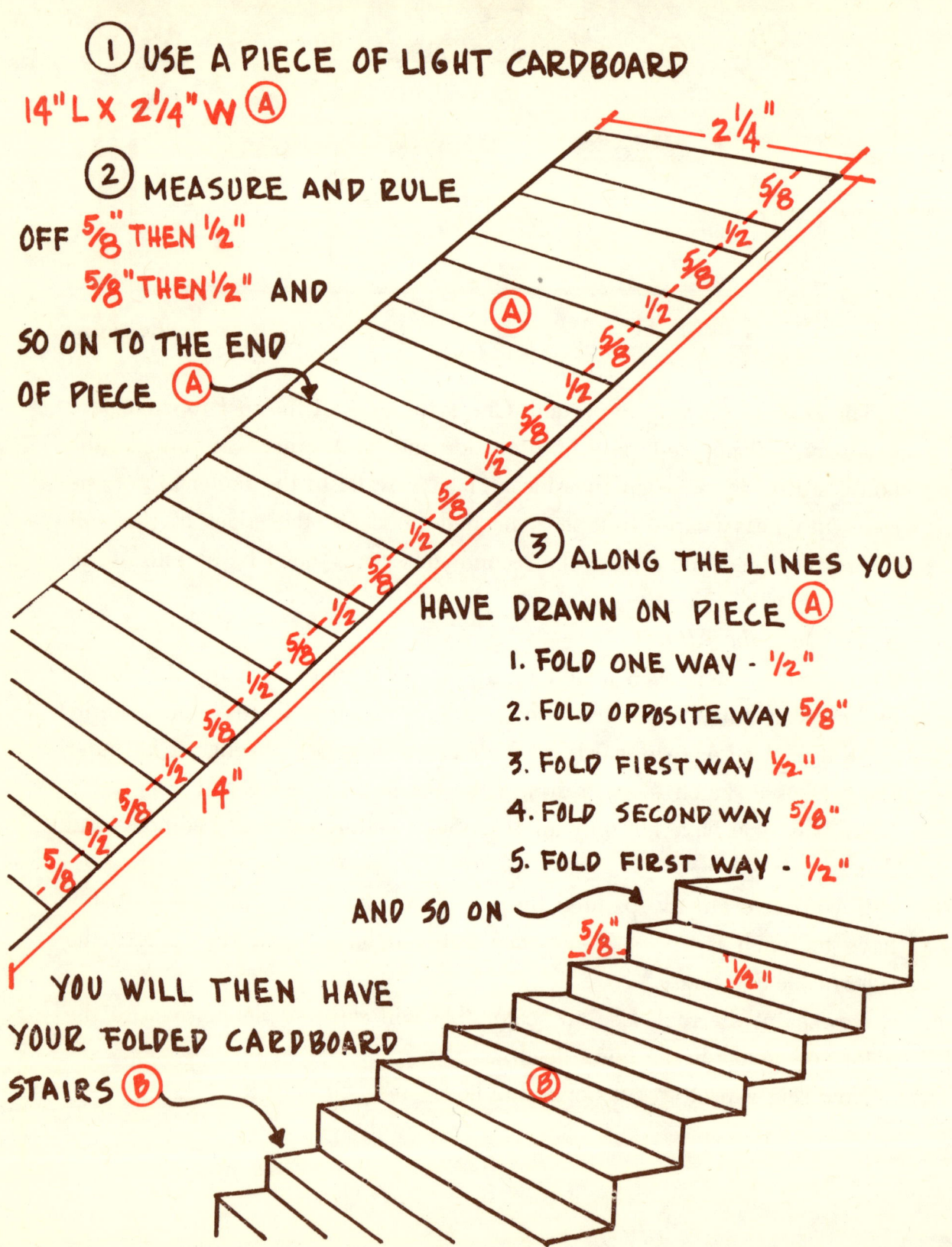

④ ON ANOTHER PIECE OF CARDBOARD 7½"L X 6"W, WITH A RULER, MEASURE AND DRAW "STEP-FASHION"

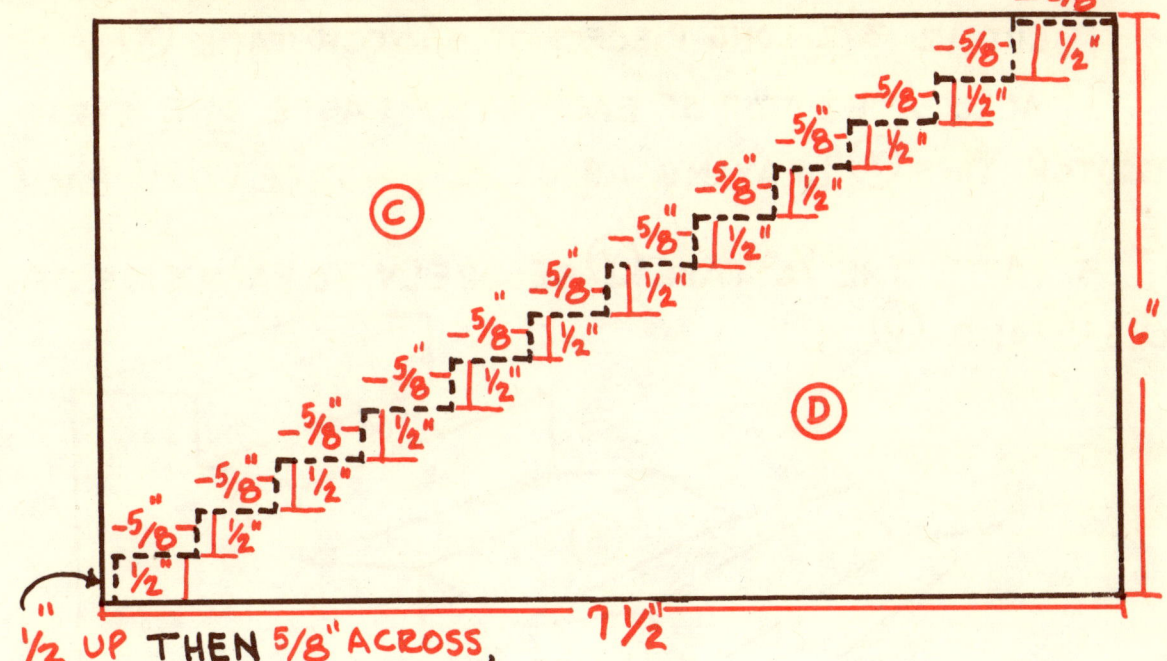

½" UP THEN ⅝" ACROSS,
½" UP THEN ⅝" ACROSS
AND SO ON, DIAGONALLY ACROSS THE CARDBOARD.

⑤ CUT ALONG THE "STEP" LINES YOU HAVE DRAWN. NOW YOU WILL HAVE TWO PIECES Ⓒ AND Ⓓ - WHICH WILL BE THE SIDES OF YOUR STAIR

169

⑥ TAKE FOLDED STAIRS Ⓑ (BE SURE THEY ARE LONG ENOUGH TO MATCH THE SIDE PIECES Ⓒ & Ⓓ.)

   1. CUT 12 3½" LONG PIECES OF SCOTCH TAPE Ⓧ.

   2. ACROSS THE TOP OF EACH STEP, PASTE <u>ONE</u> STRIP OF SCOTCH TAPE Ⓧ LEAVING ABOUT ½" OF TAPE Ⓨ ON EACH SIDE.

   3. PASTE THE ½" TAPE Ⓨ SECURELY TO EACH SIDE OF PIECES Ⓒ AND Ⓓ.

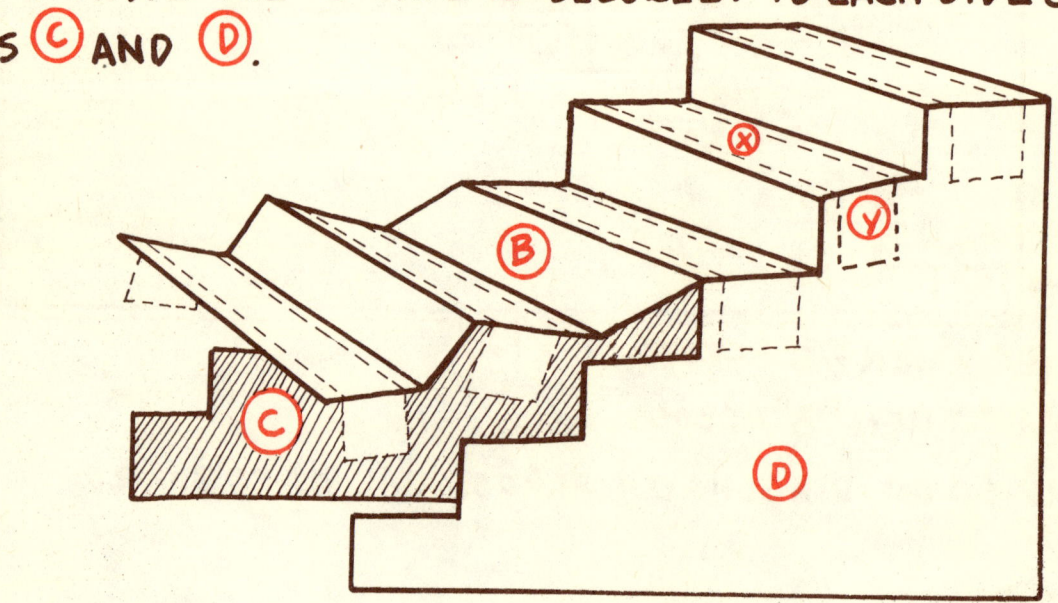

WHEN EACH STEP IS IN ITS PROPER PLACE THE STAIRS ARE THEN READY TO BE INSTALLED IN THE DOLL HOUSE HALL (SEE PAGE 159)

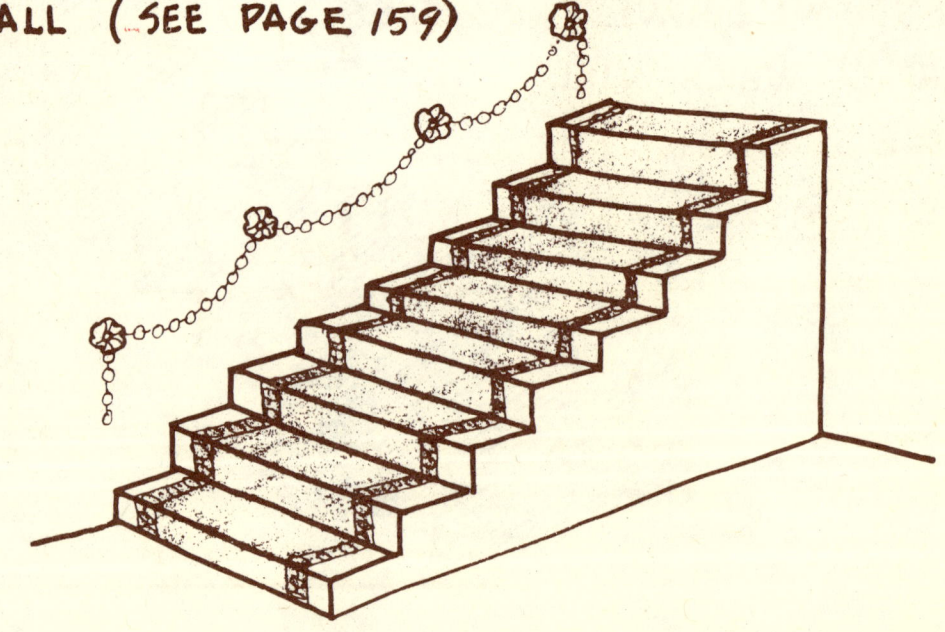

HANDRAILS
(FOR STAIRS)

USE UPHOLSTERY TACKS TO HOLD PLASTIC SODA STRAW FOR HAND RAIL.

OR USE UPHOLSTERY TACKS AND ELECTRIC LIGHT PULL CHAIN FOR STAIR HAND RAIL.

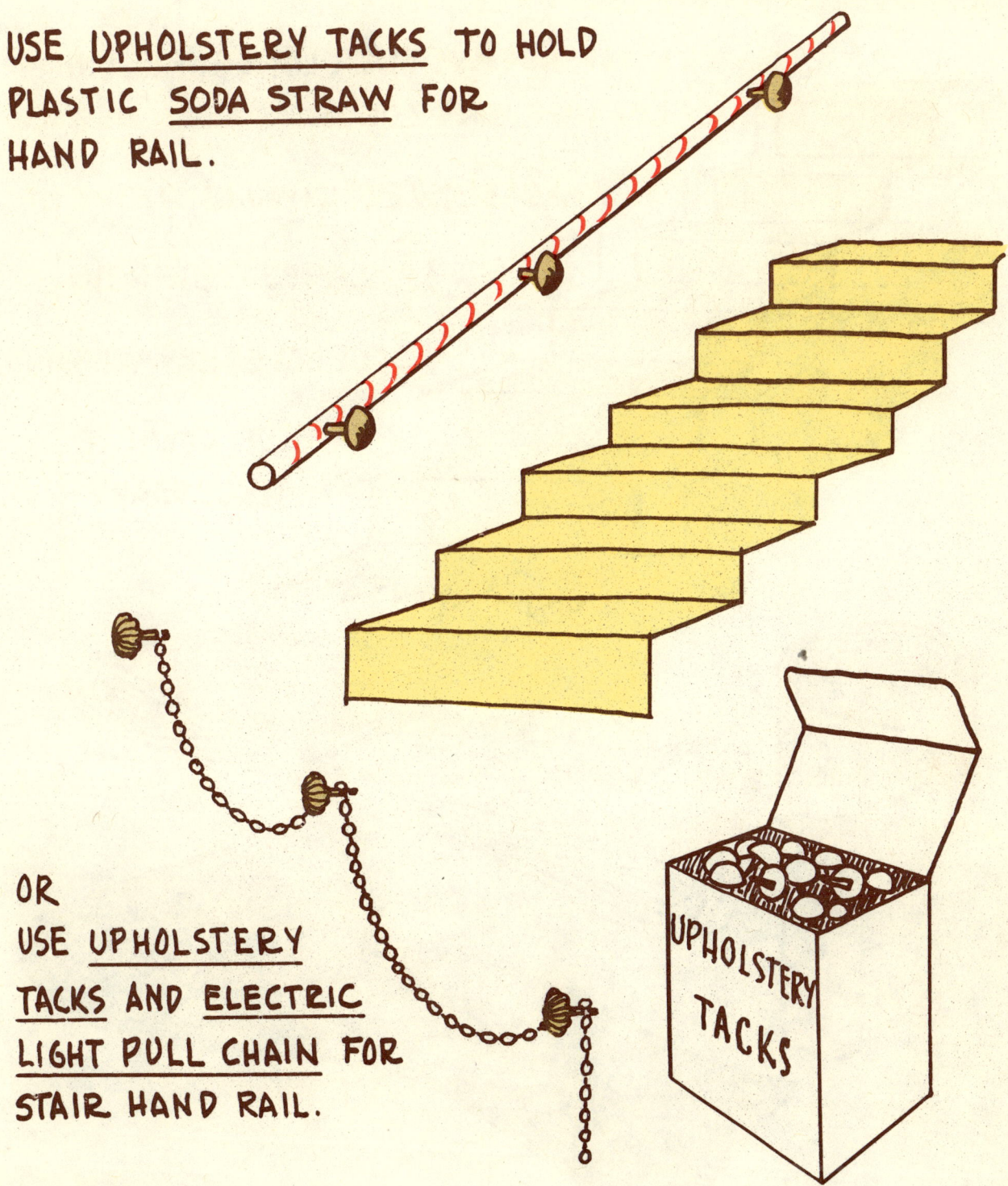

DOORS

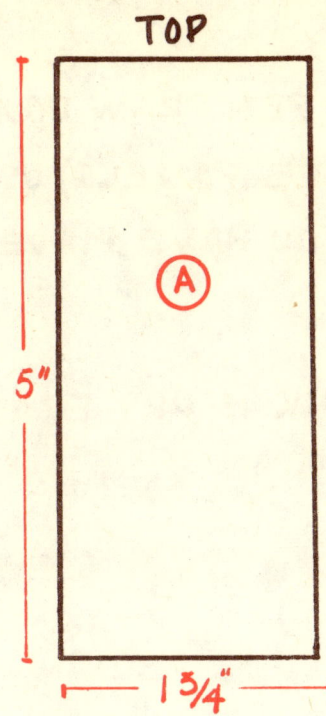

① USE ANY PART OF A WHITE GIFT BOX AND CUT A RECTANGLE 1¾" W X 5" L Ⓐ.

② TO MAKE DOOR PANELS (SHOWN IN DOTTED LINES), MARK OFF PIECE Ⓐ USING MEASUREMENTS IN THE SKETCH AND LIGHTLY DRAWING THE LINES IN THIS ORDER:-

1. FROM ⓐ ACROSS TO ⓐ
2. FROM ⓑ ACROSS TO ⓑ
3. FROM ⓒ ACROSS TO ⓒ
4. FROM ⓓ ACROSS TO ⓓ
5. FROM ⓔ ACROSS TO ⓔ
6. FROM ⓕ ACROSS TO ⓕ

NOW:-

7. FROM Ⓧ DOWN TO Ⓧ
8. FROM Ⓨ DOWN TO Ⓨ

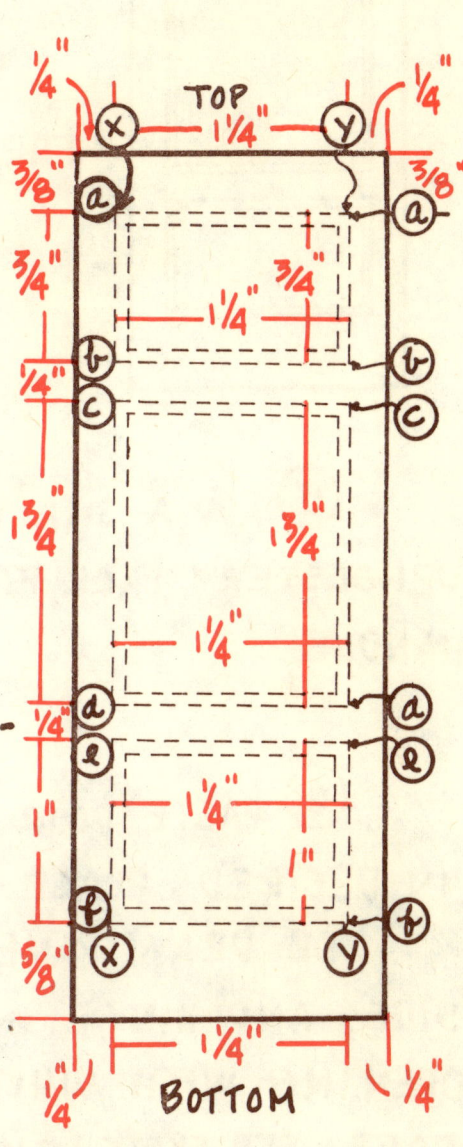

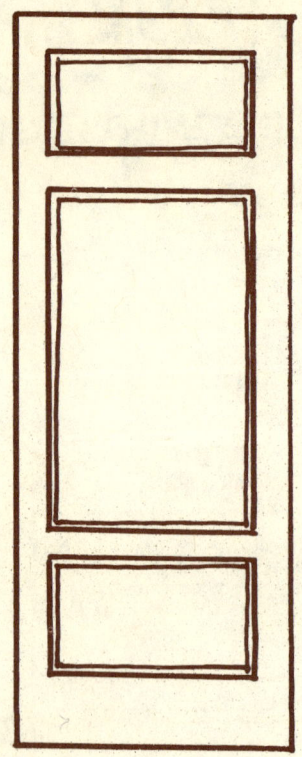

③ WITH A FLOW PEN DRAW DOUBLE LINES (TO FORM THREE PANELS) USING THE GUIDE LINES YOU HAVE MADE.

④ WHEN THE INK IS DRY ERASE THE GUIDE LINES.

⑤ ADD A SMALL BRASS UPHOLSTERY TACK FOR A DOOR HANDLE.

⑥ PASTE DOOR ON WALL IN DESIRED PLACE.
OR DRAW PANEL ON BOTH SIDES AND HINGE INTO DOOR OPENING WITH WHITE MYSTIK TAPE. SEE SKETCH #16 PAGE #161.

WINDOWS

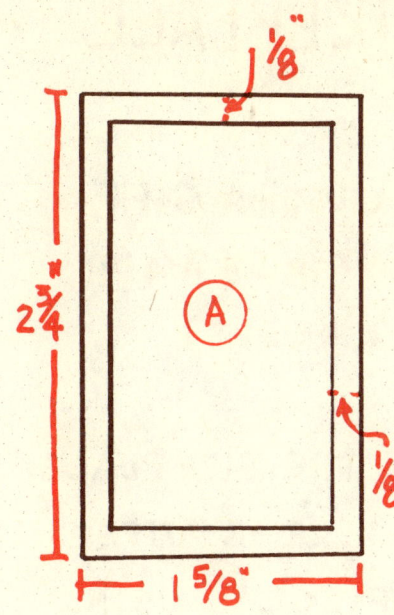

① CUT A WHITE GIFT BOX (OR TOP) INTO A PIECE 2¾" L × 1⅝" W Ⓐ.

② USING A BLACK FLOW PEN AND A RULER, DRAW A ⅛" W BORDER ON FOUR SIDES.

③ TO MAKE THE "WINDOW PANES" MARK OFF PIECE Ⓐ, USING THE MEASUREMENTS IN THE SKETCH AND DRAWING DOUBLE LINES WITH YOUR FLOW PEN THIS WAY ⟶

FROM ⓒ ACROSS TO ⓒ
　　　 ⓑ ACROSS TO ⓑ
　　　 ⓒ ACROSS TO ⓒ
FROM ⓧ DOWN TO ⓧ
　　　 ⓨ DOWN TO ⓨ

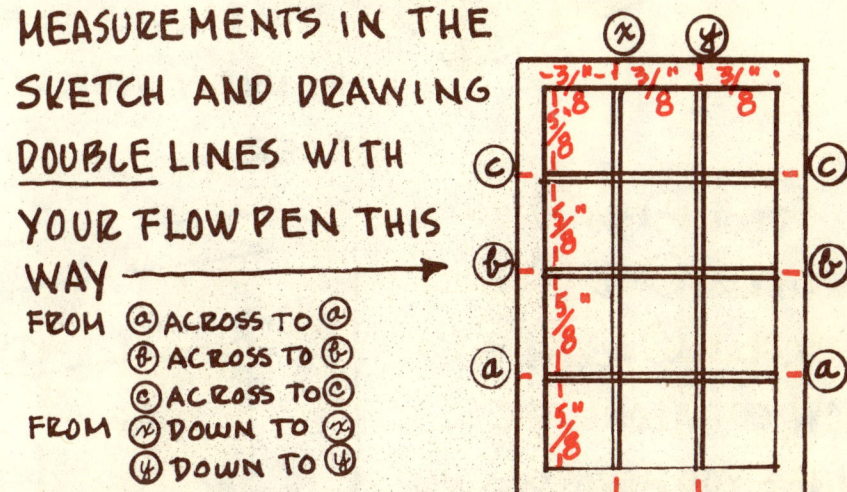

④ FOR THE OUTSIDE OF DOLL HOUSE ADD SHUTTERS TO THE WINDOWS (SEE PAGE 120)

FIREPLACE

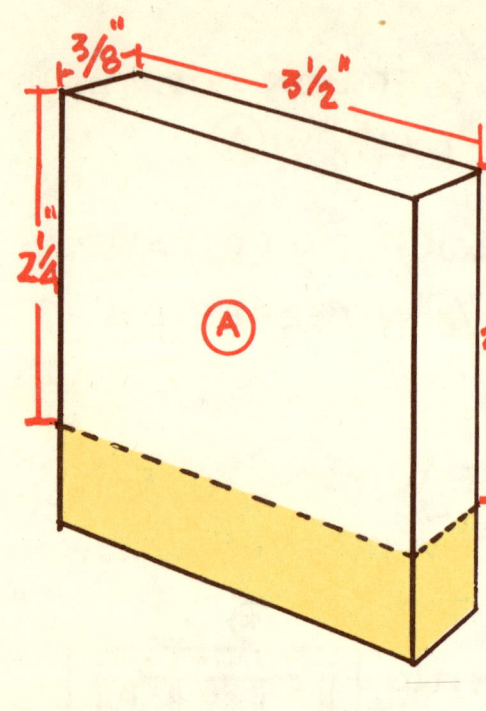

① TAKE THE LID OF A GIFT BOX Ⓐ, ABOUT 3½"W × ⅜"D × 2¼"H (OR CUT IT TO 2¼" HEIGHT).

② TO CUT OUT THE FIREPLACE OPENING Ⓑ, SHOWN HERE IN DOTTED LINES. MARK OFF PIECE Ⓐ USING THE MEASUREMENTS IN THE SKETCH AND DRAW YOUR LINES IN THIS ORDER

1. FROM ⓐ TO ⓑ
2. FROM ⓒ TO ⓑ
3. FROM ⓑ ACROSS TO ⓑ

NOW CUT ALONG THE LINES YOU HAVE DRAWN

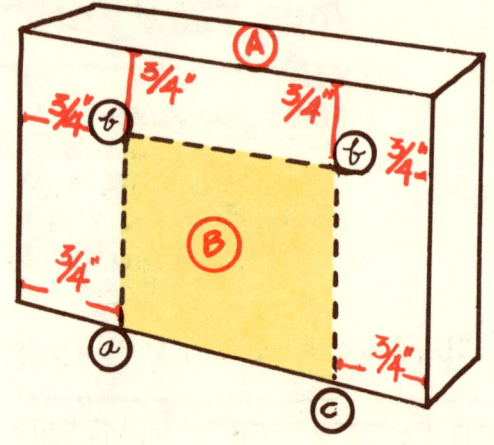

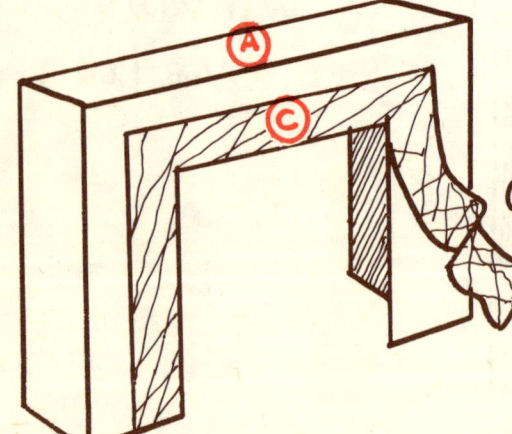

③ CUT A STRIP OF MARBLEIZED CONTACT PAPER ⅜"W × 6"L Ⓒ. PASTE STRIP Ⓒ ON 3 SIDES OF CUT OUT OPENING.

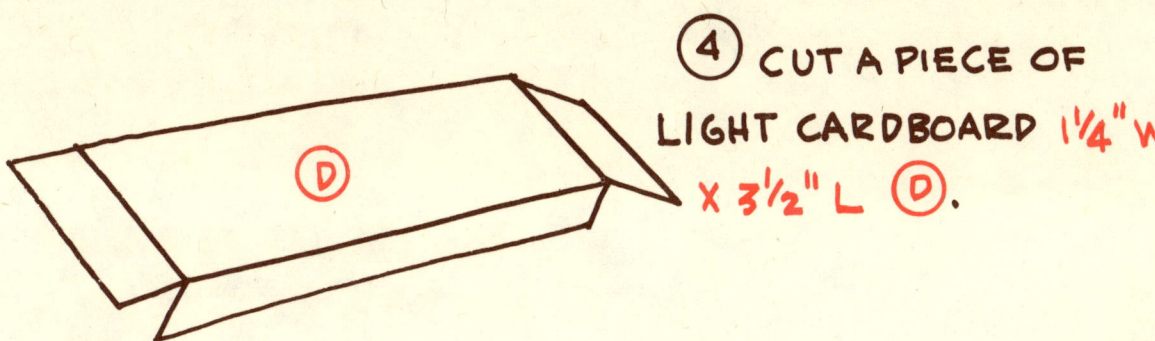

④ CUT A PIECE OF LIGHT CARDBOARD 1¼" W × 3½" L Ⓓ.

⑤ CUT A PIECE OF THE SAME MARBLEIZED PAPER Ⓔ 4" L × 1¾" W. CUT OUT ¼" SQUARES FROM EACH CORNER.

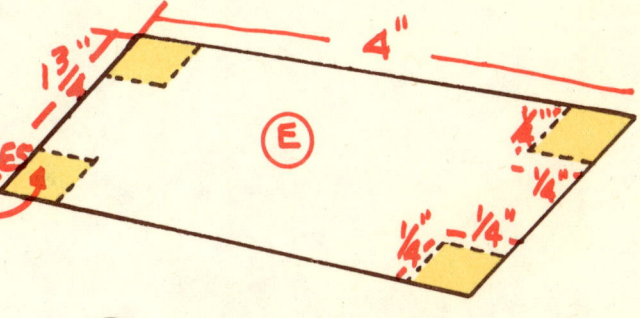

⑥ COVER PIECE Ⓓ WITH CUT OUT MARBLEIZED PAPER Ⓔ FOR THE HEARTH.

⑦ PASTE THE HEARTH Ⓔ ¼" UNDER THE FIREPLACE OPENING. PLACE THE FIREPLACE AGAINST THE WALL.

⑧ USE LAMP FINIALS FOR ANDIRONS

⑨ USE CUT SODA STRAWS FOR LOGS.

By now you have toyed with some of the mini-basics of decorating, played with many of the problems, and even solved some of them. Perhaps you have made most of the furniture, even planned a room, and also have two or three color schemes all set to go. If you have, then you are beginning one of the most exciting games—the game of creating!

How is it played? Simply, like most games; work with a few basic rules and use good tools—but remember the two most important tools for the game are your eyes and your imagination, so use them well. If you do, you will soon create *your* own color schemes, design *your* own furniture, discover *your* own way of making tables, find different materials for rugs or even a new way to make shutters. Any one of these can be *your* idea.

The idea of the game—is ideas that work.

Index

Page numbers in italics refer to illustrations.

Accent colors, 110
Accessories, 17, *46-7*
Andirons, *46*
Armoire, 79
Ashtrays, *47*
Attic, 165, *167*

Bathrooms, 143-4
Bed, 5, 76, 80, 82-91
Bedrooms, 143-4, *147*, 155, 158
Beds:
    bunk, 81, 88-9
    day or sofa, 80, 108-9, *116-7*
    master, fourposter, or canopy, 7, 76, *83-5*
    twin, *86-7*
Bedspread, 6, 7, 78, 85, 109, 110
Bench, ottoman, 77, *104-5*
Bolster, *106*, 109, 110
Bookcases, 15, 16, 109, 110, *111-115*
Books, 17, 81, 109, 110, 115
Bookshelves, 15, 16, 49, 51, 81
Breakfront, 51
Broom closet, 162
Buffet, 48, *53-5*

Cabinets:
    base (kitchen), 123, 127-9, *130-1*, 162-4
    bedroom, 79
    broom, 124, *138*, 162
    dining room, 51
    double-hung (wall), 124, *137*, 162-4
    TV, 15, *21-3*, 51, 77, 79, 80, 110
Carpeting, wall-to-wall, 10, *38-9*, 51, 110
Ceiling, 158-9, 167
Chairs:
    club or easy, 6, 7, 15, *24-5*, 49, 51, 77, 80-2, 109, 110
    dining room, 48-9, *58-61*
    side or bridge, 15, 16, 17, *26-9*, 77, 80-1, 110, 126, 128
    wing, 49, 51, *64-6*
Chandelier, *73-5*
Chest, blanket, 77, *101*
Chest of drawers, 77, 80, 82, 92-4, 109

Chest-on-chest, 81
Children's room, 155, 158
Chimneys, 161, 166
Clock:
   table, *107*
   wall, *141*
Color scheme, 7-8, 127
Commode, 78, 92-4
Crib, 81-2, 90-1
Cupboard, tall, 21-3, 48, 51, 79, 80
Curtains, 5, 6, 7, 15, *41-2*, 51, 79, 81-2, 159
Curtains, cafe, 127-9, *139*

Den, 143
Desk, kneehole, 15, 16, *18-20*, 77, 80-1, 109
Dining room, 143, 149, 152, 162
Dishwasher, 123-4, 127, *133*, 162
Doors, 143-4, 149, 152, 159, 160, *173-4*
Drapery poles, *43*, 159
Drapes, 15, *41-2*, 49, 110, 159
Dresser, 6, 51, 78, 80-1, *95-7*

Entrance walk, 148

Fireplace, 16, 49, 77, 143, 159, 161-2, *176-7*
Floors, *40*, 51-2, 81-2, 127-8, 159
Flower holders, *46-7*
Frames, picture, *44-5*

Guest room, 155, 158

Hall, 143-4, 149, 152, 155, 158-9
Handrails, 159, *171*
Hardware, 143
Headboard, 80, 109
Heating, 143-4
Highboy, 78

House (how to build it), 142-167

Kitchen, 143, 152-3
Kitchen equipment, 159, 162

Lamps, bases, 5, 6, 7, 15, *37*, 49, 77, 80, 109, 110
Lampshades, 7, 37, 82, 110
Laundry, 143
Lighting, 17, 109, 143-4
Living room, 143, 149, 152, 159, 160
Logs, *46*
Loveseat, 77, *98-100*

Master bedroom, 155, 158
Materials, 9-13, 48, 110, 127, 144-6
Mattress, 108-9
Mirrors, 6, *44-5*, 51

Oven, 124, 162
Ottoman, bench, 77, *104-5*

Painting, 158-9
Papering, 158-9
Paneling, 110
Partitions, 149-152, 155-158
Pictures, 5, 17, *44-5*, 51, 110, 128-9
Pillows, 7, 78, 109, 110, *122*
Plan, 5, 6, 14, 124-6, 143, *147*, 147-167
Plant stands, *46*, 110
Plumbing, 144

Rack, towel or tie, *140*
Range, 124, *134-5*, 162
Refrigerator, 123-4, 127, *136*, 143, 162
Rocker, 81
Roof, 158, 165-7

Rugs, 5, 6, 7, 15, 38-9, 51, 110

Scale model, 147
Sconces, *46*, 51
Screens, 15, 49, *68-9*, *70-2*
Secretary, 79
Server, 48-9, 51, *62-3*
Settee, 49, 77, *98-100*
Shades, lamp, 7, 37, 82, 110
Shades, window, 49, 128-9
Shelf, wall, 51, 129
Shutters, 49, 110, *120-1*, 128, 159, 161
Sink, 123-4, 126-7, *132*, 143, 162
Sofa, 15, 16, *30-2*, 49, 80, 109
Staircase, 159-160, *168-170*
Stools, 6, 7, 81-2, 127-8
Stove, 124, *134-5*, 143, 162

Table:
  bridge, 9, 15
  coffee, *35*, 49, 82
  dining, 48, 51, *56-7*
  drum, *33-4*
  end, 16, 17, *36*, 49, 82, 110
  kitchen, round, or covered, 49, *67*, 126, 128
  night, 6, 77, 80, *102-3*, 109
  square, 80, 82, 109, *118-9*
Terrace, 143
Tools, 9, 10, 145-6
TV, 15, 21-3, 51, 77, 79, 80, 110

Umbrella holder, *47*

Wallpaper, 7, 49, 82, 127-8
Walls, 7, 81, 110, 128-9, 158-9
Wastebasket, *47*
Window, bay, 49
Windows, 144, 159-161, *175*
Window box, 129